The Awakening

7 STEPS TO UNLOCK THE SECRET BEHIND THE LAW OF ATTRACTION

Alicia Ashley, M.A.

NEW YORK

THE AWAKENING
7 Steps to Unlock the Secret Behind the Law of Attraction

Library of Congress Control Number: 2007939432
ISBN: 978-1-60037-292-6 (Hardcover)
ISBN: 978-1-60037-291-9 (Paperback)

Published by:

MORGAN · JAMES
THE ENTREPRENEURIAL PUBLISHER™

Habitat
for Humanity®
Peninsula
Building Partner

Morgan James Publishing, LLC
1225 Franklin Ave Ste 325
Garden City, NY 11530-1693
Toll Free 800-485-4943
www.MorganJamesPublishing.com

Cover and Interior Design by:
Tony Laidig
www.thecoverexpert.com
tony@thecoverexpert.com

Dedication

This book is gratefully dedicated to the two most important men in my life.

To my dear Father, Kenneth Albert Megehee, who was the greatest example of unconditional love I have ever experienced. His love and music brought me great joy every day of his life. It was my privilege to be his daughter. The memories of his blue eyes, generous smile, and tenderness, warm my heart every day.

I love you Dad.

To my amazing son, Kenneth Michael Ashley, who is God's greatest gift to me, and my greatest gift to the world. Together we have created a bond of mutual love and respect that cannot be broken. It is my privilege to be his Mother. The memories we create every single day fill my heart with overwhelming joy. He is the music that makes me dance.

I love you Kenny.

A Standing Ovation Goes to...

❦❦❦

My Higher Power for creating the miracle of THE AWAKENING within my own heart and soul, and for giving me the opportunity to share it with the world. I am deeply humbled and forever grateful.

The amazing group of authors, experts, ministers, doctors, and teachers who generously gave of their time and brilliant wisdom to make this book a reality. Each of you opened my mind and touched my soul. I'm grateful and abundantly appreciative to share these pages with each of you:

Chellie Campbell	Dr. James Golden	Alex Mandossian
Dr. John Demartini	Mark Victor Hansen	Stephen Lewis
Hale Dwoskin	Scott Hunter	Marci Shimoff
Dr. Masaru Emoto	David Koons	Rev. Jim Turrell

All of the men and women who contributed their stories making this book more "real-world" by showing how you apply the principles in your lives everyday.

All of the men and women who have attended THE AWAKENING live seminars. Thank you for opening your minds and your hearts and sharing your stories with me. Your endless support and encouragement have meant the world to me throughout this process.

My publisher, David Hancock, who was immediately able to see my vision and make it a reality in record time. I am deeply grateful and indebted. And to the rest of the team at Morgan James who masterfully designed the cover, the layout, and the coordinated the process in light speed. I thank you deeply.

All of the additional editors who read, commented, proof-read, lovingly criticized, and supported this process. They include but are not limited to Rick Krebs, Khatia Krebs, Chuck May (spell-check Chuck!), Sue McCullough, Natalie Weiss, and Carol Mastro-Covington.

My personal Dream Team, which is an amazing group of unlimited women who I love and adore. We laugh together and cry together, through thick and thin, we're there to see each other through. I'm deeply honored and eternally grateful to each of you for the valuable gift of your friendship. You are truly treasures that I cherish every single day. My life is wonderful because it has been touched by each of you. You are all miracles in motion and the Law of Attraction in action:

Victoria Bailey, Lisa Cherney, Cloyd Cornish-Patton, Carol Mastro-Covington, Kathy Eversen, Kimiko Miyazawa, Sue McCullough, Peggy O'Kelley, Lori Palma, Lori Rae Jamieson, Khatia Krebs, Laura Lucian, Antoinette del Peral, Alexandra Teklak, Josie Weber, Natalie Weiss, Melissa Wilson, and MiChele Wilson.

Pete Nelson and his exceptional team at Everywhere Marketing, who worked with me in creating the concept for the book cover and an amazing website to support the book. I thank you all for your never ending creative genius. And I applaud you Pete for your constant guidance and direction and for seeing a picture for me that is bigger and better than I can sometimes see for myself.

To the numerous individuals who so lovingly cared for my dear son Kenny, allowing me the opportunity to focus and write with peace and joy: Art Ashley, Bonnie Philpott, Valerie and Vincent Mesa, Miles and Rita Jamieson, Carol and Winston Covington, Peggy O'Kelley, Lori Palma, and Phillip James. It takes a village and you make a difference. Kenny and I are both blessed to have you all.

Table of Contents

Biographies

The following experts, teachers, doctors, authors, and ministers have harnessed the power of the Law of Attraction. Their wisdom is found throughout the pages of this book.

Chellie Campbell created the popular Financial Stress Reduction Workshop and is the author of two books on the topics of making more money and having more time off for fun: *The Wealthy Spirit* and *Zero to Zillionaire*. She is a professional speaker, seminar leader, poker champion, and has been prominently quoted as a financial expert in *The Los Angeles Times*, *Pink*, *Good Housekeeping*, *Lifetime*, *Essence*, *Woman's World* and more than 15 popular books.

Dr. John Demartini is a world leader in inspirational speaking and an author at the forefront of the burgeoning personal and professional development industry. His scope of knowledge and experience is a culmination of 34 years of research and studies of more than 28,000 texts in over 200 disciplines ranging from psychology, philosophy, metaphysics, theology, neurology and physiology. Dr. Demartini was one of the featured teachers in the movie, *The Secret*. He is the author of over forty books. Some of his bestselling titles include *The Breakthrough Experience: A Revolutionary New Approach to Personal Transformation*, *Count Your Blessings*, and his latest, *Heart of Love*.

Hale Dwoskin is the author of the *New York Times* Best Seller, *The Sedona Method: Your Key to Lasting Happiness, Success, Peace and Emotional Well-being*. Hale was a featured in *The Secret*, and is an international speaker and featured faculty member at Esalen and the Omega Institute. He is the CEO and Director of Training of Sedona Training Associates, an organization headquartered in Sedona, Arizona. He co-founded the company in 1996 to teach courses based on the emotional releasing techniques originated by his mentor, Lester Levenson. For over a quarter century, he has regularly been teaching The Sedona Method to individuals and corporations throughout the United States and the United Kingdom. He is also the co-author, along with Lester Levenson, of *Happiness Is Free: And It's Easier than You Think* (a five-book series).

Dr. Masaru Emoto is the author of the best-selling books *Messages from Water, The Hidden Messages in Water,* and *The True Power of Water*. He is a long-time advocate for peace in relation to water. He is currently the head of the I.H.M. General Research Institute and President Emeritus of the International Water for Life Foundation, a non-profit organization. In 1992 he received certification as a Doctor of Alternative Medicine. He has gained worldwide acclaim through his groundbreaking research and discovery that water is deeply connected to our individual and collective consciousness. His work was featured in the movie, *What the Bleep Do We Know?*

Dr. James Golden served as a Religious Science minister for over twenty years and as President of Religious Science International, the governing body for the worldwide organization, for two years. He was awarded the organization's most prestigious honor, the Ernest Holmes Legacy Award. In 2003 Dr. Golden made the decision to step down from the ministry to follow his dream of offering seminars, retreats, and workshops to help attendees deepen their spirituality. He also serves as a personal mentor for dedicated spiritual students worldwide.

For more than 25 years, **Mark Victor Hansen** has focused solely on helping people and organizations, from all walks of life, reshape their personal visions of what's possible. Mark and his business partner Jack Canfield sold more than 100 million *Chicken Soup for the Soul* books in North America alone, and have over 100 licensed products in the marketplace. It is one of the most successful publishing franchises in America today. He is also a prolific writer with many popular books such as *The Power of Focus, The Aladdin Factor, Dare to Win* and others. His new book, co-authored with Robert G. Allen, is *The One Minute Millionaire: The Enlightened Way to Wealth*.

Scott Hunter, a successful business coach and speaker, has been transforming organizations for over two decades through keynote speeches, workshops, retreats, and management team coaching. Since 1985 he has helped hundreds of businesses, delivered over 1,000 speeches and worked with over 100,000 individuals. He created a 5-step system to deliver repeatable results and has been teaching that system for over 20 years. His book, *Making Work Work* has received successful reviews and garnered a following among executives, professionals, and students. He's been recognized as an "expert" on over 50 radio talk shows and has appeared on a number of television news programs.

David Koons is an internationally recognized Master of Results. With over 20 years of military, corporate, and entrepreneurial success in his arsenal, David delivers a powerful array of tips, tools and strategies to empower you to create permanent and lasting change. He is famous for saying: "You have a Millionaire Inside fighting to get out and the only person holding this Millionaire back is You!"

Stephen Lewis, founder of EMC² and Co-Author of the novel *Sanctuary: The Path To Consciousness* has been exploring energetic balancing for more than 25 years. His degrees include acupuncture and homeopathy, both of which are forms of energetic healing. Lewis's extensive studies and research led him directly to the insights upon which EMC²'s spiritual energetic balancing technology is based. Lewis's energetic balancing technology, called AIM, has been used by thousands of individuals worldwide and has earned the endorsements of Dr. Wayne Dyer, Dr. Michael Beckwith, author Kevin Trudeau, and many others.

Alex Mandossian has generated over $233 million in sales and profits for his clients and partners via "electronic marketing" media such as TV Infomercials, online catalogs, 24-hour recorded messages, voice/fax broadcasting, Teleseminars, Webinars, Podcasts, and Internet Marketing. Alex has personally consulted Dale Carnegie Training, NYU, 1ShoppingCart Corp., Mutuals.com, Pinnacle Care, Strategic Coach, Trim Spa and many others. He is the CEO of Heritage House Publishing, Inc. – a boutique electronic marketing and publishing company that "repurposes" written and spoken educational content for worldwide distribution. He is also the founder of the Electronic Marketing Institute.

Marci Shimoff is the woman's face behind the biggest self-help book phenomenon in history, *Chicken Soup for the Soul*. Marci has been on more than 500 national and regional television and radio shows. She is prominently featured in *The Secret*, and she is the author of *Happy for No Reason*. A celebrated transformational leader and one of the nation's leading motivational experts; Marci has inspired millions of people around the world sharing her breakthrough methods for personal fulfillment and professional success. President and co-founder of the Esteem Group, she delivers keynote addresses and seminars on self-esteem, self-empowerment, and peak performance to corporations, professional and non-profit organizations, and women's associations.

Rev. Jim Turrell is a musician, minister, businessman, and author. He is the Founder and Pastor of the Center for Spiritual Discovery in Costa Mesa, California. He also serves on the Board of Directors of Religious Science International and is a featured speaker at many of their national conferences. He is the author of three of books: *The Gospel of Cause and Effect, Socrates' Secret, Speaking from the Heart* and *The Secret According to Jesus*. The latter provides an entirely new approach to public speaking and composition.

Preface

I was introduced to the Law of Attraction in the early eighties when I attended the Rev. Terry Cole-Whittaker's Church of Religious Science in San Diego, CA. I embraced it and saw amazing changes take place in my life immediately. I began to expand my thinking and nurture my self-esteem. I searched for my gifts and talents in life, and was eventually able to find them. I went on a spiritual journey and felt plugged into a power greater than myself like never before.

I have used the Law of Attraction to both my delight, and unfortunately my demise. Somewhere along the path I abandoned the principles, and my life went downhill. I soon realized that my worst day when using the Law of Attraction in my favor was better than my best day without harnessing its positive power. So I decided to take the steps necessary to stay focused and create a permanent change.

I was raised by a mean, rageaholic Mother and quiet, loving Dad. How the two of them ever got together and stayed together for 48 years will forever be a mystery to me. I had two brothers who were 10 and 11 years older than me. My Mother was violent and beat me regularly. There were many occasions when I thought she was going to kill me because her beatings were so brutal.

She regularly told me the following:

- Your feelings don't matter, just do what I say.

- You're never going to amount to anything.

- Children are to be seen and not heard.

- You're lazy, stupid, and ugly.

On one occasion she was upset about the boy I was dating. She told me, "I have a gun in the trunk of this car, and if you ever see him again, I will kill you." Because of her bottomless well of anger and rage, I wouldn't have put it past her.

My brothers were not taught to treat me with respect, care, or kindness. When I was five years old, my brother Vaughn abused me on four or five occasions. Both of my brothers were allowed to boss me around senselessly and degrade me by calling me their slave.

As much as my Dad loved me, it couldn't make up for the anger and rage of my Mother. He never protected me or stood up for me enough to stop the numerous levels of abuse that my Mother and brother inflicted upon me.

As a result, I never felt truly safe or truly loved in my own home. When I say I had no self-esteem, I mean it. Low self-esteem would have been a plus for me then.

As a means of coping, I developed an eating disorder. I used food to numb the feelings of being unimportant to the people who were supposed to love me the most. My heart was broken, and I couldn't comprehend anyone ever loving me if my own Mother did not.

A pivotal moment came in 1980 when I attended my first meeting of Overeater's Anonymous. It was at that moment that I set foot on the path of self-discovery, and although I've taken a few detours, I've never wandered very far off that path.

Many of the steps I took are outlined for you clearly throughout this book. I took every one of them very seriously. I knew my life depended on it. I felt like a zero, and if I was ever going to have even a decent life, I knew I had to approach my plan for personal growth with total devotion and dedication. I have written volumes in journals over the years, as I found it the most significant step in leading me back to health and wholeness. I eventually learned to love myself enough to know that I deserved to live a wonderful life, no matter what my Mother told me.

Physical, emotional, and sexual abuse is rampant around the world. My story is a testimony to the fact that no matter what kind of abuse you've experienced, there is a way to integrate it into your life and thoroughly heal from it.

What I've learned is that whether you can relate to any of the experiences I had or not, success in life is all about personal growth and development. I could never be a success to the degree that I am today with the habits and attitudes I had back then. I continue to grow and dream new dreams. It's exciting to AWAKEN to all of the possibilities, and to know they'll become a reality.

It took many years, but I eventually forgave my Mother and my brother. Many years after that, as I continued to grow and deepen my spirituality, my forgiveness went even further to recognizing their total and complete innocence. I can't tell you the magic formula that led to me being able to achieve this, except that in the teachers I was following and the books I was reading I kept hearing about how important forgiveness was for me, and I simply decided to be open to it. I couldn't imagine it, but I never closed the door on it.

I believe forgiveness is key to using the Law of Attraction in our lives. However, going beyond that to recognizing the innocence of those we've previously resented is just icing on the cake. They were both gifts I gave myself as I became more enlightened and evolved.

I realized my life depended on me giving back the issues, that were never mine in the first place, to the people they belonged to. When my Mother told me I was worthless, I believed her. After all, she should know, she was my Mother.

I spent a lot of years blaming and it got me nowhere. Then I began to acknowledge who was responsible for what, and I asked myself, "What am I now going to do about it?" So the focus shifted from blaming to becoming. But it was only by acknowledging what happened that I could become the best me possible.

I learned that you are more than your past, you can change your future, and you're not a victim of your circumstance. No one is dealt a perfect set of cards in life. That's just a part of being human. However, what you do with the cards you're dealt makes all the difference. I had to acknowledge repeatedly, "That is what they did to me then, look what you're doing to yourself now! I couldn't do anything about it then, but I am certainly smart enough and capable enough to do something about it now! What will that be?"

As a result of my own personal transformation, I developed a passion to help others deeply transform their lives. Eventually I became a psychotherapist, and successfully guided hundreds of people through the darkness of their fears and insecurities into a better and brighter day. I find tremendous joy in sharing the intricacies and intimacies of life with those who are eager to create a bigger future for themselves and their families. To witness the totally vulnerable, gut-wrenching, as well as joyful moments of a soul awakening to its True Self is equal to watching a new life being born. It is a privilege I cherish like no other.

With the success of the movie and book, *The Secret*, people have a thirst for more knowledge and understanding of the Law of Attraction and how to use it successfully. This is one of the greatest gifts author Rhonda Byrne, and the teachers of *The Secret* could give us. However, many people have struggled with the principles and concepts presented in *The Secret* and with not being able to move forward as quickly as they hoped.

As a result I felt a strong calling to write *THE AWAKENING*. I was inspired to share the steps necessary to take people from where they are to where they want to go, even if they are just embarking upon their journey of personal growth and transformation.

Once I started writing *THE AWAKENING*, the flow of just the right people and situations unfolded before me. I knew that it was the culmination of years of aligning myself with the Universal principles of the Law of Attraction and believing with all my heart that my moment would arrive and that I would be able to seize it. Most of the time, I felt like I was so perfectly in the flow that it wasn't really my book, it was my Higher Power's.

But there were several real life moments where breakdown led to breakthrough. And I am very grateful for these because rarely is there ever a perfect path. But what we do with these imperfect circumstances is what makes all the difference. That's what makes it perfect.

In my psychotherapy practice I saw men and women who were destroyed by guilt, shame, self-doubt, resentments, and excuses, just like I was at one time. I closed my practice because I realized my love of being able to share my message with more people through public speaking. Those years were very important to me though, because what I had the opportunity to intimately experience is that we are all so alike. With little variation we feel virtually the same. If we're breathing, we have some issue to resolve and grow through. And I love that. You're not alone, and in one sense of the word as special and unique as you are, you aren't that different from everyone else.

None of us arrive…I don't care who you are, what you do, how much money you have or what kind of car you drive. The key is being committed to becoming the best you, you can be.

In spite of the odds against me, I gave it my all and I'm so grateful I did. I hope you will give it all you've got!

Introduction

"My father says almost the whole world is asleep. Everybody you know. Everybody you see. Everybody you talk to. He says that only a few people are awake and they live in a state of constant and total amazement." From the movie ~ *Joe Versus the Volcano*

Are you awake, or are you asleep? Do you live in a state of amazement or in a sleepy kind of fog? Are you living your life fully or just going through the motions day to day?

This book will guide you into the AWAKENING you long for and it will help you to accelerate your success and harness the power within you by using the Law of Attraction. Your eyes will be opened to all the things the Universe has in store for you. You will be connected to the Source of all life and divinely inspired to be who you were born to be and live the life you were created to live.

Who were you born to be? What is the kind of life you were created to live? Your current circumstances may cloud the true answer to this question.

What is the true answer and how do you discover it? The <u>true</u> answer is you were born to be awesome! You were born to express who you are and all your unique skills, talents, and abilities. You were born to succeed in all of the ways succeeding is important to you.

What is the life you were created to live? The <u>true</u> answer is that you were created to live an abundant life, rich with love, prosperity, freedom, and joy. You were created to live a life filled with confidence and the ability to soar! You were also created to do what you love to do with people you enjoy having around you.

That's not what you are experiencing now? I understand. It's very easy to get derailed along the way. You were born to be all of these things and to live a wonderful life, but at some point you veered away from the positive thinking and outlook on your life that came so easily when you were an innocent, carefree child.

Once the positive thoughts are replaced by negativity in all of its many forms, some kind of intervention is necessary to change your beliefs, thought processes, and that inner voice that tells you that you can't and reprogram it to "I CAN!"

Some of those interventions can be a book, tape, CD, DVD, seminar, or a special person you respect or love. That's precisely what this book is meant to do. It's meant to wake you up, trigger an AWAKENING in your life, reprogram your thinking, and to help you get back on the positive track so that you can stay there, attracting all the good you want and deserve.

When the AWAKENING occurs in your life, you'll know. Suddenly you'll see things around you that you'd never noticed before, and you'll feel truly ALIVE! You'll feel like the planets are all in alignment and the stars are spelling your name! You'll feel like all things are working together for your greatest good. That's what using the Law of Attraction is all about.

WHAT IS THE LAW OF ATTRACTION?

The Law of Attraction is the power you have right now to attract into your life what you think about, focus on, or put your time and energy toward, whether you consciously want it or not.

It attracts either positive things, experiences, and people to you, or negative things, experiences, and people. It attracts what you think about and focus on in your daily life.

Gratefully, author Rhonda Byrne, along with a number of authors, experts, and teachers, brought this powerful law to the forefront of our lives with her amazing DVD and book *The Secret*. She describes three steps to using the Law of Attraction, 1) Ask, 2) Believe, and 3) Receive.

While these are indeed key steps to successfully using the Law of Attraction, there are many obstacles that can prevent you from attracting all that you want in life. *THE AWAKENING* will show you how to overcome those obstacles.

The Law of Attraction is always working according to our beliefs, whether we are conscious of it or not. We all have experiences in our past that make it difficult for us to believe in our dreams. These past experiences often create the framework for Overriding Background Beliefs that do not allow us to create powerful results in our lives, and we don't have a clue they are holding us back. These beliefs get buried deep in our souls and quietly replay in our minds like a never-ending record forever sabotaging our success. But, there is help.

The human mind is amazing! It's the most incredible creation on the face of the earth. The powers of the mind surpass all the ways we're able to define it. It's actually quite incomprehensible how vast the human mind really is and how it can soak up and replay past experiences years later and use them to our glory or to our demise.

In addition to thinking, feeling, and deductive reasoning, men and women over the ages have come to realize one of the most significant abilities of the human mind is our ability to actually attract what we think about; to simply see something in our mind's eye and then create it in our reality. I know men and women throughout the ages were just as excited about this discovery as many of us are today. But before you can accomplish this, you must first reprogram your mind by putting all of *The Seven Steps to AWAKENING* into practice consistently and sustaining your focus on them over time. Your AWAKENING will occur when you apply these steps, shift your thoughts, and remove any obstacles.

Here's the best example: Imagine a beautiful Waterford crystal vase filled with the purest, clearest water possible. This vase represents you, me, and every human being alive at the time of birth. We are all born with the unlimited possibilities of love, freedom, abundance, and joy. The water represents your conscious and subconscious mind.

Now, imagine beside this beautiful crystal vase is a dirty old metal farm bucket filled with muddy, smelly water. This represents all of the negative words, situations, and events in your life that have taken place since you were conceived.

Imagine taking that dirty water and pouring one cupful into the beautiful clear water in the crystal vase. Now pour another cup in for every year of your life. It doesn't take long before that crystal clear water is completely muddy too!

This is the subconscious mind of most humans on the planet. You see it in the negativity, anger, resentment, and abuse that is rampant around the world.

Now enters another beautiful Waterford crystal pitcher filled with pure water, known as the powerful and amazing Law of Attraction. You pour this energizing water into the muddy water and it makes no difference whatsoever. You may be able to notice it at the point of entry, but seconds later there is no visible trace of it; the water is still muddy and smelly.

The key to using the Law of Attraction in your life is first being able to clear the muddy water so that you can indeed attract the things you want and live the life of your dreams.

That muddy water represents the obstacles that may be standing in your way. These obstacles literally push your good away from you faster than you can attract it, because no matter how much you believe in the Law of Attraction, you've dedicated more years to the development and grooming of these obstacles. They will override your current efforts and then you will feel that the Law of Attraction is ridiculous and give up on using it, which is a costly mistake.

You must quickly begin to eliminate these obstacles in order to create the life you truly deserve.

THE AWAKENING will guide you through *The Seven Steps to AWAKENING*, which are:

1.   Discover Your Deepest Desires

2.   Declare What You Desire

3. Believe It Is Yours Now

4. Raise Your Frequency

5. Eliminate Any Obstacles

6. Take Meaningful Action

7. Receive Your Good

While mastering the above seven steps, you can further increase your ability to attract what you desire by using *The Five Keys to Accelerate Your Power of Attraction*, which are:

1. Renew Your Beliefs

2. Expand Your Thoughts

3. Deepen Your Spirituality

4. Face Your Fears

5. Nurture Your Self-Esteem

When you dedicate the time and energy necessary to grow and develop in each of these areas you will create a whole new life, one that you love to live!

The Law of Attraction is an amazing phenomenon. It's true! If you want more money, a better body, a loving relationship, a bigger house, or a boat or car, you can have it! However, to have it all in this lifetime you must consistently focus on *The Seven Steps to AWAKENING.*

Research has shown that less than 3% of the population has clearly-defined, written goals that include a deadline for their attainment. *What does that tell you?* Most people will not take the time to sit down and write a plan for their lives that will help them fulfill their hopes and dreams. Most people will not really put forth the effort to do what it takes and stay focused on success for as long as it may take for the Law of Attraction to be activated in their lives.

To activate the Law of Attraction, most people need to experience a shift in their consciousness. Constantly bringing their past into the present dilutes their ability to create powerful results today.

THE AWAKENING is about shifting your power from your past to your present and your future. As a small child, you didn't dwell on the past. You weren't plagued with thoughts of guilt, regret, or envy. You focused on what you could achieve instead of what you couldn't. To AWAKEN you need to take the time in the present to have a mental detox, experience a rebirth of your psyche, and get rid of all the residue from your past so that you can then create a powerful new future.

Instead of living in the past, this process puts you in charge of your life, and therefore your future! It puts you in the driver's seat. You won't be controlled or reacting to the people or situations of the past that may be driving you now. This process will give you a power surge like you never believed was possible. You will take action. You will become the author of the book of your life; you will become the star of your play. You will be in the flow and creating miracles around you like magic!

You will then be one of the few people who are awake and living in a state of constant and total amazement. You will see the full spectrum of your potential and know precisely how you can actualize it.

That is THE AWAKENING!

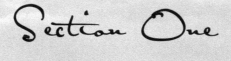

Section One

Although the Law of Attraction has been and always will be in existence, there is much confusion about what it really is and is not. In order to use it to your maximum benefit, it's critical that you know how to master every nuance of it.

In Section One we'll discuss what the Law of Attraction is and ten specific things the Law of Attraction is not. This will eliminate some of the popular misconceptions about using the law and creating powerful results. When someone gets stuck on a specific area of the Law of Attraction and fails to use the rest, his or her results will be minimal.

For example, when many people hear the words "Law of Attraction," they think it's simply positive thinking. They believe if they master positive thinking, they're experts at using the Law of Attraction and their good should be flowing to them rapidly.

However, there is so much more to using the Law of Attraction than just positive thinking. In Section One you'll find out more.

In Chapter One we'll look at what the Law of Attraction is and in Chapter Two we'll look at what it's not.

CHAPTER 1

The Law of Attraction and You

"It is the law that determines the complete order of the Universe, every moment of your life, and every single thing you experience in your life. It doesn't matter who you are or where you are, the Law of Attraction is forming your entire life experience, and this all-powerful law is doing that through your thoughts." —Rhonda Byrne, *The Secret*

You are magnificent. The ability you have to define and direct your life is remarkable. If you're living a different life than the one you want to live right now, you can change it. If you're experiencing lack or limitation in your life in any way, instead of focusing on the lack, focus on the way you want your life to be, and that's what you'll attract. If you want to have more money, a more loving and enriching relationship, better health, to lose weight, to have more fun, to improve your grades, to start your own business, or to get a promotion, you can!

The ability you have to define and direct your life is remarkable.

By tapping into the Law of Attraction, you can change your life for the better, forever. It's not like a diet where you lose weight and gain it back. If you keep your focus on the positive and follow *The Seven Steps to AWAKENING*, you will stay on a continuous path of positive attraction.

THE SEVEN STEPS TO AWAKENING

Right this moment there is a miracle waiting for you. All you have to do is step out and claim it. The miracle is your AWAKENING; your opportunity to command the forces of the Universe to operate in your favor.

I am committed to ensuring that you experience your AWAKENING and create the life of your dreams. Unfortunately, most people only tap into less than five percent of their minds, the conscious part. It's like the tip of the iceberg. The vast remaining ninety-five percent of your mind is not only below the surface, or subconscious, but because it's below the surface, most people never stop to really take a good, long, honest look at it.

In that remaining ninety-five percent lies power beyond measure for you to act with conviction, confidence that nothing can stop, intelligence enough to solve your greatest challenges on a moment's notice, unconditional love enough to heal the world and certainly any injustice you've ever experienced, and an abundance of joy that wants to scream from the mountain tops. All of this is within you, yes YOU, right now.

The Seven Steps to AWAKENING, along with *The Five Keys to Accelerate Your Power of Attraction*, are your secrets to tap into the deep well of potential you possess right now to turn your dreams into reality.

Some people go through their entire lives never living up to their full potential because they're only using five percent of their minds. That's the equivalent of purchasing one of today's sophisticated computers, preloaded with advanced applications for accounting, photo and movie editing, word processing, et. al., and then only using it to play Pac-Man.

Imagine what you'll be able to do as you AWAKEN and begin gaining access to the enormous resources of the hidden ninety-five percent of your mind! Imagine the life you will be able to create!

Here are *The Seven Steps to AWAKENING* that will take you on this wonderful journey:

1. Discover Your Deepest Desires

2. Declare What You Desire

3. Believe It's Yours Now

4. Raise Your Frequency

5. Eliminate Any Obstacles

6. Take Meaningful Action

7. Receive Your Good

Your Awakening begins when you take the first three steps and apply them to any goal or desire. But after that, you may perform the rest of the steps simultaneously, without limiting them to their order. You won't focus on Raising Your Frequency once; you'll do it repeatedly. You won't Eliminate Any Obstacle once, and be done with that; you'll keep coming back to eliminate other obstacles that may have crept up.

THE FIVE KEYS TO ACCELERATE YOUR POWER OF ATTRACTION

When you practice using *The Seven Steps to AWAKENING* daily, in partnership with *The Five Keys to Accelerate Your Power of Attraction*, your life will soar! You'll definitely see results by simply focusing on *The Seven Steps to AWAKENING*, but if you want to turbo charge your results, add *The Five Keys to Accelerate Your Power of Attraction* and you'll see amazing miracles happening in your life all the time. Here are those powerful keys:

1. Renew Your Beliefs

2. Expand Your Thoughts

3. Deepen Your Spirituality

4. Face Your Fears

5. Nurture Your Self-Esteem

When you put all of these principles into action consistently you will create the amazing results you long for.

Remember, the Law of Attraction is always at work, whether positive or negative, you attract what you think about and focus on. So why not harness the power of your mind and start attracting all that is good in life. When you do, your future will be so bright you will need to wear shades 24/7!

THE POWER BEHIND THE LAW OF ATTRACTION

Since the beginning of known time, most people have honored and respected something that they believed to be outside of themselves. For others, the belief was that this something, this Higher Power, resided within their being.

Every religion, indigenous tribe, and culture has had an awareness of a power greater than itself. This power has been called: God, Higher Power, Spirit, Universe, Universal Energy, The Divine, Infinite Power, and other sacred names.

Positive thinking alone will not bring you your desired results if while you state positive words aloud, your thoughts are negating everything you say.

It doesn't matter what term you choose to use, for they're all productive. If you have an affinity for a particular tradition such as Christian, Muslim, Jewish, or any other, use the approach that's comfortable for you. If traditions don't work for you, chart your own course. You're in charge here!

Positive thinking alone will not bring you your desired results if while you state positive words aloud, your thoughts are negating everything you say. You must learn to believe within the core of your being that you deserve what you desire. A significant part of this "believing" comes through knowing beyond a shadow of a doubt that this Higher Power wants to bring you your highest good and bring it to you fast!

Throughout this book you'll be given more information on <u>how</u> to build and strengthen your belief, not <u>what</u> to believe.

It's necessary to understand that this Higher Power may know more than you do about what's best for you. Perhaps the "specific person" you're attempting to attract into your life would not turn out to be for your highest good. Therefore, simply declaring that the "perfect mate" is on his/her way to you now might be more effective. You want to name it and claim it, not try to figure it all out. That's the task of our Higher Power.

Our responsibility is to declare our deepest desires with emotion and energy and allow this Higher Power to bring it to us in the most direct manner. We don't need to attempt to control this Higher Power – only to engage it. Thought truly does become form when we understand and utilize the Law of Attraction.

The energy that you bring forth during this process is what allows your focused thought to become reality.

When you remove the obstacles that are presented in this book, you'll find that your connection to this Higher Power is a natural evolution. This is because you're a spiritual being, having a physical experience. When we remember this, we open the door to the Divine Presence of this Higher Power. When life becomes difficult to bear, our task is to remain focused on this Higher Power and to keep our current connection strong.

We can continue to bring this awareness to a level of belief by accepting through faith that the Law of Attraction will manifest the qualities and things that we want in our daily lives. All things are possible with a strong belief in a Higher Power.

A final word: don't get caught up in what you call it or who or what it is. Just slowly begin to entertain the idea that there is something greater than you out there, and that something is there to help you AWAKEN to a new life of love, power, freedom, and joy!

THE SEEDS OF ATTRACTION

How fast does the Law of Attraction work? It works as soon as you start consistently applying ALL of the principles in this book. When you believe without a shadow of a doubt that your dreams are yours now, you become a powerful magnet, attracting your good to you with amazing speed.

I like to use the example of planting seeds of attraction. First, you find some really great, fertile soil, not sand or gravel. What kind of seed do you plant? Is it the seed of poison ivy or of a beautiful flower? Whatever seed you place in the soil is what kind of plant you'll get. Plant the seed a few inches into the soil and it sits there in the darkness and begins to germinate. You can't see it sprouting and growing, but it is. If you water it regularly and give it plenty of sunshine it will continue to grow!

But wait, it's been a week, a month, or a maybe even a few months and you haven't seen a tiny green shoot bursting through the soil to show you it's growing.

You may get discouraged and forget about it. You may neglect to water it regularly. After waiting for a while it still doesn't grow and pretty soon you say, "Forget it!" and stop watering it entirely because you've given up all hope of ever seeing your beautiful blossom.

Or, in some cases you may let the weeds grow up around it and choke the life right out of your seedling before it has had the chance to take root and grow.

Just like a seed growing in the ground, The Law of Attraction has to be planted into a mind that is positive and open to growing and changing. The seeds of attraction have to be watered by using positive affirmations and other techniques that help you to believe and stay focused on your goal.

And most of all, have patience. Because just like a seed, you are germinating! Before your goals and dreams become a reality, they're moving towards you with momentum, you just can't see them yet. During this time keep remembering, "I am germinating!" and keep the faith. Don't give up!

Sustain the daily focus you need to manifest your dreams. Not just once in a while when you remember, but multiple times every single day.

THE ORDER FULFILLMENT WAREHOUSE

As you get in the flow and stay focused, you'll begin manifesting your dreams. Manifesting is what happens when what you know becomes real in your life. The minute you begin to focus on it and believe in it, the Universe puts all things in motion to bring you your good.

When you declare your request, it's received by the "Order Fulfillment Warehouse" and all the little men begin to pull everything together to fulfill your order.

But be careful not to send in an opposing order! Don't think, "This is what I want, but I don't really deserve it." Oops! The little men in the "Order Fulfillment Warehouse" will start putting back all the things you first requested.

...have patience because, just like a seed, you are germinating!

Get in alignment with your good and stay there. Be diligent in keeping your focus and staying in the positive flow.

It's such an exciting experience to manifest something out of nothing. For this reason, I'm grateful for even some of the worst hardships I've experienced. When I see how the Law of Attraction has worked in my life, I get such a kick out of it! I love it.

I'm eager for you to know this joy as well. You are the magnificent creator of your life. When you begin manifesting miracle after miracle, you'll see the power that you and the Universe have together and you'll begin manifesting greater and greater things in your life and in the world.

WHEN NEGATIVITY MOVES IN

Life goes on while you're learning to use the Law of Attraction, yes it does. Everything won't turn up roses by tomorrow. Stand firm on the fact that it will turn up roses, but there may be a few thorns along the way.

When it seems as though you're in the middle of a living hell, remember, DON'T SET UP RES-IDENCE THERE! Your old habit may be to move right in and start telling your story of negativity to numerous friends and relatives; to just sit right down and have a "pity party" where others can pour on the sympathy for you.

But I recommend that you treat this negative situation like a fire in the middle of your house! You can throw fuel on the fire and burn your whole house down, or you can throw a wet towel on it and put out the fire.

A significant key to your success in using the Law of Attraction is to learn how to put a governor on your negative emotions. You want to learn how to decelerate your negative emotions, not accelerate them.

You can do this by stair-stepping your emotions from a lower vibration up to a higher vibration. For example, in the past you may have been quick to anger. Learn to minimize this costly emotion. If in the past you would have felt devastated by a situation, learn to minimize these emotions to being simply frustrated. In time you will be able to stair-step your emotions up to a higher level and feel a greater sense of peace and joy.

Look at the negative situation and think: "This is so underwhelming. I'm so much bigger than this little problem. HA! I'm not about to let that get me down. I'm going to play at the top of my game, no matter what!" And to get a visual working for you, imagine it as a bug on your finger and flick it right off! "Be gone! You have no power here!"

TEARS AND FEARS

You can probably look back at your life and see times when you were in the flow of attracting good into your life and loved it. It was exciting and fun to be on the receiving end of so much good. You may have called it synchronicity, karma, luck, or coincidence. Whatever you called it, you want-ed it to continue.

Then something possibly happened to take your energy off of the positive powerful direction your life was going. It could have been something discouraging someone said, a negative current event that you spent a lot of time focusing on, or possibly not getting something you really wanted. But something happened that took you down a different path where you began attracting more sit-uations and things into your life that you didn't want.

I can recall a very negative time in my life shortly after 9/11. It seemed like the whole world was marinating in negativity and fear, and I joined right in with the rest of them. I was in the middle of a very difficult divorce with an infant and was in emotional turmoil on a daily basis. I was not using the tools that I normally would to stay on the right track.

Then the big blow came. I had just received one of the largest checks ever for work I had done to the tune of $20,000. I had deposited it in my bank account and paid my bills. Approximately 10 days later, I went to my mailbox and received five bounced check notices. Alarmed, I called the bank immediately, and they informed me that my account had been levied and there was no money in my bank account at all, zero, zip, nada! My money had been taken by a creditor that came after me because I was the sole signer on a document for a piece of equipment for my ex-husband's business. I began to cry buckets of tears. I had about $110 in my wallet at the time and that was all the money I had to my name. I had visions of living on the street with a baby, and I took a nose-dive into a mental state of toxic negativity.

The next day I had to go to the county courthouse to file some papers regarding the levy. On the way into the courthouse I broke the heel of my high-heeled pump, leaving me to limp around the courthouse oddly. I was terribly aggravated by it. It was not a pleasant experience locating all that I needed there and by the time I left I was miserable, angry, resentful, and depressed.

When I returned home and entered my bedroom I was aghast! There was an unbelievable site. My jaw drops even to imagine it now. There was a three inch wide band of ants traveling horizontally around my room about four feet from the floor across two long walls.

Occasionally, there would be a few ants in the kitchen, based on what crumbs and food was left laying around for them to feast on. But there had never been ants in my bedroom! The line of ants was so thick and black that it almost looked like a perfectly straight line had been painted on my bedroom wall.

I realized immediately that I was creating a huge negative mess in my life and had to get back on the path and begin attracting my good again, otherwise what would be next? I eventually got my positive focus back, but it took quite some time to clear out all of the negative emotion – and all of the ants!

How did I get my positive focus back? I practiced steps 4, 5 and 6, which you will learn more about in their respective chapters. I focused on raising my frequency, eliminating any obstacles, and taking meaningful action. I also expanded my thoughts by using affirmations religiously and writing in my journal daily. I deepened my spirituality by focusing on gratitude, especially when it didn't appear there was a lot for me to be grateful for. I had gotten myself into quite a negative spiral, so I had to practice these steps without fail before I saw the changes that turned my life around.

OUR GOOD ISN'T ALWAYS WHAT <u>WE</u> THINK IT IS

There will be times when all that you want does not show up on your doorstep, nor is it presented to you on a silver platter. You'll wonder: "What went wrong?"

On the other hand, sometimes it will seem as if it dropped right down from heaven into your lap, and that is such an exciting moment!

David Koons, an internationally recognized Master of Results with over 20 years of military, corporate, and entrepreneurial success has an excellent philosophy on this:

"A lot of times people will say, 'I didn't get what I wanted. It didn't go the way I planned.' My response? I say, 'Thank God it didn't go the way you planned.' Sometimes good things don't happen to allow great things to occur. For example, think of past relationships when they ended that you might have cried over. Now, looking back, you're grateful that they're gone."

What is your greatest good is not always what you think it is. You might think you blew it, you're off track, or that you're not quite awake yet, but that isn't necessarily true. When you can't figure out what's going on, don't give up!

Here's a story about two dear friends of mine that testifies to the fact that your good isn't always what you think it is:

Sometimes good things don't happen to allow great things to occur.

My friend Lisa's husband, Greg, closed his chiropractic office after being in business for less than two years. She had been the sole bread winner throughout the four years he was in chiropractic college.

Now let's just pause for a moment here. Imagine your husband/wife quits a great job and decides he/she wants to go to school to be a doctor. You say, "Great honey, that's a wonderful goal. I'll support you all the way. I love you. The four years will go by fast, and we'll be all the happier and more successful down the line." You work hard, support him/her while they study endless hours and lower your standard of living dramatically to make ends meet. And then when it's all done and the ink is barely dry on the diploma on the wall, he/she says, "This isn't what I expected it to be and I don't want to do it if I can't care for patients in the way I know is best for them." This occurred after all of the major expenses involved in chiropractic college, and setting up an office.

I was absolutely amazed at the sense of peace and calm Lisa had when she told me about this situation. She didn't judge her husband, complain about him, change her tone of voice an inkling, or give any clue that this wasn't business as usual. She was in total and complete acceptance over the situation. While my jaw dropped open, she was as happy and calm as she could be.

Three months after Greg quit his job to go to chiropractic college, Lisa was laid off and started her own marketing consulting business, Conscious Marketing. She was able to build a successful business under some of the most stressful situations imaginable.

When I asked Lisa how she was able to maintain such acceptance, here's what she had to say:

"I had faith in God's plan. If my husband felt an overwhelming desire to close his doors, then that must be his path. Logic, and my ego, might say he gave up too soon; he needed to have thicker skin, or just try harder. However, my heart, my higher-self, just wanted him to be happy and I was willing to stay centered in my faith and watch how things were going to unfold.

It wasn't always easy. I wanted to focus on changing him, but in the end maintaining my connection to the Source is what made me feel peaceful. As long as I focused on my self-care, I knew everything was going to be okay and that he would take care of what he needed to do.

When I fast-forward a short one year later, I can see how God's plan was abundantly clear. Greg wound up getting a great job back in his old industry. We decided we were ready to start a family. I got pregnant immediately and the health insurance we had fully covered the cost of our daughter Bella's birth.

After only a few months on the job, Greg realized that his heart remained with the chiropractic field. He had a newfound conviction and inner strength and he was ready to go back. Within a few weeks of this awareness, the company closed their Southern California location and they gave him not one, or two, but six months of severance pay. That six months of severance pay allowed him to open a new practice with a substantial safety net.

I'm glad I didn't waste a lot of time worrying or complaining about this situation, because in the end, there was nothing to worry or complain about! In the end it was all good. Just goes to show you it's not always what you think it is."

So, if things don't go as you expected, remember something better is usually on the way. The more deeply you accept this, the faster your good will come to you.

OWN YOUR POWER

Right now, in this very moment, no matter what the current conditions of your life are, you have a tremendous amount of power. Power is your ability to act. To use the Law of Attraction means that you must own your power. To own your power means that you have a choice in how you direct your power, including what you think and how you act. Stand firm in your ability to use your power to make your life better for yourself and those you love. If the conditions of your life aren't what you want them to be, it points to the fact that you possibly don't own your power.

If you do not own your power, who does?

If you do not own your power, who does? To receive the maximum benefits of using the Law of Attraction, you need to get in touch with your dreams, own your power and make them a reality.

You'll experience THE AWAKENING in many areas of your life at different times. One of the first awakenings I experienced was in my early 20s. My mother was a very controlling and domineering woman. It seemed like she had it in for me at a very early age, and that she wanted to destroy anything positive I felt, had, or experienced.

She had ideas about how I should live my life and I disagreed, but I was terribly afraid of her. She was mean, angry, and at times, quite violent. I felt like I had to please her in order to get the slightest amount of love or approval. I had totally given her my power.

Then one day it happened. It was one of the most brilliant realizations of my life. I realized that if I ignored my dreams and desires and lived my life the way my Mother wanted me to and I didn't like it, I would hate myself and my life. I would feel like I sold out, like I settled, and I couldn't live with that.

On the other hand, I realized that if I lived my life the way I wanted to and didn't like it, I could live with it. I would know that I had done the best I could do, that I had given it my all and I followed my heart. And that is exactly what I chose to do.

Get in the flow and own YOUR power today!

My Mother insisted that I become a secretary. I didn't want to become a secretary. I have tremendous respect for secretaries and I was a secretary every summer through high school and college. I enjoyed it and I was quite good at it. But I didn't want to do that for the rest of my life.

Anytime anyone went against my Mother they experienced a lot of wrath, so it wasn't an easy thing to do. But I knew it was my life and I had to live it. I didn't want to live a life filled with regrets because I let her tell me what to do and who to be.

The Law of Attraction won't work for your highest good if you're following someone else's dream for your life! Don't let others decide what's right for you. The truth is they don't really know what you should do with your life. They know what they want you to do. But they don't know what your deepest desire for your life is. Follow your heart, and it will lead you to your bliss. Follow someone else's advice for your life when it doesn't really fit for you, and it will lead you straight to misery and a lot of sessions in your therapist's office.

As I look back now, I realize I would be cheating the world of the real Alicia had I followed my mother's commands. I would be unhappy and unfulfilled and you wouldn't be reading this book right now. I would be in Oklahoma making coffee and taking minutes for some very important board meetings. That wouldn't be me owning my power. That would be me giving my Mother all MY power. I wouldn't have had the freedom to make my own choices or had the opportunity to build the life of my dreams.

Instead, I decided to take my power back and follow my heart and I've never looked back or regretted it for a moment. I live a glorious life of love, power, freedom and joy. I like the woman I am today and I have no regrets.

Get in the flow and own your power today!

Using the Law of Attraction is one of your best advantages to creating a great life. Before I define *The Seven Steps to AWAKENING* to help you maximize this powerful law, it is important to know exactly what the Law of Attraction is not. That is the topic in Chapter Two.

CHAPTER 2

What the Law of Attraction Is Not

"Desire is the starting point of all achievement, not a hope, not a wish, but a keen pulsating desire which transcends everything."

—Napoleon Hill

As we go forward through *THE AWAKENING*, we'll examine all of the many amazing aspects of the Law of Attraction. It's there for you to use at will. You don't need to get anyone's permission or approval to begin using the Law of Attraction now.

Since many are not familiar with the law, I want to touch briefly on some of the ways that people are confused in regards to the Law of Attraction, and how it works in your life. Once you understand these key points, you'll be better able to understand exactly what the Law of Attraction is.

1. IT'S NOT JUST POSITIVE THINKING

Many people think that positive thinking is the basis of the Law of Attraction, and they're <u>way</u> off track. Certainly, positive thinking is one of the basic fundamentals of the Law of Attraction, but at the same time there is so much more! We'll be discussing the other key elements throughout the book.

Marci Shimoff is the woman's face behind the biggest self-help book phenomenon in history, *Chicken Soup for the Soul,* and is prominently featured in the film, *The Secret.* Her comments on this topic say it very well:

> "The Law of Attraction is not just positive thinking. It goes far beyond that. It's when you have a deep knowingness inside, not just a thought that what it is you're wanting is going to happen, and that energy propels your intention forward."

In this comment, she's addressing the fact that you can think positively all day long, but unless you develop the ability to believe, without a shadow of a doubt, that your desires are yours now in spirit, you won't ever see them in reality.

The Law of Attraction is much more than positive thinking. Those who have mastered it have connected to a deep level of spirituality in one way or another. Alex Mandossian, generator of over $233 million in sales and profits for his clients and partners via "electronic marketing" media such as TV Infomercials, online catalogs, 24-hour recorded messages, voice/fax broadcasting, Teleseminars, Webinars, Podcasts, and Internet Marketing, said succinctly:

"The Law of Attraction is where science and spirituality meet."

When you connect the two, you'll have the power to move mountains and enjoy the journey along the way.

A commitment to positive thinking will definitely put your life on a higher level immediately. But, if you don't focus on both the scientific and spiritual aspects of the Law of Attraction, you'll create random, haphazard results.

Simply having positive thoughts and doing little else is not going to create what you desire. You need to take action.

2. IT'S NOT MAGIC

The Law of Attraction isn't like wishing upon a star. It's not magic. When you're in the flow, however, and have removed many of the internal obstacles we all face, let me assure you, it will feel like magic. Your good will line up at your front door and come to you so fast that you and everyone around you will wonder where it was hiding! So trust me, it will be worth all of the time it takes for you to thoroughly do all of the exercises presented throughout this book to get those obstacles out of your way.

But, it's not magic. Rigorous honesty, consistent effort, and a powerful focus are all required to attract your good to you.

3. IT DOES NOT REPLACE TAKING ACTION

Believing in the Law of Attraction doesn't replace taking action. Many people don't have what they want (even though they believe in a Higher Power and in the Law of Attraction), simply because they DO NOTHING! Yes, the universe is ready to give you what you want, but you have to get up and go get it! You have to do what it takes to achieve your goals and dreams.

Every person I interviewed for this book underscored the importance of action in one way or another. Hale Dwoskin, the author of the *New York Times* Best Seller, *The Sedona Method: Your Key to Lasting Happiness, Success, Peace and Emotional Well-being,* and teacher from *The Secret,* didn't mince words at all when I spoke to him about the significance of action:

"Simply having positive thoughts and doing little else is not going to create what you desire. You need to get into action. Get off your butt and go do the things that are in the direction of achieving your goals. Getting into action keeps the energy flowing. It also helps bring up whatever inner obstacles you have toward creating what you choose. As you let them go into action, you're naturally and intuitively guided to what's right for you."

David Koons hit the nail on the head by identifying what most people do:

"I say, 'consistently take action,' and I should put an asterisk by action and add 'right action.' When you consistently take 'right action' it starts snowballing, and you gain momentum. That doesn't happen when you inconsistently take action. You know the starters and stoppers. They start and then take a couple of days off."

You still have to follow all of the "old school" rules and set goals, make plans, and take action. But, when you do these under the umbrella of the Law of Attraction, the results flow and the process is exciting. If you create a compelling desire, believe it without a doubt, raise your vibration, and do all of these consistently – not like the starters and stoppers – you'll see results. Each of these will be discussed at length in upcoming chapters.

4. IT'S NOT A GIMMICK

There are many people who say that the Law of Attraction is just the latest self-help gimmick, like eating soy or low-carbs used to be in the health industry. They believe it's just another way to capitalize on people looking for some "feel good" way to approach life.

Rev. Jim Turrell is a musician, minister, businessman, and author. He started his studies of the Science of Mind® in 1972, and is the author of four books: *The Gospel of Cause and Effect, Socrates' Secret, Speaking from the Heart* and *The Secret According to Jesus*. He touched on the kind of people who discard the Law of Attraction when he said:

"Most people who don't believe in the Law of Attraction, the ones who are the naysayers about it, have said that it's a gimmick. Most of those people are tied into the world in a very empir- ical way, which means they only believe what they can hear, see, taste, touch, and smell."

Using the Law of Attraction creates powerful results in people's lives. You'll read many stories throughout this book where people have turned their lives around by using it. But no, there is no stamp of certification the Universe places on a person or situation to indicate it did its work right there on that particular day.

I'm also aware that there is an element of fear involved in this process. What if Hank believes the Law of Attraction, starts talking to all of his friends about it, and then he's in a car accident? He has to ask himself, "How did 'I' create that?" He didn't have anything to do with why that happened. It wasn't "his" fault. A high level of honesty and personal responsibility is required that most people are either incapable of, or unwilling to face. It's easier to just put it down and say that the Law of Attraction is just the latest gimmick.

5. IT'S NOT A CRUTCH

Many people who are afraid to get on board and use the Law of Attraction to their greatest benefit say that it's just a crutch. They're the kind of people who will say, "Anything that makes your life better is a crutch." I've heard people say that going to church is a crutch, listening to motivational tapes is a crutch, believing in God is a crutch, and so on.

Literally, a crutch is something you use when you have an injury to your foot, ankle, or knee, which are all parts of your body that will not heal if you continue to walk on them without assistance. When you use the crutch, the injured area has the opportunity to heal, and then you no longer need the crutch.

This example shows that a crutch is something you use for the short-haul. When you use the Law of Attraction to your maximum ability, it will become a significant part of your life, and a very exciting one. It's not something you'll use to get your life together and then forget about it. At least I hope you don't, because if you're not directing the Law of Attraction where it works in your favor, then it can also work against you.

6. IT'S NOT ALWAYS FAST

Yes, the Universe loves speed and won't hold you back in the slightest way once you're in the flow!

The Universe wants to bring you your good— yesterday!

There are several reasons that manifesting your good isn't as fast as you would like it to be.

You have to decide exactly what it is you want, and that isn't an easy task for most people. You also have to declare it in a manner that the Universe takes notice. You can't decide and write it down on a Post-It note and never look at it again. You must believe, without a shadow of doubt, that what you want is already yours. You need to raise your own personal frequency so that you're vibrating at a higher level. You need to remove any internal obstacles, such as Overriding Background Beliefs. You need to take consistent and meaningful action. You also need to get in the flow of receiving.

None of these are easy. They're simple and anyone can do them, no matter what their current circumstances may be. But, depending on where you are in your own process of AWAKENING, it may take longer than you thought it would.

If you've never stopped to take an honest look within yourself or done any soul-searching, it may take you longer to get into the flow, but don't dally. Be like a sponge and attend, read, listen, or watch anything and everything you can that will help you to develop a deeper sense of awareness of yourself and your connection to the Universe or God (of your own understanding).

Possibly more significant than any of the above is the fact that you don't always know what's in your best interest. In the grand scheme of life, what you want may not be the best thing for you to actually get. This is why it's so great that there is a time delay.

Trust that the Universe wants you to be happy and to live the life of your dreams every day! You do your part and The Law of Attraction will do its part.

7. IT'S NOT ALWAYS EASY

Most of us are "easy addicts." If it's not easy, we don't want to do it. Our culture has gone overboard in trying to make everything fast and easy. Daily, we're seduced by fast and easy. You see claims all the time that say, "Try this weight loss method, it's easy," "Try this strategy to earn money, it's easy." The same claim is repeated for many other things as well. The truth is that anything worth having is worth the effort it takes to get it. It's not always easy.

Most everything we really want, but don't already have, is outside our comfort zone.

While it takes effort, it's definitely not struggle and misery. If you're in misery, you're off track and you're not in alignment with your highest good. Marci Shimoff describes this as a "redirect":

> "The people who are the happiest and most able to use the Law of Attraction are those who see potential struggle as an opportunity. If something "bad" happens it's only to redirect them; it's to point them in a different direction, to show them a lesson they need to learn."

As wonderful and important as redirects are, they're not always easy. We can't always see the big picture to know what's going on in the grand scheme of things.

With practice, using the Law of Attraction will become easy. You'll get in the flow and feel like you're in heaven. It's like learning any new skill or habit. It takes focused effort at first, and then it will become as natural as breathing. One thing I know for certain:

8. IT'S NOT ALWAYS COMFORTABLE

Putting the Law of Attraction into action isn't always comfortable. For a while, the actions you need to take may feel very awkward. That's because they're outside your current comfort zone.

When we constantly seek comfort we do ourselves a disservice, because most everything we really want, but don't already have, is outside our comfort zone.

How big is your comfort zone? To achieve all that you want you'll need to expand your comfort zone and learn how to be comfortable doing what isn't comfortable for you right now. While comfort is wonderful, our comfort zones keep us stuck. You'll never meet a successful person who said their path was a smooth ride, perfectly plotted from point A to B, and comfortable every step of the way! No! You'll hear about the sacrifices they made and the many ways they had to expand their comfort zone to overcome the fears that crop up to hold them back.

Rev. Jim Turrell addressed this so poignantly:

"Of course, expanding beyond your current comfort zone means that you're eventually going to wind up in the scariest place ever, which is the unknown where you have no references. You have no reference points that you can look back upon to figure out where you are. But, that's when you're at the ultimate place of growth. If you can get comfortable with the unknown, then the sky's the limit. You can accomplish anything you want, and you can accomplish it very quickly."

If you keep doing what you're doing, you're going to keep getting what you're getting.

There are forces within us that keep us in our comfort zones at all cost. To consider moving into the unknown is unspeakable. David Koons talked about one inner drive we must all address:

"We all have this visitor called 'the ego.' The ego is part subconscious mind, part conscious mind. Its sole mission is to keep you safe. The important thing to understand is that safe to the ego means nothing changes – nothing. That means not an increase in your finances, not a decrease in your finances, not an increase in your health, not a decrease in your health – nothing changes."

If you want to make changes in your life, you'll need to step outside your current comfort zone, because as the saying goes, "If you keep doing what you're doing, you're going to keep getting what you're getting."

When you get out of your current comfort zone, it expands. You create a larger comfort zone.

9. IT'S NOT ABOUT BEING MATERIALISTIC

Many people have heard about the Law of Attraction and their ears quickly perk up. What gets their attention is all of the things people can attract to them using the law. This is very true, and it's a wonderful benefit of using the Law of Attraction.

Although this is a wonderful benefit, the Law of Attraction isn't about being materialistic, trying to get as much as you can, and never giving anything back. A generous spirit of giving puts you in the flow faster than anything else can.

What you'll find is the more you deepen your spirituality (as described in Chapter 12), the more material things you'll attract, but the less it will really matter to you!

Dr. James Golden served as a Religious Science minister for over twenty years. In 2000 he was awarded RSI's first presentation of its most prestigious honor, the Ernest Holmes legacy award. He elaborated on the downside of wanting more "stuff":

"Wanting something just for the sake of wanting it is not good. Not that a fancy house or car is bad, it's just that we're very likely to have a string of those things over and over and over again. If you get the fancy house, there is just something else that you want. If you want the fancy car, you are going to want something else immediately thereafter. It's not that there is anything wrong with any of these things in particular. What's wrong is a person does not understand that their happiness and their fulfillment have nothing to do with gaining more things."

For many people, their worth is tied to material things. Dr. John Demartini, world leader in inspirational speaking, author, and one of the featured philosopher/teachers in the world-renowned movie, *The Secret,* told an excellent story about the seduction of the material world. You'll see how when we only focus on "things" we miss out on a lot of success and joy we already have in our lives.

"This man comes up to me and says, 'Dr. Demartini, I want you to help me to become successful.' I said, 'Great! Where are you successful now?' He said, 'Well, no, I'm not. I want you to help me become successful.' I said, 'I know. So where are you successful?' He said, 'Dr. Demartini, you're not hearing me. I'm not, I want to be!'

I said, 'No, you're not hearing me. You already are. Tell me where you are?' I made him take a closer look at his life. He said, 'Okay I have successful relationship with my wife.' I said, 'Okay, can you see that that's one of your successes?' He said, 'Yes, we've been together for ten years and we have a great relationship.' 'Okay, what's another success of yours?' 'Well, okay, my son and I get along great and he's in baseball and I'm the coach and we may win the pendent this year.'

I said 'Okay, that's two. Can you see that that's a success?' He said, 'Yes, I can. Number three, we're planting a beautiful flower garden and we may get yard of the month this summer.' I said, 'Great, what's the next one?' 'Well, now that I think about it, my mother-in-law lives with us and most people don't get along with their mother in-law. We have a great relationship. She's like a real mother to me.'

I said, 'Can you see that that's a success?' He said, 'Yeah.' 'That's really good. What else?' 'I'm a lay minister on Wednesdays and Sundays at the church and I've always dreamed about doing that since I was about 20. I guess I'm a success there.' I asked him, 'Can you see that you have a lot of successes?' He said, 'Well yeah, I guess I do.'

I said, 'In order for you to feel like you're not a success, you must be comparing yourself to somebody else. Who are you comparing yourself to?' All of the sudden he said, 'This guy up on the hill is a big doctor. He has a big practice, a big home, and a lot of cars.'

I said, 'All right, how's his relationship with his wife?' 'Well, they're having some problems.' 'Does he have kids?' He said, 'Yes.' I asked, 'Does he have a son?' 'Yes.' 'How is his relationship with his son?' 'Well, he's a teenager and they're having problems with him. He's on drugs and giving them a hard time.' I said, 'What about the yard?'

He said, 'Well, they have people who take care of it. I don't think they even notice it.' 'What about the mother in-law?' 'Well, they moved out of the state to get rid of her.' 'What about the church?' 'I don't think they even go.'

I said, 'I have one more question. Would you trade places with this guy in order to have all of his wealth, home, cars, and his success in business? Would you do that if it meant having the same relationship and spiritual dynamics he has?' He said, 'Absolutely not!'

I said, 'Can you see that you have a hierarchy of values that are different from his and what's important to you is family and spirituality? What's important to him is business and finance. He has achieved in those areas because that's his dominant thought, and you've achieved in yours and those are your dominant thoughts. To expect yourself to be something that you're not is unrealistic and you're going to beat yourself up. The reality is that envy is ignorance and imitation is suicide.' He stopped, he reflected, he had a tear in his eye and he started realizing that he already had success. He just didn't realize the form it was in."

Marci Shimoff also made a key point regarding happiness and material things:

The Law of Attraction is where science and spirituality meet.

"I believe the highest use of the Law of Attraction is to put you in alignment with your greatest good, not just to bring you material things. I have nothing against material things. I think material things are wonderful. But when people are looking for their happiness and fulfillment from material things, they won't find it. You can never get enough things to make you happy! It's obvious. If things like fame, success, and money were the key to happiness, we would have a lot more happy people in Hollywood."

Marci added:

"We are very misdirected when we think that all these things are going to bring us happiness. In reality, happiness is what brings us those things. It's that inner feeling of joy and of love that allows the outer things to show up much more easily."

10. IT'S NOT SECULAR

The Law of Attraction isn't secular, it's spiritual. Secular means pertaining to worldly things or to things that are not regarded as spiritual, or sacred. The Law of Attraction is deeply based in the spiritual realm.

As Alex Mandossian mentioned earlier, "The Law of Attraction is where science and spirituality meet." There are plenty of people who activate the Law of Attraction in their lives, focusing on the scientific aspects of it without ever making a connection to a Higher Power. And they certainly receive noteworthy benefits.

However, when you plug into a Universal power or Divine Energy of your understanding and deepen your spirituality, you'll accelerate your power of attraction tenfold.

David Koons states it clearly, "A person's understanding or beliefs about God and spirituality are an individual preference. Whether you call it God, Life Force, or Higher Power doesn't matter. From my experience, It is there and It is serving us. The Law of Attraction is based on an understanding that there is a Greater Intelligence out there, there is an Energy Field out there that has our greatest good in mind."

Words well-said by Chellie Campbell, author of *The Wealthy Spirit* and *Zero to Zillionaire,* on the sacred nature of the law include:

"God is the ultimate source. God is the ultimate light of love. When people are tapped into the prevailing force that binds all of us in humanity together, it's all a part of God. That is what the Law of Attraction is all about."

WHAT THE LAW OF ATTRACTION IS NOT

Now, you'll be better able to understand exactly what the Law of Attraction is as we move into the next seven chapters on *The Seven Steps to AWAKENING.*

Before we move on, here is a quick recap of what the Law of Attraction is not:

1. It is not just positive thinking

2. It is not magic

3. It does not replace taking action

4. It is not a gimmick

5. It is not a crutch

6. It is not always fast

7. It is not always easy

8. It is not always comfortable

9. It is not about being materialistic

10. It is not secular in nature

In Section Two we will examine *The Seven Steps to AWAKENING.* Get your pen and paper ready, as there will be much for you to write about as you clarify and discover your deepest desires.

SECTION TWO

The Seven Steps to Awakening

The following seven chapters address *The Seven Steps to AWAKENING.* They're the specific steps you'll focus on every day, throughout the day.

As you deepen your awareness in each of these areas, you'll AWAKEN to a whole new world.

You're an amazing miracle. Tapping into the Law of Attraction will allow you to fully realize the perfection that you already are. Feel it. Believe it. Live it.

CHAPTER 3

Discover Your Deepest Desires

∽☾∾

"When your desires are strong enough, you will appear to possess superhuman powers to achieve." —Napoleon Hill

The Seven Steps to AWAKENING are:

1. *Discover Your Deepest Desires*

2. Declare What You Desire

3. Believe It Is Yours Now

4. Raise Your Frequency

5. Eliminate Any Obstacles

6. Take Meaningful Action

7. Receive Your Good

BUT, I DON'T KNOW WHAT I WANT!

This was one of the most challenging issues I faced regularly with my clients during the years I spent as a psychotherapist. When someone is unhappy, trying to figure out what will make them happy isn't always an easy task.

The reality is that you are the expert on the topic of you, only you know how to make you happy. Everyone else can guess, and at times they'll have some very good guesses, but their suggestions won't necessarily be what's right for you.

I'll never forget the day that Laurie came to my office for the first time. She was a beautiful young woman with fair skin and blonde hair that cascaded over her shoulders like Rapunzel. She was there because her grandfather had recently passed away. This was a catastrophic event for her since she was very close to him and she wanted counseling on how to work through the grief and painful sadness she was experiencing. She would talk of wonderful weekends spent making waffles with him, a ritual she adored. She talked of his joy and laughter and the love he gave her. Now all of that was gone and her world was tremendously shaken.

You must discover your deepest desires if you are going to use the Law of Attraction to its fullest magnitude.

As she progressed through the stages of grief, over time we eventually began talking about what would make her happy in her grandfather's absence. For weeks her answer was, "I don't know."

When someone says they don't know what they want, it's only a half-truth. Yes, that's a very strong statement for me to make. However, I firmly believe that you know and can access this information fairly easily over time just by being tuned in to what makes you feel good and deepening that awareness.

Most of the time the reason someone says they don't know is they're currently feeling some sort of fear. They're afraid someone will say, "You can't do that!" or "Who do you think you are?" They have possibly been criticized for saying their desire or something close to it before, and now they don't want to risk the criticism by saying it again. Perhaps they don't have a clue "how" it could happen. Since the desire seems so big that they may not know where to begin, they just set the desire aside and say they don't know.

Laurie eventually saw that she really did know what she wanted. She really wanted to begin her own family and start having children. This seemed too soon. She and her husband had been married less than a year at that time and it scared her to say it, for fear of his reaction. Despite her fear, her desire was great enough for her to approach the subject with her husband. He handled it very well, and it wasn't long before she was pregnant and happy as she could be.

You must discover your deepest desires if you are going to use the Law of Attraction to its fullest magnitude. When we discover our deepest desires, we create a deep sense of happiness and joy that can sustain the inevitable ups and downs of life. When we haven't discovered our deepest desires, we wander around through many random jobs and people which lead to hit-or-miss happiness.

FIND YOUR JOY AND FOLLOW IT!

There was a time in history when finding happiness was not on anyone's radar screen. It didn't even enter their minds to find happiness. Food, shelter, clothing, and staying alive were their only priorities. For some people, it's not much different today. They eat, sleep, work, eat, sleep, work, and continue this routine over and over all of their lives not realizing that there is so much more to be had in life, or that it's theirs for the taking.

For those who are ready to define a new life and who want to make happiness, love, freedom, abundance, and joy all apart of your lives, I, along with all of the experts and individual stories presented throughout this book, am here to say you can be happy! You can have an exceptional life and you can be happy.

Dr. James Golden is a minister that I met when I attended the silent retreat he and his wife Leslie offer. It was truly a life-altering experience for me, and I will continue attending them annually. It was so amazing! You will find many of his comments in Chapter 12, Deepen Your Spirituality. However, there was one brief dialogue that is so profound I want to share it with you word for word here. It went as follows:

Alicia:	Dr. Golden, what creates happiness and fulfillment?
Dr. Golden:	Knowing the Self. Knowing the True Self, period.
Alicia:	What is the True Self?
Dr. Golden:	The True Self is God. In particular it's God as expressed through the individual.
Alicia:	When someone knows the True Self, the God within them, and themselves as an individual, they achieve happiness.
Dr. Golden:	Yes.
Alicia:	But that sounds so easy, Dr. Golden.
Dr. Golden:	Of course it is. Why would it be complicated? What it takes to actually do that is not so easy. But many beliefs and ideas have to shift and change for that to come to pass. The truth itself is simple.

I realize this poses many questions for us all and I hope you will continue to explore the answers to each of them. For now let's consider this, I believe we get a glimpse of that True Self he is referring to when we find our joy and follow it. Some people discover their joy early in life and follow it, leading them to an abundant life filled with joy, prosperity, and love.

Others don't find their joy and follow it until later in life. I have two dear friends who discovered that they had amazing artistic talent for painting in their early 40s. To see them find this joy and begin to follow it is truly a thrill. I have another dear friend who has always known her joy was dance, and not until her late 40s did she begin to follow it.

How do you find your joy and follow it? Ask yourself the following questions:

1. What do you do that you enjoy the most?

2. What do you do that you love so much that you could do it for endless hours and feel energized instead of depleted?

3. What do you do that others say you are amazing at? You might not think it's so amazing because it comes so naturally to you.

4. What do you do that is easy for you and may be difficult for others?

5. When you were a child, what did you do that brought you the most joy?

When someone knows the True Self, the God within them, and themselves as an individual, they achieve happiness.

Your answers to these questions will point you in the direction of your joy. Then you must follow it. It doesn't help to know your joy and do nothing with it; you must follow it and see where it leads you. My friend Cathryn, who discovered she has incredible talent in oil painting, followed her joy and began taking art classes and entering her work in art shows and competitions. She took a business class for artists who want to make a living selling their artwork, and she painted some pieces that friends commissioned her to paint and was paid well for them.

After several years she has set a goal that she eventually wants to earn her living doing what she loves most – painting. She found her joy and she is truly following it.

What's your joy? Are you following it to see where it leads you? If you're happy in your life, you're probably experiencing some aspect of following your joy. If you're unhappy in your life, finding your joy and following it will lead you to peace and fulfillment.

YOU ARE A DIAMOND IN THE ROUGH

Discovering your deepest desire is like finding a diamond in the rough. You are that diamond. David Koons explains the process you need to go through to make that diamond ready for show:

"When people say, 'I don't know what I want.' I say that's a great place to start and then I ask, 'If you did know, what would it look like?' Knowing what you want, getting clarity, discovering your passion, getting focused, all of these are practices. Sure, we would like to get the email from God laying it all out for us. Chances are that's not going to happen.

I like to remind people that it is like mining for precious stones. You pull this rock out of the ground that you think is a diamond. Well, that diamond certainly isn't ready to go in the display case today, is it? We want to get that diamond, cut it, shape it, and polish it over and over again with a polishing cloth.

Focus is a practice. Clarity is a practice. The more clarity we have, the more we can focus our energy on discovering what it is we want. Once we focus our energy, we will be able to take better actions. When we talk about focus, we talk about action.

First let's be really clear about what it is we want or as clear as we can be today. Over time that image will become clearer. We'll correct. We'll continue. We'll focus our energy again and take another action until we discover our deepest desires."

When we can identify exactly what will make us happy, then we've hit the target. We have to look for it everywhere and constantly evaluate what brings us joy. It's like the philosophy behind *The One Minute Manager*, by Ken Blanchard. He says, "Catch someone doing something right and then praise them." In order to catch that someone, you must first look for them; if a manager is always looking for what people are doing wrong, they're never going to find people doing things right.

It's the same way with discovering your deepest joy. If your antennae are only up for what you don't like, you'll never find what you do like. You have to look for it and then acknowledge it.

My process of discovering my deepest desires relating to my career was a meandering one. There were two things I knew were very important to me, and the first one was freedom. I did not like to "have to" stay in an office all day long. I like the freedom to come and go. If I wanted to go on my son's field trip, I wanted to be able to go without asking permission. That doesn't make me very employable does it?! I realized that I really liked being self-employed.

The other thing I was certain of was that I liked to travel. The work I do speaking and training across the country satisfies that desire tremendously. I knew there was more to the formula, but it came a while later. I was seeking the clarity to see exactly what the rest of the formula was and it came to me one year over Thanksgiving vacation.

I had business to conduct in Florida and decided to take my son with me so that we could enjoy the holiday with friends who lived there. It was a slow week at the hotel where I was working and they generously gave me a suite with adjoining rooms. My friend and her two children came to stay with us for one night while I was there doing business. That meant that the kids had their own room and we adults had our own room. Sounds like the perfect way to travel with kids, doesn't it?

My son, Kenny, and I had arrived at the hotel and we were on our way to our rooms. This particular hotel has a very large atrium that is just beautiful. It was a very open feeling as we went to our suite. Kenny skipped ahead of me with his key in hand feeling very happy, independent, and eager to get to "his" room.

It was in that moment that my heart felt so full of love, joy, peace, and happiness that I noticed and acknowledged it immediately. I was so excited! Inside I said to myself, "This moment is pure happiness and joy! There isn't anything I could add to this picture that would make me any happier than I am right now. More money wouldn't make me happier; to lose weight wouldn't make me happier; to have a soul mate wouldn't make me happier; there isn't anything that needs to be removed from this picture that would make me any happier. This is a perfect moment of happiness."

I examined that moment closer to gain clarity on what it was that made me so happy in order to duplicate it any time I wanted to. Here is what I discovered:

Freedom

I had the freedom to be where I wanted to be and I wanted to be right there, right where I was, right in that very moment.

Travel

I love to travel. I love to see the world. My son and I had flown from California together and had a great trip. We were getting out of our everyday routines and seeing another part of the country and it was an extra special experience.

Speaking

I love speaking, training, teaching, and facilitating. And I knew I was going to be doing that the following day. I enjoy helping people improve themselves, whether it's in their personal or professional lives.

Luxury and beauty

I loved the beauty of the hotel, the beauty of our suite, and the beauty of the view we had from our suite. I loved the luxury of having someone else cook and clean for us. There was a peace of mind in all of this.

My son

I got to be with my son and soak up all of this with him; watching him skip in such a happy-go-lucky manner made me so very happy. I feel blessed to be in beautiful, luxurious hotels all the time, but not with him, and that made a big difference to me.

Friends

My dear friend, Laura, was on her way with two of her children, Philip and Ali, and I was so excited to spend time with them. We have roots that go way back. We knew each other in high school and were roommates in college. They are like family to me and it meant the world to share the experience with them. We had access to the concierge lounge and the kids were overjoyed at being able to go get cookies and milk before bed. I loved sharing these experiences with them.

It was great to be able to see and identify the components of that magical moment. What I've realized since then is that any blend of these makes me very happy. Since then I've identified two others, education and spirituality. I love to learn and I love to grow spiritually. Anything that helps me do either of these is wonderful.

Watch what goes on in your everyday world and soon you'll gain the clarity to find the magic formula of people and situations that fill you with joy.

EXPLORE YOUR VALUES

In some way the list I discovered was connected with my values. Although my family didn't have a lot of money when I was growing up, we always took a summer vacation. So, travel was something I valued from an early age. Do you know what you value?

Dr. John Demartini has a process he uses to help people identify their values. As you identify your values, you'll be better able to determine what your deepest desires are. He recommends that you write down three things for each of these questions, look for the common threads between them, and then prioritize them. This will give you a great list of your values based on what your life demonstrates.

1. How do you fill your space?
2. What do you spend your time doing?
3. What do you spend your energy on?
4. What do you spend your money on?
5. Where are you most organized?
6. Where do you have the most discipline, focus, and reliability?
7. What do you think about most?
8. What do you visualize or dream about most?
9. What do you talk to yourself inwardly about most?
10. What do you talk to others about most?
11. What brings a smile to your face the most?
12. What are your three top goals?
13. What most inspires you?

What brings a smile to your face the most?

When you do this exercise on paper, it will point you in the direction you need to go in order to determine what it is that you really want.

Alex Mandossian decided it was family he valued. Below he explains the Mandossian Hierarchy of Roles:

"The reason I chose teleseminars is because I wanted my kids and wife to recognize me when I am old. Many of my friends travel 225 days out of the year. There is nothing wrong with it. It is tough to have a family life while working like that. I can't have a family life with a four and six-year-old and a wife of ten years if I am traveling 225 days a year. I am not present for the school fundraiser, the bowling, or the miniature golfing.

I have the Mandossian Hierarchy of Roles. My top role is father and husband. Then it is employer, trainer, and student. I could have been public speaker, which is more fun for me, but it clashed with my highest role of father and husband. This was not my number one role until my wife taught me how to make it so. She didn't threaten to leave me. She showed me what I could have with a vivid vision of parallel realities of men and women we knew. She showed me the dedicated family men and how they ended up, and then she showed me men who loved their families, but were not dedicated to being with them and how they ended up.

By acting like Charles Dickens's Scrooge, I went into the future to find out what happens if I had continued to do what I was doing, and I chose teleseminars versus public speaking. Instead of traveling 225 days out of the year, I travel 70 days, which I still consider a lot. Most of my work is done at home. I made it a choice. I believe it was William Shakespeare who said, 'He who makes a decision against his will, is of the same opinion still.' I knew I would be of the same opinion, if it were against my will. I looked at both visions. I did not like the vision of my kids not talking to me. There was a time I did not speak to my dad when my dad had divorced my mother. It was not fun. There was a healing process I had to go through. I did not want my son or daughter to not speak to me because he or she did not recognize me. It is a difficult choice. It is very seductive to go make money at a public speaking event."

WHAT DO YOU WANT?

As I walked through the above steps myself, I found them very valuable. I also chose to look at them from a different perspective, and was able to go to another level of clarity. I looked at them from the perspective of what I "wanted" instead of what already is. If your current conditions are really low compared to what you know you're capable of creating, then looking at your world from this point of view will inspire you.

1.   How do you want to fill your space?

2.   What do you want to spend your time doing?

3.   What do you want to spend your energy on?

4.   What do you want to spend your money on?

5.   Where do you want to be most organized?

6.   Where do you want to have the most discipline, focus and reliability?

7.   What do you want to think about most?

8.   What do you want to visualize or dream about most?

9.   What do you want to talk to yourself inwardly about most?

10.   What do you want to talk to others about most?

11.   What do you want to have that brings a smile to your face the most?

12.   What do you want your three top goals to be?

13.   What do you want to be most inspired about?

FROM ACTRESS TO BOOKKEEPER TO SEMINAR LEADER

Chellie Campbell's process of discovering her deepest desire is a great story with many twists and turns over a series of years that eventually led her to her current career.

"I wanted to be an actress as I was growing up. I did shows in high school, and in college. I declared a drama major and then I came to Hollywood to be a star. That didn't happen, but what did happen was I got skilled at being in front of people. I learned the dynamics of an audience and a rapport between the audience and a performer.

I had a great time being a team. When you get a group of actors together and they're doing a performance it's a team sport. It's a team creation. I loved all the energy around it. In between acting jobs I used to take secretarial jobs to eat because my mother said, 'Oh, you want to be an actor? Well learn to type, honey.' So I did. I would sing, I would type. I would sing, I would type. Then one of the typing jobs took over my life. They kept promoting me, it was fun, and I enjoyed it.

The people were great. They were all having a good time. They offered me to go full-time permanently. I just said, 'Oh no. How do I give up show business?' My friend Gay had a wonderful bit she did with me. I was tortured about giving up show business. She said, 'Chellie, what is it you really like about show business?' I said 'I like the sense of creating with a team. I like the fun. I like the acknowledgement and applause. I like the money.'

She said, 'What is it that you enjoy about this bookkeeping job you've got working in this office?' I said, 'I really enjoy the team spirit of the group I'm working with. I like that we have an ultimate goal that we're working for. I like the acknowledgement and applause that they give me. I like the money.' She said, 'It's the same list.' I learned then to look at the underlying value. What is it you're really wanting and getting?

I made the decision to quit acting and never looked back. I eventually became a partner and then sole owner of a business management firm. But what I saw people doing with money appalled me. The wealthy people had no spirit and the spiritual people were broke! And everyone was responding from fear of financial insecurity.

After having studied the Law of Attraction all these years, I knew the spiritual relationship between money, belief in self, and making things appear that we wanted to appear. I started reaching out to my clients and saying, "You know, this is what I see you doing with money. You could make an adjustment here and have a better result. People started doing what I told them, doubling their incomes, paying off debts, starting businesses and all those kinds of things.

I said, 'Wow, this is really working!' People said, 'You've got to teach this.' Three people in the same week said that. I said, 'Okay.' I designed a workshop. When I designed my workshop, I didn't know how to design a workshop. I started looking around. Who else has a workshop? How did they run it? What did I like and what didn't I like? Let's see what I want to put in it. How do I make it my own? What do I think are the key elements that are going to make somebody happy, joyful, and rich?

I designed my workshop and started teaching it. Soon it took over my life. I loved it. I got rid of the bookkeeping service, I sold it to someone and I started just teaching the workshop.

Suddenly I saw that I was where I wanted to be all those years ago when I said 'I want to be an actress.' What happened was I needed all the acting skills. Then I became a bookkeeper to learn all the financial skills. I could help people master money in their lives and be happy, joyous, and rich. I loved doing that.

I was still communicating with audiences. I was still designing programs and writing scripts. I was doing all of this and fulfilling myself in every way that I wanted to when I had envisioned it as being an actress. My whole life had been leading me to this result that I could serve and empower people around the issue of money. I just want the whole world to be happy, joyful, and rich. That's what my work and my life are all about."

DISCOVER YOUR PASSION

Alex Mandossian has a four-step process that helped him and many of his students discover their passion:

1. Ask yourself what you're really good at doing. Write it down on an 8½ x 11 sheet of paper. If I am very passionate that day, I write it down on an 8½ x 14 sheet of paper. I write and write.

Ask people who know you what they think you are really good at.

2. Ask people who know you what they think you are really good at. I ask people who like me and even people who don't. I make a second list of answers from people who really know me well.

3. Compare both of your lists, what you think you're really good at and what others think you're really good at and see what overlaps. Pick three things that overlap on the lists. Put those three things on an index card. Ask, "Am I really passionate about these three things? Would I do these things for free? Even if I was starving, would I still be willing to do these things for free?" If the answer is yes, then it makes the list of three. If not, remove it from the list of three.

4. This step is unique because it involves monetization of your passion. From the list of three, choose the one thing that will make you your first dollar the fastest. This is very important. Choose the one thing that will make the first dollar, not the first thousand or million dollars. Therefore, you will get some positive reinforcement as fast as humanly possible. When you make the first dollar fast, the second dollar comes even faster.

The geometric progression gets faster and faster. Anything I've done in the market place, like co-inventing the audio generator, inventing the ask methodology, or becoming a tele-seminar marketer, or having over 11,000 students, I've done by using these four steps.

The first dollar is so important to me. When you make the first dollar, you go from amateur to professional. An amateur doesn't make money. An amateur is not bad, he just doesn't make money. He could be a hobbyist. If you like to knit, you don't make money as a hobby. If you do it professionally, you make money from it. A professional makes money, which is a form of success. In my mind, professional and amateur statuses are miles apart. Zero to one dollar is not miles apart, maybe inches or centimeters apart. I trick my mind into exalted status by turning pro. I turn it into a passion, which then becomes a business. I recognize I am best at the electronic marketing industry, which involves direct response marketing.

YOUR PASSION LIVES IN YOUR HEART, NOT YOUR HEAD

Each of these exercises will help lead you to deepest desires. It's as though you're on a treasure hunt in search of what you truly want in your life. As you search, it's important to look in the right place. Make sure you look in your heart, not your head!

Another great question I want to ask you is "If you could do anything you wanted to, without the possibility of failure, what would it be?"

"If you could do anything you wanted to, without the possibility of failure, what would it be?"

Hale Dwoskin talks about letting your heart lead the way. He says, "Follow your heart, not your head. We have all these beliefs and concepts based on the past that are very head centered; even those of us who are very emotionally based have them. If you let your heart be your guide and you allow your heart to be the arbiter of what you attract into your life and you do that with as open a heart and mind as possible, then the results are very profound."

Following your head disconnects you from your true essence or your heart as Hale Dwoskin states above. Your true essence is connected to your Source, your Higher Power and your passion and purpose flow from that connection. In your head is where the Overriding Background Beliefs reside that prevent you from realizing your greatest good. It's where the ego works diligently at keeping you safe and remaining at your status quo.

Following your heart is where true inspiration blossoms and dreams are born. It's where you feel the most joy, love, and passion.

DARE TO THINK BIGGER THAN YOU THOUGHT YOU COULD

The bigger you dream the more exciting it is to think about your dreams becoming a reality. Little dreams produce little excitement. Big dreams produce big excitement. The more energy and excitement you have for something the faster you attract it.

One of the steps I took several years ago was to write out what my life would be like if I tripled my income. Thinking about this and sitting down to write about it was completely exhilarating. My excitement reverberated off the page. My heart sang while writing about it and thinking about it. It wasn't long before I sealed the deal on the largest contract I had ever had in the history of my business. Here's the sweet spot—I knew it was coming all along, so as happy and grateful as I was, I wasn't really surprised.

Another example that is currently in motion is my intention to take THE AWAKENING seminars around the world. It's easy for me to write this now, but when I set this goal many months ago, it got caught in my throat! I was born on a farm down a dirt road in Luther, Oklahoma with a population of 496. It never entered my mind to travel internationally until my late 20s. So it's not as though I had any comfort zone established for this.

Nevertheless, I declared that this was my intention and I knew I would have the honor to present the information contained in this book, and more, to men and women around the world. I bought an international map and hung it across from my desk in my office and I highlighted the cities that I most wanted to visit. Just going to the store and buying that map was exciting. Looking at it and thinking about all of the people I will meet and the many possibilities I will experience makes my heart soar with joy.

Dare to think bigger than you thought you could.

Just days after I made that declaration, I received an invitation to attend a conference in Amsterdam, where one of the topics on the schedule was the Law of Attraction. I had never received an announcement about international seminars or conferences before then. Even though it was nine months away, I knew attending was clearly the next indicated step for me to take THE AWAKENING around the world. So without a moment's hesitation I signed up! It's still a few months away, but I know it will be an AWAKENING within itself.

Dare to think bigger than you thought you could. Do not settle for something that doesn't put a smile on your face, a song in your heart, and the amount of money in your bank that satisfies you. Rev. Jim Turrell spoke eloquently on this topic:

"If you look at most people with wealth, not all of them, but certainly a good deal of them, basically dominate in their fields or disciplines, and that's kind of why they're so successful. But, there's another reason why people reach the top, and it is because they express their originality.

At one time I was a professional musician and a lot of people would have what they call 'cover bands,' which is a band that would play the music of other stars. You could make an okay living covering other people's music, or imitating other people's success. Eventually, to have real success, you have to dare to be yourself, which means you have to get to the original 'you;' the 'you' that the world has never seen before."

DON'T TRY TO FIGURE OUT HOW

One of the most challenging stumbling blocks on the path to believing is trying to figure out "how" manifesting our good is going to happen. This prevents us from dreaming big dreams and really getting excited about all the possibilities of our new lives.

Marci Shimoff sums it up well:

"One of the big things that people get hung up on is that they try to control the 'how's.' They try to control how it's going to happen. You can't know how something's going to unfold. You can just know what your soul is longing for. Then let the Universe unfold it in a way that's best for you. Your job is to stay on course with the feeling of it manifesting and let the details take care of themselves."

When you get caught up in the "how" of attracting the amazing life of your dreams, you have just stepped out of your business and into your Higher Power's.

Remember to mind your own business. It's not your job to worry about how it's all going to happen. Your job is to discover your deepest desires, declare them, stay focused, feel good, and take the next indicated step.

When you entertain the idea of how it's all going to happen, you may get sidetracked and settle for something less than you really want. You don't want to do this. You want to have goals, dreams, and desires that excite and inspire you to take action! Settling isn't exciting or inspiring!

In this step all you're doing is dreaming and putting it down on paper. You don't need to concern yourself with all of the steps it's going to take to make it all happen. You have to let go of worrying or wondering how it's going to happen. If you get into worrying and wondering, it will hold you back, because you'll be filled with trepidation. Stay focused on what you want and let go of how it's going to happen.

THE PROOF IS ON THE PAPER

Throughout *THE AWAKENING* there will be many processes and exercises that will help you to increase your power of attraction. It's very important that you actually write each of these down.

The exercises mentioned in this chapter will help you discover your deepest desires. But don't think about doing these in your head, put them down on paper. So, if you haven't already, stop now. Get your pen and paper. It doesn't need to be anything fancy at all. As a matter of fact, I don't like to use the really fancy notebooks because then I think I have to write neatly and say things perfectly and my perfectionism takes over and defeats the whole process.

Any kind of notebook or paper will work just fine. When you do these processes on paper, it gets the thoughts and feelings out where you can look at them and work with them.

YOU HAVE PERMISSION

This step is a tough one for many people because they've never been given permission to dream! I'm not only giving you permission to dream, or recommending that you dream, I'm insisting that you dream! Don't look at the current conditions of your life, because they could hold you back from dreaming about the life you really want to live and <u>deserve</u> to live.

It may help you to go to a park, coffee shop, or somewhere you can just let your mind expand and the ideas flow. But whatever you do, dream big dreams! People who don't dream or have little dreams are more prone to unhappiness and depression.

You're entitled to live a wonderful life! You deserve it!

The direction you'll receive in the remaining chapters of *THE AWAKENING* will give you the confidence that the dreams you have can become reality. Your life was meant to be magnificent in every way. That doesn't mean problem-free in every way, because we all know that some of our greatest problems have given us our greatest growth.

Don't let the dreams of others stifle your ability to dream. They may have different dreams and that's perfectly okay. But don't let them dictate what your dreams are going to be. You're entitled to live a wonderful life! You deserve it!

Lastly, listen for anyone who tries to "should" on you. They might say, "You should go for this," "You should do that," or "You shouldn't talk like that," etc. Don't let people "should" on you. *THE AWAKENING* isn't about what you "should" do, or what anyone else thinks you "should" do. This is your life and *THE AWAKENING* is about what you want to do, what you want to feel, what you want to have. You have permission to have it all!

This step is simply doing what it takes to discover your deepest desires. Our next step in Chapter 4 is where you send it out into the Universe and it begins making its way back to you.

CHAPTER 4

Declare What You Desire

> *"There is enough for everyone. If you believe it, if you can see it, if you can act from it, it will show up for you. That's the truth."*
>
> —Dr. Rev. Michael Beckwith

The Seven Steps to AWAKENING are:

1. Discover Your Deepest Desires

2. *Declare What You Desire*

3. Believe It Is Yours Now

4. Raise Your Frequency

5. Eliminate Any Obstacles

6. Take Meaningful Action

7. Receive Your Good

DECLARE IT A SUCCESS

The way that you declare your deepest desires a success involves several things:

1. State what you want clearly in the present tense.

    Write your desires down in what I call "Power Statements" or affirmations. A Power Statement is your desire written in the present tense, as though it's already yours. As you write them, make sure they include an emotion you want to feel. As you read them, the emotion or feeling words increase your vibration just by reading them.

Mark Victor Hansen, co-author of the popular *Chicken Soup for the Soul* books and prolific writer with many popular books such as *The Power of Focus, The Aladdin Factor, Dare to Win,* and others, described affirmations like this, "Affirmations are the words you say to yourself and repeat so often that you believe. Then you go achieve." You say them until you believe them at the depth of your being.

Here are some examples: (Insert your name in the space)

"I, _____, now enjoy owning my own business that provides me with all the freedom and money I desire."

"I, _____, am happy and grateful that my income abundantly exceeds $100,000 each year."

"I, _____, am excited that I am in a wonderful relationship with an exceptional person."

"I, _____, joyfully take all of the steps necessary to weigh my perfect weight of …"

"I, _____, am now a powerful magnet attracting all my good to me with speed and precision."

"I, _____, am open and honest as I gratefully explore all of the possibilities for my new life and Awakening.

You can't get caught up in the details of life and lose your focus.

2. Keep your focus on your desires.

Focusing on what you want is critically important. Write your Power Statements on index cards, and keep them with you so that you can review them a minimum of three times each day. Always review them first thing in the morning, last thing before you go to sleep at night, and at another time mid-day. Distractions have been the downfall of many a desire. You can't get caught up in the details of life and lose your focus.

3. Set the intention of making it a reality.

You may think that by the time you get to this point that the intention of making it a reality is a given. Well, it's not. Many people will write down their deepest desires and look at them like they're a good idea. This is your life; these are your deepest desires. They're way more than a good idea! They're the very essence of what will bring you peace, love, joy, happiness, and abundance. As you look at them, state your intention to make them a reality. Every time you see something that is a goal of yours say, "That's for me. There goes my car. That's the healthy fit body that's for me. I can have that too."

MORE ON POWER STATEMENTS

I was introduced to affirmations, also know as Power Statements, in the early 80s, and it wouldn't be much of an exaggeration to say that they saved my life. I had such painfully low self-esteem that I had to begin there before I could even discover my deepest desires. I've written a Power Statement for almost everything you can imagine, large and small, spiritual and material, from powerful to peaceful, and they work. Please don't underestimate the value of these statements. Sometimes the simplest solutions are the most helpful.

I recommend that you write your Power Statements and say them. Write them in a notebook 10 or 20 times each. Say them out loud in front of a mirror. Exclaim them while you're power walking or driving in your car. Say them with genuine feelings of gratitude and excitement as if they're already a part of your reality. These simple actions will cement your new Power Statements into your subconscious mind. You want to place as much energy and focus on these statements as you possibly can. Eat, sleep, and breathe them!

I also recommend that you say and write your Power Statements in the first, second, and third person. For example:

1. I, _____, now have all the power I need to make my dreams a reality.

2. You, _____, now have all the power you need to make your dreams a reality.

3. He/She,_____, now has all the power he/she needs to make his/her dreams a reality.

Try writing and saying your Power Statements in many different ways. There is no one way that is perfect for everyone. You will develop your own preference. I like to use the word "now," because although this is the step in which we are declaring what we desire to the Universe, the way we declare it sets the stage for the next step of believing. Here are several ways to begin writing and saying your Power Statements:

I am...

I am powerful.

I am joyful.

I am wealthy.

I am healthy.

I am successful.

I now...

I now take action to fulfill my dreams.

I now have the power to make all my dreams come true.

I now focus on all of the good in my life.

I now have the courage to follow my heart.

I now love and nurture myself daily.

I am happy and grateful now that...

I am happy and grateful now that my body is healthy and fit.

I am happy and grateful now that I own a big, beautiful home.

I am happy and grateful now that my life is filled with love and joy.

I am happy and grateful now that I have an abundance of money in my life.

I am happy and grateful now that I get to travel in luxury around the world.

In this very moment...

In this very moment I am filled with gratitude and joy.

In this very moment I am attracting everything wonderful into my life.

In this very moment I experience peace of mind.

In this very moment confidence fills my entire being.

In this very moment I know my deepest desires are becoming a reality.

I am becoming...

I am becoming financially free.

I am becoming fit, healthy, and strong.

I am becoming a successful business owner.

I am becoming wealthy and wonderful.

I am becoming a person who radiates peace, love, and happiness.

I am in the process of...

I am in the process of creating the marriage of my dreams.

I am in the process of building a successful business.

I am in the process of forgiving everyone for everything.

I am in the process of transcending all my perceived limitations.

I am in the process of becoming all that I can be in every area of my life.

Thank you for my...

Thank you for my healing.

Thank you for my new car.

Thank you for my beautiful, big home.

Thank you for my growing retirement account.

Thank you for my abundant energy, vitality, and well-being.

Chellie Campbell is a firm believer in Power Statements as well. She stated, "We have to start inputting into those 60,000 thoughts that we're almost helpless to having every day. We have to create better thoughts. The way you have better thoughts is you repeat positive statements endlessly until they become the new CD that plays in your head over and over. Things like, 'People love to give me money.' 'Money flows to me easily and effortlessly.' 'Something wonderful is coming to me today, I can feel it.' Then you have to juice up your feelings so that you don't just say them, you feel them."

LYNNAE SHARES HER JOURNEY TO DRIVING PINK

Here is what I know to be true for me:

If I can imagine it, I can achieve it. If I can dream it, I can become it.

I became aware of this about 17 years ago, although my journey in Mary Kay has been for the past seven years.

The success I have had in Mary Kay, and in my life, is in direct relationship to what I feed into my daily thoughts about me. Daily I must quiet the committee in my head that attempts to fill me full of lies like "I am not good enough, I am crazy, no one likes me, and what do I have to offer?" The strongest belief that I have is that it's not okay to be in my own power; I'm supposed to stay small; I shouldn't play out of the lines of safety. My list is endless.

A Power Statement is your desire written in the present tense, as though it's already yours.

It's hard to admit, but sometimes that chatter never stops, even when I sleep. So, in spite of that scary place between my ears, I know that everything is energy, and to change that I must stand in my new belief that my own awareness is my answer to change. I like to say awareness is 95% of your ability to change. The ability to admit that this is going on in my life allows me to make the shift. Sometimes it can be done very quickly. That's the amazing thing about energy, it moves and recreates in the present time very fast. Just talking about it sets the new thought process in motion. The new awareness attracts what I can believe in the present time. Other times change has not been fast because I still need to learn something from this experience. I know it's a process, so I am okay with that. I just validate myself.

To make these changes over the past 17 years I have done the following:

1. Saturated myself with like-minded people.

2. Created situations that support my new growth.

3. Sought many avenues to encourage this Awakening.

4. Done body work to receive the new beliefs on a cellular level.

5. Had coaching on a mental and spiritual level.

6. Done a lot of reading, prayer, and mediation.

7 I also share with others what I want. I can not keep it to myself for fear that I will look stupid. I must speak it out loud to own it.

8. I have created a personal connection with the God of my understanding.

9. I have a deep sense of gratitude for being alive.

10. I also have to acknowledge all the emotions and beliefs I have that will sabotage my efforts. I do this by being conscious of my feelings that direct my thoughts.

This is your life and these are your deepest desires.

My favorite time to attract is while I am asleep. When I lay my head down, I visualize what I am working on and ask the energy to heal and change while I am in this effortless state. A lot happens for me while I am sleeping.

I have found the tool of writing and drawing the new pictures is fun for me…I know that when I am serious and try to make things happen, nothing will attract and shift. In the place of ease and no effort, anything is possible.

My process to becoming a Cadillac Sales Director in Mary Kay started with a very small vision. When I wanted more for myself, I was taught to take a look at my deserve level. I had to be honest with myself. My deserve level was so low, even though I truly thought it was high. I eventually learned that I deserved way more!

Self esteem is a strange thing. I can present myself to others that I am confident and strong. But I am great at pretending. The steps I took to increase my deserve level came from the place of personal awareness. I am determined and not afraid to face it and continue to raise my bar. I accepted that the Universe wants it all for me. I am just now learning to receive it in bigger gifts. Every time my deserve level has increased I have turned more of myself over to my Higher Power, God.

I had to learn to connect to that inner being of myself. I have learned to value my God given gifts, my goodness, the direction, meaning, and purpose in my life. I have trusted my ability to see in front of me and set an intention. If it is in my highest good it will manifest. As I have done this, I have found my passion.

I use all of my senses to mock up and create the new picture. I can visualize it in my mind before it has manifested. I like to feel it. Getting behind the wheel, driving a friend's Pink Cadillac, taking pictures of me in the car. Practicing what it's going to feel like when people stare and wave and congratulate me. Placing pictures of me and the Cadillac everywhere so that I am reminded of what I am attracting. I fill my subconscious mind acting as if it has already been done. I have to affirm myself and the new pictures daily, sometimes minute to minute, and constantly remove myself from negative people.

Then reality comes—the action plan—the roadmap of what I needed to do to make my experience real. I make graphs and charts and write out exactly what I need to attract. I create visual tools, vision boards with the end results on them, white boards that I could draw lines to be filled up by the deadline. I know that if I don't create the space I can not receive it. I rarely know where it is going to come from, but day by day the miracles happen. I never underestimate the power of what some might call a miracle. I just know that it has been provided, due to my openness and commitment to not give up.

I am motivated and every cell of my body has an overwhelming sense of fulfillment when I stand in my power.

Doing this requires that I trust the process knowing that the universe will provide. What I think about I bring about. I had to fully step out, throw my heart completely over the line and everything into what I believed I could do. There was no going back, no room for doubt once I set that in motion. I told everyone. I let everyone into the process; I know that the excitement and belief helps create that attraction. I kept that space very clear from negative people who weren't willing to believe in my dream. I just needed to work and take action and know that my efforts would be blessed.

The end result is I am driving pink. The most important and rewarding part of this process for me is what I have been able to do for others. I have attracted this into my life, which allows others to step into that space as well. The gift of stepping into my own power allows others to find their greatness. I am motivated and every cell of my body has an overwhelming sense of fulfillment when I stand in my power. I have to be true to me so that I can be of service to others. I have to give it away in order to keep it. I am like an open channel, knowing that anything can happen in love and honesty, loving others and accepting others just the way they are.

To all the extraordinary people before me, "I thank you for awakening your seed of greatness and teaching me the power to create my future."

JENNIFER WANTED A BETTER CAREER

My story is truly amazing and I do believe it is God given! I had been working in the fitness industry for 15 years as an instructor and personal trainer. While I enjoyed my lifestyle, clients and utilizing my gifts, I was tired of living paycheck to paycheck. I knew that if my family needed me, I would certainly not be able to assist them.

At the time I was working in an exclusive fitness club and began to take notice of the clientele who seemed to have the kind of careers that enabled them to support a higher standard of living. They all seemed to be in outside sales.

I have always set goals and used affirmations to reshape my point of view. I wrote out five goals and affirmed them as if they were happening in my life at that very moment. I placed them on my mirror in my bedroom so that I could see them each day. I prayed and asked God for guidance. I actually purchased a desk, computer, and brief case to prepare for my new career.

For two years I interviewed with various companies, was offered positions, and kept relying on my intuition for the one that was for my highest good.

I met someone at the fitness club that worked for a nearby mortgage banking firm and they encouraged me to work for them. I knew nothing about the industry, but I began to ask and interview everyone I knew. I was constantly reminded, "There is no reward without risk!" So I took the leap!

My second year in outside sales I grossed six figures and my success continues to climb! I purchased a beautiful home on a hill with an ocean view and have been able to give generously to the many charities I support. I thank God daily and maintain an attitude of gratitude.

If I remember that this house is His, that I work for Him, and that I am simply here to help someone else, my life is filled with joy! I continue to use the Law of Attraction as my vision and abundance grows!

BARBARA SAYS "I DO" TO STARTING HER OWN BUSINESS

Some 15 or more years ago when I was practicing psychotherapy, I had an amazing woman client. She was a very astute woman who was working with a major real estate developer and she wanted out of the corporate arena. She came to me to assist her in facing her fears and making the transition. After months of counseling and lots of great ideas that she failed to follow-through on, I told her in a fit of frustration, "Barbara, you have to just f-ing do it!"

The following week when she returned (yes, she actually came back!) and she brought me a plaque with that quote engraved on it. It was a pivotal day for Barbara, who today is one of the nation's most successful wedding planners. She said that my kick in the seat of the pants was just what she needed after going in circles most of her life.

She faced a lot of fear in leaving the corporate environment. "You know you're going to have a salary, you know you're going to have benefits, you know you're going to get that vacation, including savings plans and matching funds. It's not easy to leave that. You have to take a leap of faith. It's a major, major thing. Once I started moving forward it just snowballed. It was just amazing!"

Barbara's career path led her through a couple of other businesses before she landed on wedding planning. "You have to trust your gut. I tried a few different things that didn't gel for me, but I kept knocking on doors and finally the right one opened."

"You need to experience the downs and the ups." I've often said, you need to have as many downs as highs so you that you can know what the difference is. If you go along in an equator type fashion, you don't know how wonderful the highs and the lows both are. You have to have them both.

Once Barbara decided on a direction, she used vision boards and affirmations to declare her desire. She said:

"I used them both regularly. Actually, I did a vision board that was sort of shaped like steps. It was very interesting. I bent the paper and had all these different things on it that I wanted. I included a car, just the way I wanted my yard to look, and a slim body type.

Then at one point I looked at them and I thought, 'Hey, I've gotten these. They've come true.' I finally took them off and I made a new board. I really do keep the board going all the time. It's sitting in the corner of my bedroom. I don't look at it all the time, but my subconscious notices it.

A few years ago I stopped doing what I call my smaller services. Now, I only do full service wedding planning. That was a leap of faith because when most people start out they are doing smaller services where they are not handling everything. I took the leap and turned these weddings down. I started saying 'I'm not available, I only do full service wedding planning.'

It was very frightening to turn business down. I would hang up the phone and think, 'I could have had income there.' Then I said, 'No. My goal is to do full service weddings and I'm holding out for them. I have to make space for those weddings because if I take small services, they're going to take the place of the full service weddings that I really want.' I took the plunge.
Guess what? I have more full service weddings than I would ever imagine, calling continuously. I left the space open and it was filled with the kind of weddings I wanted.

The minute you begin this process the Universe is aligning itself to bring you your desires.

I have also defined my ideal bride. My ideal bride is a career minded, well paid, professional woman in her 20s, 30s or 40s. She's a confident decision maker, well educated with refined taste, but with an adventuresome spirit, good manners and a sense of humor. Her budget is $125,000 plus, and she and her family are willing to spend freely, though not necessarily extravagantly, for my full service wedding planning services, which will aid her in achieving a wedding congruent with the groom's and her social or professional standing. That's who she is."

Once you have discovered your deepest desires, you must declare them to the Universe so that you can summon them into your life like Lynnae, Jennifer, and Barbara. Know that the minute you begin this process the Universe is aligning itself to bring you your desires. How soon they reach you depends on how fully you practice all of the remaining steps and *The Five Keys to Accelerate Your Power of Attraction*. Once you declare what you desire, your next step is to believe it is yours now. When you know without a shadow of a doubt that what you want is yours in consciousness it will manifest in your material world. The depth of your belief accelerates your ability and speed to attract what you desire. We will discuss this further in Chapter 5.

CHAPTER 5

Believe It Is Yours Now

⌘

"What the mind of a man can conceive and believe, it can achieve."

—Napoleon Hill

The Seven Steps to AWAKENING are:

1. Discover Your Deepest Desires

2. Declare What You Desire

3. *Believe It Is Yours Now*

4. Raise Your Frequency

5. Eliminate Any Obstacles

6. Take Meaningful Action

7. Receive Your Good

BELIEVE IT AND YOU WILL ACHIEVE IT

There are two things that turbo-charge your Attraction Quotient: The emotion you add to your desires, and your ability to believe that what you want is already in your life. If you believe 100% without a shadow of a doubt that what you want is already yours, and you continue taking the next indicated step, you're in the flow and your Attraction Quotient is skyrocketing!

1% DOUBT AND YOU'RE OUT

Believe without a doubt that what you want is yours now. The miracle of manifesting is that even though you don't see it instantly in your life, just like the seed that is growing beneath the soil, even though you can't see it, your good is on the way.

Mark Victor Hansen speaks about believing very convincingly. Read this everyday and I guarantee you will learn to believe! He says:

"Your greatest obstacle is always yourself, getting you to believe. You can't even have 1% doubt. With 1% doubt you send out an inharmonic resonance that will come back wrong. With 1% doubt you are out! Even 1% of disbelief takes you out of the game. It puts you right out of business. Have certainty! John Kennedy had certainty even though there was no NASA when he said 'Let's land a man on the moon.' He said to Wernher von Braun, 'You go figure out how to do it.' Then he put it together, made a program and man walked on the moon."

THE THREE STAGES OF BELIEF

To some, this may seem like the most daunting step of all. How can you believe in something unseen and unknown? The process of believing is one that occurs in stages for many. You can traverse through these stages right now as you read them, or it can take some people years to make it through them all. The good news is that you decide. You decide how quickly you want to believe. You have the power. As Mark Victor Hansen said, "One percent doubt and you're out!" You may want to focus on expediting your journey through these stages PRONTO!

One percent doubt and you're out!

Here are the Three Stages of Belief:

STAGE 1 - I can have a wonderful life.

This stage is about giving yourself permission to live a glorious life and attaining your deepest desires. It's about coming to terms with the fact that it's okay to want a great life and that you can have it all. You may also take the Power Statements we discussed in Chapter 4 and apply them the same way, "I can enjoy owning my own business that provides me with all the freedom and money I desire."

STAGE 2 - I will have a wonderful life.

This stage is about the actual possibility of you having all you want. Now that you know you can have it, will you? Yes! When you own your power, you'll know, without a doubt that you're going to create a great life. "I will have an income that abundantly exceeds $100,000 each year."

STAGE 3 - I now have a wonderful life.

This stage is about the possession of that wonderful life now! It's about declaring that all of your hopes and dreams are yours now. They may not be manifested in your world yet, but they're already a part of the Universe's plan to push your good towards you. When you're in this stage, you're attracting your highest good in the most expedient manner.

There will likely be some obstacles you'll need to remove before you can believe wholeheartedly and start attracting your good. But you don't have to wait until they are all gone to begin the process.

THE CONTINUUM OF BELIEF

As I have used the Law of Attraction over the years and watched my clients, friends, and colleagues use it, I see that there is a direct correlation between how big, amazing, and exciting the goal is and how much the individual is able to actually believe with 100% confidence they will attain it.

I call this varying range of believing, the Continuum of Belief.

In the area of wealth, for example:

Maybe it seems outlandish for you to believe you could make $500,000 a year or own a $4 mil-lion mansion. It may seem ridiculous for you to dream about driving a BMW, wearing a Rolex, and dining in the finest restaurants. You may roll your eyes at the thought of flying around the world in a spacious first-class seat and staying in the very best hotels.

On the Continuum of Belief, your belief level that you could ever attain this level of affluence and wealth is very low. Yes, you may think it would be great and at some level want it, but you couldn't begin to believe the possibility of it being a reality in your life. As far out as these things may seem to you, I encourage you to think big! Do not limit the Law of Attraction, because it knows no limits.

Do not even come close to settling for rhinestones because the Universe is waiting to give you diamonds!

It may still be a stretch for you to believe you could make $200,000 in a year, but you believe you deserve it and with effort you believe you could make it a reality. Maybe owning a home worth a million dollars is a huge leap from your current apartment, but it's within your comprehension.

Neither one of these is better than the other. It's just playing a different game in life. Some people want to play a big game in life and others are quite satisfied playing on a smaller field. That's wonderful. This is part of the beauty of life and what makes the world go around.

But if your smaller game means you struggle to pay your bills and you can't afford some of the simple necessities of life, that's a whole different issue. Don't settle for struggle and frustration. That's not getting in the flow, being in your power, or using the Law of Attraction to the best of your ability. You're a miracle, and your life was meant to be magnificent. Do not even come close to settling for rhinestones because the Universe is waiting to give you diamonds!

So let's go back to you making $200,000 a year and moving into that beautiful million dollar home. On the continuum, you have a very high level of belief. The more you believe it's yours now, the sooner you'll actually receive it.

Can you go from your small apartment to a spacious million dollar home and go from $50,000 a year to $200,000 a year or more? Yes, you can!

AWAKEN TO A DEEPER LEVEL OF BELIEF

The more you believe the more you will achieve. So what steps can you take to help you believe? Here are several tools and strategies that will help you believe your good is yours now:

1. Deepen your spirituality.

Our aim is to believe, without a shadow of a doubt, with unwavering faith, and complete and total confidence that our good is wanting to meet us just as much and just as quickly as we want to meet it! To believe with that much conviction requires establishing a current connection with the Universe or Higher Power of your understanding at this point in your life. You'll continue to grow in your awareness, but you just need to begin somewhere.

Marci Shimoff discusses what she's found to be true about the underlying beliefs of happy, successful people. "I've found in my research that happy, successful people have an underlying belief that the Universe is out to support them; that this is a benevolent Universe; that the energy of support and love is primary; that God is a loving God. They do not believe we're on this reward and punishment system. They believe that anything that happens to us is to direct or redirect us towards our highest good."

When you focus on developing that kind of belief system, you can't help but soar! In spite of what you may think now, or may have thought in the past, the Universe is conspiring for you!

We will discuss further ways you can deepen your spirituality in Chapter 12.

2. Create a dream board.

A dream board is piece of poster board that you craft or construct. You glue pictures onto it along with phrases that inspire you and help to keep you focused on your dreams. For years I would hear this and think, "That's a really good idea, I should do that," but I wouldn't do it. All of these really good ideas are useless unless you DO them. I finally did several of them and started manifesting what was on them like crazy.

One of the most exciting things I manifested was that I wanted to stay in a castle, so I put a picture of a castle on one of them. In less than a year after making the board, out of the blue came an opportunity for me to go to France and the chance to stay in a castle. It was an absolutely amazing experience! Some people would say, "It was a once in a lifetime experience," but not me. I believe, "It was the first of many lifetime experiences just like it." The board helps you to sustain your focus and helps you to believe in and allow your good into your life.

Alexandra Teklak is the creator and CEO of Aquamantra. She uses the Law of Attraction in her daily principles to create the milestones she needs to take her company to the next level. Aquamantra is natural spring water labeled with "I AM LUCKY," "I AM LOVED," and "I AM HEALTHY."

Alexandra knew her water tasted great because the water itself is affected by the powerful messages altering its frequency and its flavor. Also, when she did demonstrations at markets, expos, and fairs, people always commented on how delicious and smooth the water was.

Alexandra thought, "If there was a way to prove it, then Aquamantra's credibility would increase in an over-populated bottled water industry." Shortly thereafter, Alexandra received an article about the Berkeley Springs International Water Tasting Competition. Her intuition nudged her to enter all three of her waters. To hold her intention on her waters winning the competition, Alexandra created a vision board.

The more you believe the more you will achieve.

She used graphics from the previous year's winner, placing the gold medal over her "I AM HEALTHY" bottle, a bronze medal over her "I AM LOVED" bottle, and a silver medal over her "I AM LUCKY bottle." Then she wrote "Aquamantra Sweeps Berkeley Springs International Water Competition." She printed it out and placed it near her computer monitor. For two months leading up to the competition, Alexandra visualized the excitement she would feel winning the competition and receiving the coveted awards.

Alexandra was sharing her water with all of the stars at the Academy Awards in Hollywood the same weekend the water tasting competition was taking place back east, and in all the excitement, she actually forgot about the water competition.

A couple of days later she received a press release stating, *"What people are calling the Academy Awards of Water, more than 200 people watched as 12 judges spent hours tasting more than 100 waters from 23 states and 12 foreign countries."*

As she read this, her first thought was that if she was receiving the press release, then she most likely didn't win. But, as she raced through the letter, she came to the winner of her category, Aquamantra's "I AM HEALTHY" tied for the gold medal, the first tie in years. Elation and ecstatic energy burst through her body as the information settled, Aquamantra really won! She quickly glanced at the vision board she made for herself and it was the gold medal that was placed on the "I AM HEALTHY" bottle. What a victory. Now Alexandra shares her story everywhere she goes as a testament to the power of a vision board to help you turn your dreams into your reality.

3. **Place pictures and reminders all around you.**

These reminders can be pictures or phrases. I suggest you place them in locations where you'll see them the most. In your kitchen, on the refrigerator door, on the bathroom wall, inside your medicine cabinet, on your computer, in your wallet, in your car, anywhere you'll see these reminders throughout the day.

Marci Shimoff recalls a time when she used pictures to her disadvantage and then later to her advantage. She described how, "I actually remember when I was quite young and used the Law of Attraction and didn't even know it. I was in the 8th grade and my girlfriends and I had wanted to lose ten pounds, so we each put a picture of our worst selves on the refrigerator. It made me so depressed, because every time I'd walk by the refrigerator, I would get this picture in my mind of myself at my worst. It made me open up the refrigerator and eat more ice cream. I thought, 'This doesn't work. Something's wrong with this picture!'

Always have one or more Power Statements you are focusing on.

Instead, I put a picture of my head on a great body that I cut out of a magazine, and every time I walked by the refrigerator I got that visual image in my mind of myself at my best or my ideal. It made me not want to open the refrigerator because that was the picture that I had so my actions became in alignment with that picture. That's the Law of Attraction."

4. Focus on 1 - 5 Power Statements every day.

Always have one or more Power Statements you are focusing on. Repeat them to yourself out loud regularly throughout your day, especially before you go to bed at night and first thing in the morning. There are 101 Power Statements in the back of this book to give you some ideas. They need to be stated positively. Believe and Declare that something is true for you now. Here are some ways to begin the sentence:

- I am…
- I am now…
- I am happy and grateful now that…
- In this very moment I…

Refer back to Chapter 4 for additional information on using Power Statements.

5. Visualize your "Three Minutes of Magic" every day.

Create a three-minute scene for every one of the desires on your index card. Imagine it as all-out, over-the-top, fun, exciting and engaging all of your senses. Studies have shown that the mind cannot tell the difference between what is imagined and what is real. So when you spend quality time visualizing your "Three Minutes of Magic," your mind believes it's true. This process raises your frequency and you attract your good in lightning speed!

6. Take additional steps that bring your dream closer.

If it's a new car you want, go and test drive the car of your dreams. If you want designer clothes, go and try them on. If you want a nicer home, go and look at nicer homes. If you want to own a nicer watch or jewelry, go and try them on. Whatever it is you want, put the energy of that all around you and you will increase your Attraction Quotient.

As you experience each of these, say to yourself with enthusiasm: "This is for me!" "This or something better is now mine!" "I deserve to own this or something better right now!" "I am ready to own this now!" "Just as I am seeking this, it is seeking me now!" "I am happy and grateful this is now mine!" "Thank you, thank you, thank you!"

It's done unto you as you believe. What you contemplate, you become. It's as simple and as uncomplicated as that.

7. Connect with like-minded people.

Get support from people who are on a similar path. When you see other people believing in and manifesting their dreams, it supports you in believing in and manifesting yours as well. Also, they'll help you to stay on the path and not get derailed. In the event that you do derail, they'll be there to help you get back up and keep believing. Through my website www.TheAwakeningBook.com you'll be able to find information on THE AWAKENING Mastery Community where you will be able to participate in teleclasses and attend seminars where you can connect with others who are experiencing their own AWAKENING.

Marci Shimoff presented her strategy for continuing to grow on a daily basis. She said, "My strategy to stay focused on my inner knowingness has been to surround myself with people who will remind me of that, to surround myself with books and with lectures. I'm a perpetual student. I continue to go to things that will remind me of what I believe is true and on target in life and to support my expansion and to support my ability to use the Law of Attraction every day."

8. Read, listen, watch, and grow.

Just as Marci mentioned above, remain a perpetual student. No one ever "arrives." There are always more ways to learn and grow. Your local library is one of the very best resources you'll find. There's an overabundance of books, tapes, CDs, DVDs, and videos on a variety of spiritual and personal growth topics. Spend some time reading daily, reviewing your index cards with your Power Statements, and affirming your beliefs. Positive change occurs when you are diligent in being a student of your own personal growth. The more deliberate and dedicated you are to self-development, the quicker you'll see positive results in your life.

AS YOU BELIEVE

Dr. James Golden touched on a key point to believing. He said, "Some of the greatest beings have said it as simply as possible. 'It's done unto you as you believe. What you contemplate, you become.' It's as simple and as uncomplicated as that."

Next, we'll be taking a closer look at the scientific aspect of the Law of Attraction and how you can raise the frequency of your vibration. This is a critical step in order to attract what you desire. Thoughts are energy and you must raise the frequency of your thoughts up to the same frequency as your desires.

CHAPTER 6

Raise Your Frequency

"Discover within yourself that beliefs are just that – beliefs- not truths. Recognize that any belief is just a memory based on what was, rather than what is." —Hale Dwoskin

The Seven Steps to AWAKENING are:

1. Discover Your Deepest Desires

2. Declare What You Desire

3. Believe It Is Yours Now

4. *Raise Your Frequency*

5. Eliminate Any Obstacles

6. Take Meaningful Action

7. Receive Your Good

YOUR VIBRATION IS A FACT, NOT FICTION

If there is anything that's been a secret about the Law of Attraction, it's this little known fact: Your thoughts and feelings are energy, and they vibrate at a certain frequency. Based on that vibration, your thoughts and feelings attract people, places, and things that vibrate at that same frequency.

When I was introduced to the Law of Attraction in the early eighties, no one mentioned this critical point. It's a key success factor to how quickly and how much of your deepest desires you actually attract.

Dr. Masaru Emoto, author of the best-selling books *Messages from Water*, *The Hidden Messages in Water*, and *The True Power of Water*, is known for his work with the vibration of water and how water crystals change when positive or negative words are placed on the container holding the water. The crystals from water in a container labeled with positive words such as love, gratitude, and joy, are beautiful and inspiring in their formation. The crystals from water in a container labeled with negative words such as hate, anger, and fear are fragmented and disturbing in their appearance.

Here is his perspective on you and your vibration, "Everything is created from vibration. If you are positive and optimistic and only have this level of vibration, then you will create a reality that is positive and serving. If you are negative and pessimistic and have that level of vibration, then you will create a reality that is negative and obstructive. When things resonate with the same or similar vibrations, they attract each other. To the people who do not believe this, I would say this is not an opinion—it is physics! It's a fact that everything is created from vibration."

The way this frequency works within the Law of Attraction is that 'like attracts like.'

Each expert I spoke with was emphatic that we attract what we send out. Are you attracting what you want? If not, it may be time to examine the vibrations you are sending out.

You may be familiar with the characteristics of a tuning fork. When a tuning fork is struck, it begins to vibrate. The interesting thing is that when that vibrating tuning fork is brought near an un-struck tuning fork, the un-struck tuning fork also begins to vibrate. Likewise, when we strike our "internal tuning fork" with the energy of ideas and emotions, we resonate with people, places, and things of like vibration and they're drawn to us.

Initially, this fact may seem a little "out there," just as many new ideas are. This clearly is not a new idea however, it's a fact that most of the population is unaware of or has not known how to use in their own lives.

EVERYTHING IS ENERGY

There is so much more to energy than most of us ever considered! David Koons explains this phenomenon further:

"Everything in the world is energy and all energy has a frequency. It vibrates at a certain level, and based on that vibration it creates a frequency. The way this frequency works within the Law of Attraction is that 'like attracts like.'

We see the visible spectrum as only one small sliver of the frequency and wavelengths out there. At one end of the spectrum you have radio waves and microwaves. At the other end of the spectrum you have gamma rays and x-rays.

For instance, certain animals can see in infrared, the human eye cannot. What does that mean? That means there is more to this world, more to this Universe than just what we can see. These frequencies we send out attract like frequencies.

For example, I served eight years in Marine Corp Special Forces. I had the honor of rising from the rank of Private all the way up to the rank of Captain and leading hundreds of Marines on missions from jumping out of airplanes to swimming miles in the ocean, all under the cover of darkness.

One of my jobs in that eight-year period early into the unit was being a radio operator. If I wanted to talk to someone at the other end, someone that could help me, provide support, or re-supply, I had to know on which frequency to contact them. Then I had to go to my radio, dial in that frequency, and an amazing thing happened - a connection occurred. What I put out came back to me in a response from the other party.

It's no different with the Law of Attraction. You might not be aware of the frequency you're sending out. On the surface you may be affirming certain things, but underneath there is doubt, or worry that is really getting the majority of your attention. Whatever frequency you're sending out attracts to you the same. You're connecting with the Universe and it's sending back to you people, places, circumstances, and opportunities of a similar frequency.

The Law of Attraction is where science and spirituality meet.

So if you're sending out doubt, if you're sending out fear, if you're sending out insecurity, or lack of self-confidence, you're going to manifest these all around you. If you're not sure of your frequency, look around you. Look at your results. They are the greatest indicators of the frequency you are sending."

ANYTHING IS POSSIBLE

I will repeat Alex Mandossian's comment, "The Law of Attraction is where science and spirituality meet." When you put these two together, anything is possible! That's a phrase I encourage you to repeat as you consider attracting your goals and dreams - ANYTHING IS POSSIBLE!

Mark Victor Hansen elaborated on that fact:

"We're at a brand new time in history. There's no limit. Imagination creates reality. That's why the Law of Attraction is so good. Napoleon Hill explained it like this: Every signal you send out finds a matching signal. That means that if your head was like a radio station and you tuned into the frequency of abundance you're only going to attract abundance. If you tune in to negativity or go in between stations you get static. That's the 1% doubt and you're out! You have to go back to the station and get clear. You have to say 'I'm rich' or 'I'm healthy.' It doesn't matter that you are poor or have a cold. You just have to tune into the station and stay focused there. It's the station that you're successful, healthy, and wealthy. It's the station that you're attracting only the right people to you.

What you want to do is raise your vibrations. Read books and listen to recordings by people who are maintaining a high vibrational state. There are a lot of good minds out there. You have to hang around someone who's resonating on a higher level than you are; someone who is already on the vibration you want to get to."

GOOD VIBRATIONS!

Since these vibrations we send out into the Universe bring like vibrations back to us, we want to make sure we're sending out good vibrations all the time! The best way to raise your vibration is to feel good! Connect to the precise feelings you'll have when you manifest your dreams and you'll feel an abundance of joy and excitement. Get as excited and feel as good as you will when your dreams are right before your eyes. Go places and do things that make you feel good. Treat yourself with kindness, make sure that you look your best and feel your best as much as possible.

Marci Shimoff explains it very clearly:

The best way to raise your vibration is to feel good! Connect to the precise feelings you'll have when you manifest your dreams and you'll feel an abundance of joy and excitement.

"The Law of Attraction works on the principle of feeling good. The better we feel the higher we vibrate. The higher we vibrate the more good we attract to us. We're just energy beings. We're drawing people, places, and things to us all the time based on our energy. Feeling good is a much higher energy than feeling bad. So you want to focus on feeling good! The Law of Attraction is not about struggle. We are definitely a society that is about struggle. Let me struggle to make this happen. The people I've seen who use the Law of Attraction most successfully do so in such a way that they have aligned themselves with an energy of fulfillment, happiness, and joy, and then miracles have happened."

Regarding our vibration, Alex Mandossian added, "I was taught that the Law of Attraction is the result of the Law of Vibration. Everything is energy. When my thoughts are vibrating with something else at the same level, we naturally attract each other. If I am vibrating at a level of consciousness about a certain object or objective, I can attract that.

Part of feeling good is getting into the spirit of allowing yourself to feel good. Some people live in such a rush with pressures coming at them from every angle that they've actually forgotten how to feel good, if they ever knew how to in the first place.

Mark Victor Hansen discussed this clearly. He said:

"Once you figure out what you want, you must get definite with the infinite. You must make sure you are allowing. The way you know if you're allowing is if you're living in a spirit of joy.

If you're not joyous, then your inner emotional guidance system is telling you, 'You screwed up!' Everybody resonates it from their core. They know whether something fits for them or not. They must learn to pay attention and listen to that."

To keep your good vibrations going, do at least three things for yourself each day that make you feel good. These things can be anything such as dancing to your favorite music in the living room, reading a favorite book, napping, cleaning out a drawer that bugs you, lolling (shamelessly doing nothing), getting a massage, or anything that brings you joy.

Take the time to raise your frequency and feel good!

THE ENERGY OF EMOTION

All of life is energy. Science has told us that "Energy can never be created or destroyed. It always has been and always will be. It is always moving into form, through form, and out of form."

One of the forms energy takes is emotion. I'm sure you've experienced the low energy feeling of disappointment or sadness, and likewise the high energy feeling of joy and excitement.

The most important thing about emotions is that they're the "juice" that revs up your Attraction Quotient. If you're aiming to attract more good in your life, it's not just all of the good and positive <u>thoughts</u> you think that are important, it's all the good and positive <u>feelings</u> you can feel that turbocharge your ability to be a powerful magnet.

The most important thing about emotions is that they're the "juice" that revs up your Attraction Quotient.

You can think, "I am worthy of my highest and greatest good. I always have been and always will be," all day long and still feel disappointment and fear if your bank account is upside down. To harness the power of emotion in this example, you need to find something to make you feel great to take your mind off of your troubles.

At times when I have struggled financially I would pack a lovely picnic lunch, and my son and I would go to one of our beautiful parks or beaches and have a good time together. I would have to force myself to go have fun, because the situation looked so depressing. But I knew that just hanging around being depressed was not going to do a single thing for me except make me feel more depressed.

When I train executives in public speaking, one of the things I teach them is to, "Fake it until you make it, and act like you love it!" In a way, that is exactly what I am asking you to do. Find something, anything, to be excited about and build upon it each day. It may seem awkward at first if you're facing a lot of challenges, but stick with it and do not give up. You'll turbocharge the speed with which you attract your abundance.

Let's examine the energy of emotions closer. There is a continuum of emotions and it begins at the lowest level with guilt and shame. These vibrate at the lowest frequency all the way up to love and gratitude, which vibrate at the highest frequency. There really isn't a neutral emotion, since all emotions are either positive or negative.

THE ENERGY OF EMOTION CONTINUUM

NEGATIVE AND SELF-DEFEATING					POSITIVE AND POWERFUL				
1	2	3	4	5	6	7	8	9	10
Guilt	Anger	Stress	Lack	Disappointment	Comfort	Joy	Confident	Abundant	Love
Shame	Hatred	Powerless	Regret	Frustration	Acceptance	Peaceful	Excitement	Contentment	Gratitude

The more you think about, relish in, and share love and gratitude, the higher your Attraction Quotient will be. The more you torture yourself with guilt and shame, the more likely you are to attract situations into your life that you do not want.

The more you think about, relish in, and share love and gratitude, the higher your Attraction Quotient will be.

With a solid belief, confidence, and intention you can create your desired life by understanding and utilizing energy and emotion. The shortest distance between what you wish for and what you get out of life is the powerful use of your emotions. They are vital tools for attracting your intended outcome.

You want to do everything possible to keep your emotions in the highest range where you feel good, experience joy, and share your gratitude. It's your daily pursuit of happiness that will make you soar. If you aren't happy you'll not be in the flow.

David Koons offered his comments on the correlation between thoughts and feelings, "We don't always get to choose our thoughts. But we do get to choose what to do with them. Thoughts become our feelings. They guide our feelings. If you want to know how you're thinking, look at how you're feeling. Based on that, that's where we start utilizing the Law of Attraction. We have these thoughts. We have these feelings. That's the true frequency we're sending out to the world."

Make certain your true frequency is high and find reasons to be happy!

EXAMINE WHAT MAKES YOU FEEL BAD

It's very important to take notice of the people and situations that make you feel bad. If you feel unhappy, mad, sad, etc. then you're sending out a low vibration and you'll attract it back.

To look at what makes you feel bad is called "contrast," and it helps you eliminate what you don't want, therefore allowing you to focus completely on what you do want.

Noticing the contrast is what we all naturally do to decide what we really want and like in life. When you go to a restaurant, you know the foods you really like to eat by contrasting them with what you don't like. When you listen to music, you become aware of the kind of music you prefer when you hear music that you dislike.

You want to quickly acknowledge what makes you feel bad or what you don't like, so that you can move on to focusing on what makes you feel good and what you do like.

HOW HIGH IS YOUR ATTRACTION QUOTIENT?

Your Attraction Quotient (A.Q.) is your ability to attract what you want in your life. If your A.Q. is high, then you're a powerful magnet, bringing all the good you desire straight to your doorstep. Yes, you're always attracting something, but in the context of THE AWAKENING, I'll be referring to your A.Q. in relation to the good that you attract. If it's low, you'll be attracting more of the things you don't want.

THE KEY TO INCREASING YOUR VIBRATION IS TO CREATE
AND CONNECT TO POSITIVE EMOTIONS ALL DAY, EVERYDAY.

POSITIVE EMOTIONS

=

HIGH VIBRATIONS

=

HIGH ATTRACTION QUOTIENT

It's critical for you to be aware of how high your Attraction Quotient is at any given moment. Spend time throughout the day checking in with yourself about how you're feeling. Scan your body for any uncomfortable emotions you may be feeling; you may feel a tightness in your chest or butterflies in your stomach. Ask yourself why you're feeling this, where did these feelings originate? It's only through your awareness of these feelings that you can take the steps needed to raise your A.Q.

IT ALL BEGINS IN CONSCIOUSNESS

It all begins in our minds, whether we are aware of it or not. Stephen Lewis, founder of EMC² and Co-Author of the novel *Sanctuary: The Path To Consciousness* says:

"Frequencies exist in consciousness before they exist in the material world. This is a fundamental of quantum mechanics and quantum physics.

When something exists in your consciousness, it may or may not exist in your material world. However, if it exists in your consciousness, it will exist physically, emotionally, or whatever it may be, in a physical, measurable world.

First, everything takes place in consciousness. The stuff we call DNA just tags along almost as an addendum. We create our world with consciousness, everything is consciousness."

MIND OVER BODY

Here is a shocking example Stephen Lewis shared with me that demonstrates the power that your consciousness, or mind, has over your body:

"Researchers conducted tests on people with multiple personality disorders. They began by performing routine physical examinations on each person. The first person changed his personality while he was being examined. This was a man who was an insulin dependent diabetic. Diabetes is diagnosed by a glucose monitoring machine. When he changed personalities, his blood was no longer diabetic. It did not happen in the 120 days it takes to make new blood cells, but instantly he was not diabetic. They assumed the machine broke. They went and got a new machine. It reported the same change. It couldn't be that every machine broke at the same time. The new personality had no need to create the imbalance of diabetes or the frequencies that create the diabetic state. Studies like this have been duplicated repeatedly. It is not understood medically, but it is obvious. Things exist in consciousness first and your body follows suit. When he switched back to the original personality, he became diabetic again.

Everything about people, for better or for worse, is created by consciousness. That is the basis for the Law of Attraction."

Most of us have absolutely no clue about the power we have to change our lives.

Most of us have absolutely no clue about the power we have to change our lives. This example shows how absolutely mind-boggling our capabilities truly are. My goal in THE AWAKENING is to give you access to the amazing power you have right now to change your life for the better.

Stephen went on to explain:

"When you speak of medicine, you don't deal with consciousness, you deal with the physical world initially. Whether it is the flu, cancer, or depression, you deal with it first in the physical world, and consciousness is never addressed; that's called diagnosis and treatment, and hopefully results in a cure or repair, and it's a good thing.

However, when you speak of a healing, you are dealing with something existing in consciousness and understanding that it will cease to exist physically if it no longer exists in your consciousness.

Everything that exists, exists at a number of levels. You can focus on the physical aspect of it, the emotional aspect of it, or the spiritual aspect of it. It just depends upon how you wish to address it. There is no distinction between physical, emotional, and spiritual. They exist as one entity. We only separate them for purpose of conversation. But that separation is artificial. There is no division."

HEALING THROUGH WATER

Our bodies are made up of 70% water. Physically we are more water than anything else. Dr. Masaru Emoto is proving that what we think, say, and feel is not pointless information. He believes that the vibration of our thoughts, words, and feelings shape our existence.

One of the most profound studies Dr. Emoto discussed was his findings on Alzheimer's disease. He has had the opportunity to successfully heal patients with various disorders through using Hado water, or water that has been imprinted with a positive vibrational frequency. In his studies, he learned that the disease we know as Alzheimer's stems from the emotions of sadness and loneliness. These emotions attract aluminum that collects in the pituitary gland and the hypothalamus part of the brain, which regulates memory.

He said, "When negative emotions become deeply prolonged, suppressed, or intensified by other factors, such as sadness and loneliness, they disturb the elemental balance and attract stress vibrations such as aluminum, viruses, and bacteria. Due to the highly polluted water many drink and bathe in, people are more and more susceptible to accumulating toxic heavy metals such as aluminum, which will affect one's memory function."

AWAKENING YOUR CONSCIOUSNESS

On the subject of consciousness, Stephen Lewis said:

"Some sabotage themselves by making sure they are never satisfied because they are incapable of being grateful for what they have. They are never satisfied because they have subconscious imbalances. When something becomes conscious you can deal with it.

Consciousness is not a numeric state. Consciousness is a state where you are aware of yourself or not. It is a relative state. You have met people in your life who are incredibly conscious and other people who are unconscious.

The question is what is consciousness? Consciousness is very simple. It is the degree to which you perceive yourself and your interaction with everyone and everything in the universe."

IT'S ALL IN HOW YOU CHOOSE TO LIVE

We live in a world that focuses on negativity everywhere we turn. I asked David Koons what he recommends to his students and he replied,

"The first thing we have them look at is their environment. What is the environment you wish to live in? Do you wish to live in a negative, non-supportive environment? Do you want to be a victim and react to life? Do you want to live in a non-loving home? Do you want to live in a hostile universe?

First and foremost, you have to make a choice. What kind of environment do you want to live in? We learn from research that our environment is one of the primary influences in our life. It affects how our children turn out, it affects how we react and respond each and every day.

What does a positive, supportive environment look like? We read books that are empowering, we feel inspired when we're done. Choosing what you expose yourself to, choosing who you talk to, and who you associate with, making a conscious decision to separate yourself someone who just starts verbally regurgitating all over you by saying, 'Oh, this is horrible, this is terrible, I can't believe they'd do that. They're jerks. This is stupid.' Separate yourself. Make a conscious decision to walk away.

We all become a product of our environment. Surround yourself with pictures, songs, music, artwork, and all those things that you feel good about. Treat your body like the temple that it is and only allow positive visual, auditory, and kinesthetic things into your life that support you in moving toward your ideal life."

VIBEOLOGY

So, what's your vibe? Your emotions, both positive and negative, vibrate at a certain level of energy. What you want and don't want is vibrating at a certain level of energy. All that is good in the world is on a high vibration or frequency. The sooner you raise your vibration, the sooner you'll attract your good.

Ask yourself these questions:

1. What are three things I can do for myself each day that make me feel good?
2. What makes me feel bad or unhappy?
3. What people do I interact with on a daily basis that could interfere with me keeping my vibration high?
4. What steps can I take to separate myself from these people who lower my vibration?
5. What kind of environment do I choose to live in, supportive or non-supportive? Define specifically what that would look like.

We are completely responsible for creating our reality by the frequency of the thoughts and feelings we focus on. Raise your frequency now by focusing on high vibration thoughts and feelings that will create a wonderful reality for your future. The Power Statements in Appendix 3 at the back of the book will help you do this.

In Chapter 7 we will look at removing some of the obstacles that can possibly prevent you from increasing your Attraction Quotient so that you can be a powerful magnet of attraction.

CHAPTER 7

Eliminate Any Obstacles

"Are you interested or committed? When you are interested, you'll do what's convenient, when you are committed, you'll do what it takes."

—*John Assaraf*

The Seven Steps to AWAKENING are:

1. Discover Your Deepest Desires

2. Declare What You Desire

3. Believe It Is Yours Now

4. Raise Your Frequency

5. *Eliminate Any Obstacles*

6. Take Meaningful Action

7. Receive Your Good

LIFE HAPPENS

When you practice *The Seven Steps to AWAKENING*, miracles will begin to happen. You'll be able to create amazing results using the Law of Attraction. That doesn't mean that you won't be met with any issues, obstacles, or problems. It's possible that you won't, but if you do, don't let them take you off of your focus. Don't give in to them. How you face these challenges is what makes all the difference.

In Section Two you'll be presented with *The Five Keys to Accelerate Your Power of Attraction*. Within those five chapters, we'll examine several common obstacles in depth such as negative thinking, living a stress-filled life, low self-esteem, fear, and self-sabotaging belief systems. In this chapter I'll be touching on a variety of additional obstacles that you may encounter as you are learning to master the Law of Attraction.

As I was talking with each of the experts I interviewed, they all agreed that obstacles are a normal part of the process for everyone. They were no strangers to obstacles themselves. They all spoke with candor as we discussed how they handled the obstacles that were a part of their journey. And they spoke with compassion and encouragement for those who are new to using the Law of Attraction.

You'll find some powerful exercises within these pages, so once again, have your pen and paper nearby.

SELF-CRITICISM

Marci Shimoff touched on her own challenge with self-criticism and how she overcame it. "One obstacle for me was being negative towards myself. And of course, however we judge ourselves, is how we will also judge others. I was very critical and hard on myself and on other people. As I've had more compassion for myself, I've found I've had more compassion for others. The more I'm able to come up with compassion for others, the softer and more compassionate I am on myself."

"The idea that being hard on ourselves is going to motivate us is completely backwards. On the contrary, the more we are able to love ourselves and others, the more the Law of Attraction works."

I want to put her next comment in flashing neon lights on the front of this book, *"The idea that being hard on ourselves is going to motivate us is completely backwards. On the contrary, the more we are able to love ourselves and others, the more the Law of Attraction works."*

That's worth repeating. Please read it slowly and carefully and let it sink in to the very depths of your soul. "The idea that being hard on ourselves is going to motivate us is completely backwards. On the contrary, the more we are able to love ourselves and others, the more the Law of Attraction works."

Learning to love and accept ourselves just as we are right now is the perfect foundation upon which you can build a fabulous, joy-filled life.

Most divorce decrees state "Irreconcilable Differences" as the cause, but in reality if you traced many divorces back to their true origin you would find judgment and criticism festering at the core. We cannot love and accept others when we cannot love and accept ourselves.

I was recently talking with the owner of an exclusive personal training fitness center. He said that no matter the shape or the size, he has never met a woman who was happy with her body. I'm certain this doesn't come as a surprise to you since every single magazine has one to five articles in it showing women how to firm up and trim down. And even though there are thousands of books written on the topic, authors keep pumping them out and people keep buying them. This is an issue so common we practically yawn over it. But if we look at this closer, it should astound us! It has become not only acceptable to judge and criticize ourselves mercilessly, but it's the norm. I know there are some of you who have escaped this tragedy. Congratulations, you are the exception to the rule.

We must learn to love and accept ourselves as we go through this journey called "life." When I teach presentation skills, I have a disclaimer at the bottom of the self-evaluation pages and it reads verbatim:

REMEMBER:

You are never allowed to be critical or judgmental of yourself. To improve your performance, simply ask these questions:

1. What can I do better next time?

2. What would help me to do that?

You are never allowed to be critical or judgmental of yourself.

I wish we were all born knowing this disclaimer! I'm not talking about the kind of acceptance where you relax and say, "Oh well," when you don't land a pivotal sale for your company, or when you fail to meet a critical deadline. You don't just ignore these.

The kind of acceptance I'm talking about is acknowledging that you did the best you could "this time" and to improve you must kindly ask yourself, "What can I do better next time?" and "What would help me to do that?" This will generate the kind of response that will motivate you to keep moving forward.

You'll notice the question doesn't read, "What <u>should</u> I do better next time?" Or, "What <u>should</u> help me to do that?" Anytime you hear yourself using the word "should" towards yourself or others, be reminded that it carries a tone of criticism with it. So here's the key, don't "should" on yourself or others! Say that real fast ten times and you'll get the point even more clearly!

YOUR FUTURE IS NOT YOUR PAST

Yes, history does have a way of repeating itself, however when you're diligent in focusing on all of the concepts and principles contained within *THE AWAKENING*, you'll be putting your past behind you and creating a wonderful new future.

Too often it's as though we get in the car and start to drive down the street, and instead of enjoying the landscape that's unfolding before us, we're looking in our rear view mirror at our past. If you spend all of your time looking back at your past, you're going to make a mess out of your present moment and your future.

When you're creating an exciting future using the Law of Attraction, you want to focus on all of the wonderful opportunities and possibilities before you, not on your past. This can be a major obstacle for many people.

Hale Dwoskin gave this moving perspective on how your past colors your current reality, he said:

"Belief systems play a critical role in utilizing the Law of Attraction. What happens is when most people try to attract what they want, subconsciously they believe they can't do it, or have it. They look into their past experience, as opposed to what's really possible now. They find themselves simply referring to their past failures and that's what they attract. If you believe you're going to fail, those beliefs color how you perceive reality. They also are filters through which you see the world. No matter how hard you try to think and feel positively, if you're not dealing with the underlying belief systems of your past that say you can't or you don't know how or you're afraid, it will never happen for you."

∽∾∾

Letting go of the past is critical to your success in using the Law of Attraction.

∽∾∾

We'll take extensive time to examine Overriding Background Beliefs in Chapter 10. Letting go of the past is critical to your success in using the Law of Attraction. It's impossible to focus on all of the positive and powerful things developing in your life and be agonizing over your past at the same time. With that faulty strategy, your past will win and your future will fail.

THE GIFT OF THE PRESENT MOMENT

On the flip side of living in our past is when we get too involved in worrying about our future. I've heard it said that if you've got one foot in the past and one foot in the future, you're going to fall flat on your bum today!

Rev. Jim Turrell, had this to say about how important it is for us to stay in the present:

"Of course, you go through your day and you have problems that are immediate and perhaps problems that might be 48 or 72 hours or more away. If your mind is always thinking about the future, even about the near future, you can't possibly be available to anyone in the here and now, if you're out there wondering about the future.

You have no presence in your life today. Instead you just have episodes replaying over and over in your mind. In addition to not being present, this makes you pretentious. You pretend to be available. We all know people like this. You go to them and they pretend to be available to you, but you know in the back of your heart they're not really there for you. It's not like they don't want to be there for you. Their mind is some place else.

So, being fully present in the here and now is what activates the Law of Attraction."

IT DOESN'T HAVE TO BE "HARD" WORK

There are many influences on us throughout our youth that form our thoughts and feelings about love, life, and success. Unfortunately, they're not always the best influences on the beliefs we form that carry us into our adult years.

Alex Mandossian spoke frankly about some of the obstacles he faced regarding work. He said:

"One of my obstacles had to do with my beliefs. I had certain beliefs about success as a child and they continued into adulthood. It was only 5 or 6 years ago, that these beliefs were dissolved and redefined. That belief was called the Calvinistic or Protestant ethic. I call it the Middle Eastern ethic because I come from Middle Eastern roots. I am Armenian and speak Armenian. The Calvinistic ethic says that if I work hard, I will become more successful. I bought into it and started living it. That was my belief for success. I felt I could only be successful, if I really worked hard. If I don't work for it, there's no way I can be successful. If I was successful and did not work hard, I had better feel guilty about it. This Calvinistic ethic of needing to work harder, to make more money, to become more successful was a limiting belief that I had to learn to override.

I had to override it in business because there was no leverage with this belief. I found the opposite to be true. Since the year 2001 the more free days I have, the more money I have made. The more rejuvenation time I take, the more successful I am because I have had more time to rest.

I was able to overcome this by working through it and approaching it as practice. For example, when I go to the gym, I am going to practice and see if I can lift a few weights. I have to rest and rejuvenate because I am breaking down the muscle fiber. The muscle grows during rest. I brought this idea into my business.

Also, the fear of losing my family was inspirational to me. When I was living in Manhattan, I was working 16 hour days with the threat of losing my wife, Amy, Gabriel, my son, and Brianna, my daughter. The fear of loss is a functional fear which made me practice implementing free days. It took about 3 years for me to have my first official free day, without sneaking in an email, or making a call without someone knowing. When it comes to work, I almost have an addictive behavior.

The moment I had my first free day, I worked through that experience even though it was inspired by fear of loss. After the free day, I woke up at 4 a.m. and sent an email out. It was four hours after my official free day was over that I realized I had done it. I decided to do another one a week later. I realized it was not so hard. I made my executive assistant into my personal coach. I started to visualize 365 pieces in this puzzle which is representing the number of days. Ninety of those pieces, I painted as free days and put them in my calendar. I have been doing that now for the past few years. It has been the most amazing and rejuvenating experience. I dissolved the belief that you have to work hard in order to be successful. By having my first free day a few years ago, nothing bad happened. Now it is a part of my monthly and quarterly planning."

One of the many wonderful things about using the Law of Attraction to create results in your life is that it doesn't have to be a grueling process to achieve a high level of success.

CONFLICTING VALUES

A significant part of the processes you'll go through in this book will lead you to your AWAKENING. A component of AWAKENING is honesty through self-examination. Many people have conflicting wants and values. In order to create the life you want, you'll need to get real with yourself and make certain that your wants and your values are in alignment. If watching TV in your spare time is more important to you than reading books or listening to information that will help you, your values may be off kilter because you're not using your spare time to feed your soul.

Dr. John Demartini spoke about the conflict many people have between what they say they want and what they actually value. He said:

"I've asked people by the thousands, I mean thousands, 'How many of you want to be wealthy?' They all put their hands up, everybody. Then I ask them, 'How many of you are wealthy?' About one or two percent raise their hands.

When we look closer at their values those who were in the wealthy one or two percent had money as one of their top four or five values. The rest of the group has wealth as number seventeen or thirty on their list of values. It's so amazing!

As long as wealth is way down on their value list, it's not really important to them. The second they get money, they'll spend it on immediate gratifying and depreciating assets that will never build wealth. They never save their money. They're going to live in la-la-land, fantasizing that they're going to be wealthy someday. The reality is that they're living according to their current values. They don't realize it, but they're setting themselves up for failure expecting to get wealthy, when they don't really value it."

VALUE RESTRUCTURING

I thought this was such a great example. So many people say they want one thing, and then go in the opposite direction. I asked Dr. Demartini, "What do these people do then if they really do want to be wealthy? How do you help them raise this value from thirty to one of their top four or five values?"

While he is specifically addressing this regarding money, he did say that this process would work just as precisely with any other issues a person was facing. He explained further:

"What you do is list the benefits of saving money and building wealth. You ask the question, 'How is saving money and building wealth going to help me in my life?' You ask that general question and then you answer it between 200 and 1,000 times. They will find that when the 'why' is big enough, the 'how's' takes care of themselves.

Answer that question over and over again, possibly hundreds of times, until your brain sees the benefits of doing that which you desire. If you don't have a big enough reason for doing it, you just won't do it.

Let's say we want to have wealth, but we also want to keep our families. We ask, 'How is saving money and building wealth going to help our kids, my family, our children's education, our children's clothes, our children's health?'

We link it to whatever we want also applying our values. We do the other 200 links and I guarantee I've done this hundreds and hundreds of times. If you take a person through this process, and it may take hours or days for them to complete it, but the second they do, they see things differently and act according to those new things. They take action. I've seen people that have not been able to save money for years, literally in five hours of work, done. They save money and their whole financial future changes right then and there."

I can hear many people saying right now, "List 200 to 1,000 things! No way! I'm not going to do that. That's too much work." If these thoughts were anywhere remotely in your mind, then don't hesitate to write down a shorter list of 20 things that you and your loved ones will miss out on as result of having a precarious financial future. That won't take long at all. And when you're done with that list you'll be glad to start shifting your values around by listing the 200 – 1,000 great things that money will do to help you and your family.

If your health or weight is something that's currently an obstacle for you, apply these same steps. Ask yourself "How will losing weight or taking better care of my body help me to live a happier, more energetic, successful life? Make a list of 200 to 1,000 things, as Dr. Demartini suggests, and you'll have a new perspective on your health, fitness, and vitality.

Once again if that long list sounds too daunting, go for the short list of 20 things you and your loved ones will miss out on, or inconveniences you'll have to go through, as result of having problems with your health and being overweight.

LIFE'S AMAZING LESSONS

Using the Law of Attraction and the principles contained within *THE AWAKENING* puts you at an advantage. However, it doesn't mean that things will always go perfectly. You must be committed to the vision you have for your future and maintain persistence until you reach your goals.

Don't let anything deter you from achieving the life you want to create. The desire that is planted within your heart is one that you must work toward fulfilling. There are many more obstacles than we can discuss within the confines of this book, but none of these obstacles are bigger than you. No matter what, you can overcome.

However, it is important to recognize that what appears to be negative, or an obstacle in your life, isn't always bad. In Chapter 1 we discussed that your good isn't always what you think it is. As I reflect on some of the greatest obstacles in my life I am grateful for them. Was I at the time? Not always. But I've found that the miracles are always there when I look for them.

These lessons are very important in helping you to own your power, develop determination and become the best person you can be. There's a saying, "Kites fly highest against the wind," and I believe it is true for humans as well. Adversity can present you with amazing lessons that take you to the next level of personal growth. If you look at these experiences negatively and resist them it is possible you will miss the lesson and prevent your growth. Then you will have to go through a similar kind of experience again and again until you do. In other words, if you don't learn the lesson from the experience the first time, you'll have to keep re-experiencing the lesson until you get it.

An excellent example of this is people who bounce from one damaging and hurtful relationship to another. They don't stop long enough to examine the last one and learn the lesson before they are on to the next destructive relationship. This can go on for a lifetime.

Even greater growth comes when we can look at all situations and suspend judging them as good or bad and just enjoy them, or learn from them. Many of the situations we judge as bad are incredible opportunities for growth and take us on to much greater levels of abundance, happiness and freedom.

Reflect on some of your greatest challenges and try to see the lessons hidden within them.

Even greater growth comes when we can look at all situations and suspend judging them as good or bad and just enjoy them, or learn from them.

BEGIN ANEW

Here is a story of a man, Felipe, whose life was shattered and the determination he had to begin anew:

"I was married 24 years when the unraveling of the closest relationship I'd ever known was fatally struck. One day my wife told me she was finished with our marriage and asked me to leave. Within 28 days from that horrible moment, she filed for divorce. At 44, I thought my life was as secure as it could be. Great health and an awesome network of friends and family were at the top of my list of blessings. I had a great life with things both material and immaterial to go with it.

But when the divorce hit, it was like an extremely cold bucket of jagged edged ice thrown into my face of complacency and comfort. The reality of being alone and the fear that accompanies divorce set in immediately. I recall feeling like an instant loser and the fear of the unknown was heavy upon me. I felt uninformed, isolated, rejected, and pitied.

I often asked myself, 'How could this be? How could I have let my life partner down so much that she couldn't stand to be with me one more day?' I don't think I will ever have the answers to some of my questions. I don't think I am meant to. I have learned over the course of the last 18 months that many of us, not just me, are faced with these types of questions everyday.

I have a tremendous faith in God. I believe in a God that is interested in being intimately involved in my life. I began working on my new life, picking up one vital broken piece at a time. My attitude was hungry for deeper meaning and significance at this point.

I met a young lady who introduced me to a movie called, *The Secret*. She told me that maybe the film could be of some encouragement and support to me as it had been for her.

It mentioned many of the feelings already in my heart, just not as well-connected or verbally expressed. To know that you have influence over what happens to you and those around you rang very loud and clear into my soul. I immediately began using the Law of Attraction.

I've learned how to view the obstacles in my path as leaps of growth, each time making me more of a winner than ever before.

I made a fresh start and each day I learned a little bit more about how to take my life by the shoulders and shake it for all it was worth, and to live life to the fullest. I dreamed of not fearing anything again, to live as one who deeply appreciated the life God gave for me to live; one filled with purpose and joy!

I reached into my soul and found courage dormant there ready to be unleashed to go back out again and take risks of being loved again, making more investments in people, attempting new ventures in business, and learning a little more each day in such a way that giving it back to the benefit of others would be the only obvious thing to do.

I would also ask myself, 'What was I attracting all these years?' I realized that most of the negative things in my life had 'option boxes' for me to select from. Was I willing to take personal responsibility for my part in life, or would I go on blaming others for the things happening to me?

The biggest difference, as I see it, between those who move forward and regain a sense of normalcy and a sense of balance in their lives and those who are lost in their 'what if's' forever, is the power to overcome the constant barrage of negative thinking we all face.

It is clear to me; my character is under construction, and under new management. My confidence has increased and my creative resource is only growing bigger and better each day. I've learned how to view the obstacles in my path as leaps of growth, each time making me more of a winner than ever before!"

In Chapter 8 we'll discuss how you can harness the power of focus and begin taking meaningful action towards your new life and aspirations.

CHAPTER 8

Take Meaningful Action

"The way to get started is to quit talking and begin doing."

—Walt Disney

The Seven Steps to AWAKENING are:

1. Discover Your Deepest Desires

2. Declare What You Desire

3. Believe It Is Yours Now

4. Raise Your Frequency

5. Eliminate Any Obstacles

6. *Take Meaningful Action*

7. Receive Your Good

CREATE THE VISION, THEN TAKE THE ACTION

One of the most valuable steps to your success is to get a clear vision of what you're aiming to achieve. You began this in Chapter 3 where you focused on discovering your deepest desires. I like the very unique way that Alex Mandossian looks at this process:

"When I start with an idea, goal, or intention, I like to call it a vision. I make this vision as clear as possible, like a jigsaw puzzle with many pieces that make up the picture. The vision is vivid, clear, and pre-painted on the cardboard pallet. It is whole and not broken up into little pieces, yet.

Once the vision is clear in my mind, the steel blades of the jigsaw come down on the cardboard pallet. It is then broken into pieces and turned into a jigsaw puzzle. Each of the pieces represents the different action steps that need to come together to make the vision whole again.

The goal is to make the vision clear and colorful.

My greatest obstacle has been lazy thinking by not creating a vivid vision and painting it on the cardboard pallet. The steel blades come down and chop up the pieces. As I am putting the pieces together, I am creating the vision at the same time. I have blank pieces that I am mashing together until they fit. I become really frustrated because they don't.

What happened is the vision is not clear and complete. The steel blades came down too soon. As a result, there are obstacles that cannot be overcome. If I am painting as I am going, the vision is changing.

The goal is to make the vision clear and colorful. I pre-paint it in my mind so I can learn how to get from point A to point B. I know all of the pieces fit. I know they belong together because they were clear in my mind before hand, not during, or after.

SET GOALS, MAKE PLANS, TAKE ACTION

Once you have a clear vision in place, begin identifying the goals and plans that will make your vision a reality. I must credit Brian Tracy with what has become my mantra, "Set goals, make plans, take action! Set goals, make plans, take action!" It circles through my mind repeatedly throughout every business day. This means a lot to me because I've been the person who was paralyzed in inactivity, not so much by overanalyzing, but just not knowing who I was, what I was supposed to do, or what would make me happy AND financially secure. Let's examine each further:

SET GOALS

In this step, all you're doing is taking what you declared in step two and putting it down on paper as a goal. The key here is to be as specific as you can be by defining what, how much, and by when.

MAKE PLANS

This is where you turn goal into an action step in your calendar or on your daily to-do list. Schedule it into your day just like you would any other appointment.

TAKE ACTION

Do it! Don't make excuses, just do it. Remember, you're always creating either results or excuses. And excuses don't get you very far. Go for results.

PRIORITIZE

Some of the most talented people have a great office. It's organized and efficient. There's no dust anywhere. They also have great marketing materials and jazzy websites. But, they're not progressing in their careers or they're struggling to get by financially in their own businesses.

Procrastination and lack of prioritization takes over and encourages them to do everything other than what they really need to be doing. If one of your goals is to create a more prosperous future for yourself, a daily question you want to ask is, "What is my greatest income earning opportunity right now and how can I focus solely on that?" Or, if you're working for someone else, the key question is, "What is the most important priority to my boss and how can I focus on excelling at that?"

The priority is what you want to focus on, not the marketing materials, or the fancy office, or any other accoutrements, you'll have plenty of time to focus on that later.

ARE YOU THE FROG ON THE LILY PAD?

As David Koons and I were talking about action he told this story:

"It reminds me of the old riddle, you have two frogs sitting on a lily pad, and one decides to jump. How many frogs are on the lily pad? There are still two frogs. One <u>decided</u> to jump, he didn't jump. He hasn't jumped yet.

You can think about it all day long, but until you take the action, you're not going to create that symphony of activities of the universe conspiring toward your success. The action is absolutely essential to validating the Law of Attraction. Otherwise, you haven't completed the formula."

You can think about it all day long, but until you take the action, you're not going to create that symphony of activities.

Think of all the good ideas you've had that you didn't take action on and pick any one of them. Imagine how different your world would possibly be right now if you had followed through on it with blazing action? Guess what? You can still do that! Don't just sit on that lily pad of yours, go do it!

THE RULE OF FIVE

Success leaves clues and I think it's important to observe what helps successful people take action. Alex Mandossian has a great technique that he shared:

"Writing down a goal can make a huge impact. I utilize a system that Jack Canfield taught me. It is called the 'Rule of Five.' I write down five physical things that I need to do. Every time I do those physical actions, I put a check mark by the action on my white board. These are little visions that can be executed and developed. I take a digital snap shot of the x's on the white board. I literally have thousands of snap shots of these pictures.

I feel that I have attracted success in my life because I have done these little things. They have been the structure to my success. I have been keeping these photos for a keepsake for my kids. I am going to put these pictures online. I remember the day when I started audio on the internet in 2001, surveying my market instead of telling them, teaching my first tele-seminar because it was written down. It is a great way to look at your history. If your life is worth living, then it is worth journaling. This is Law of Attraction to me."

The Rule of Five is a great system. Let's take it a step further. After you have your list of five action items, start with the one that's the most important and don't go on to anything else until that one is complete. Then go down the rest of your list.

As you move down the list and complete the tasks at hand, remember to reward yourself for a job well-done. You've got to acknowledge your progress and find your own way to applaud yourself so that you continue to move forward. Sometimes the perfectionist in us makes it feel like it's never good enough. Refuse to give the slightest thought to this idea! Acknowledge your progress and give yourself a reward for action taken. It could be something simple like a massage, or something grand like a trip or a desired material item. Remember the size of the reward isn't what counts; it's the great feeling that you've accomplished something and you're creating forward movement in your life.

INSPIRATION AND INTENTION

Marci Shimoff spoke to me about the importance of inspired action. She said, "Taking action for the sake of taking action is useless. It's taking action from a deeper foundation of knowing that it is the action you're led to take. It's being in touch. It's action that's inspired. Once you know what the outcome is you desire, let's say it's a career that you're wanting. When you know inside that the career you love is going to happen for you, you automatically take the right actions and the inspired actions to make it happen. It is coming from a place of inspiration, rather than from a place of "I have to.""

A dear friend of mine, John, shared his story of success and the power of intention. He said:

"I had validation of my worthlessness, punctuated by humiliation and hopelessness. A dark cloud of despair colored every aspect of my life a dingy grey, we were bankrupt!

After the company I worked for folded in the aftermath of 9/11, I found myself over fifty, unemployable and broke. Never in my wildest dreams did I imagine that one day I'd be accepting food from neighbors just to feed my family, or selling my wife's wedding ring to help make a past-due mortgage payment, allowing our family to stay yet another month in our home.

Financial fear; I lived with it every day. But the spark of the Divine was fanned into a burning fire by the clarity of my conviction that this place, to which I had sunk, financially and emotionally, was definitely NOT congruent with God's plan for my life. God, after all, wants us to be rich! Faith played a huge role in transforming our lives - faith, backed by intention.

It all began when I took a class on prosperity at our church. As part of our class assignment, one night we all constructed a "Dream Board" made from pictures and words cut out of various magazines, depicting what we wanted our lives to look like. The "Dream Board" I made that night still hangs in my office today, because the love and vision of an abundant life that my classmates all saw for me that night, at a time when I was struggling to see anything but a wasted life, was the turning point in my journey to hope and healing. I had a Vision!

Now it was time to couple vision with the power of intention, and I intended to get myself free as fast as I could. My clear intention was to build my own business, one that would give me both financial and time freedom for the rest of my life….and to do it fast!

Momentum is built by consistently taking action.

Momentum is built by consistently taking action. Focused only on what I wanted to happen, ignoring all else, I started what I knew was a business with powerful potential, and threw myself into action for 16 hour days. Within one year, I had replaced my previous income from the lost job. Within another year we were enjoying a very comfortable lifestyle. After just one more year, the momentum I had built made each month's check like winning the lottery!

Today, we are truly blessed. This past Christmas I did something I had always dreamed of doing…I bought my wife a new car for Christmas. Took her to the dealership and let her pick out exactly what she wanted, chrome wheels and all. I travel regularly to Europe and throughout the United States to help others achieve their own dreams of starting and running their own successful business from home.

Today, I don't work nearly as much as I did at the beginning of this journey. In fact, I took time off lately to pursue a dream I've had since I was a teen-ager, getting a private pilot's certificate. What a thrill last week to fly my wife over the lights of Phoenix at night in our own small plane. Next month we're going to Hawaii for almost a month of rest and FUN! Life is good. Very, very good! And the power of intention and taking action has really paid off."

I actually stayed at John and Merilee's house a couple of times during their rebuilding years and John left the house around 4:30 – 5:00 a.m. every morning to go get a cup of coffee and returned shortly thereafter to his office and began making phone calls and continued well into the night. I saw his dream unfolding. I saw his sacrifice for his vision. His inspiration was a burning flame and it took hold, caught fire, and spread throughout his life and transformed his vision into reality.

It was an awesome experience to watch their lives take on such a dramatic change in that amount of time. It was because of John's dedication, desire, drive, inspiration, and above all, action, that made his life what it is today. He did something! He created something! He gave his all, and all that the world had in store for his family has come back to him.

THE NEXT INDICATED STEP

You don't have to know the whole plan from A to Z, but you do need to have an idea what the next indicated step is for you to make your dreams come true. When we begin thinking too far out of the moment, sometimes the magnitude of our actions and the thought of change can paralyze us. By simply focusing on the next step and not looking miles down the road, you feel a calm sense of power at making your dreams come true.

Think of this step as your flashlight in the darkness. As you move your light, you can see just a few feet ahead. By keeping your light focused on the immediate path before you, you're not overwhelmed by the big picture.

Chellie Campbell explained it very well, she said:

"The Law of Attraction is where we start. The Law of Attraction says 'What you focus on is what you create.' Edgar Casey years ago said 'Thoughts are things.' For me, it was just like the world opened up. I said 'Oh, what I focus on, what I think about is what leads me to take action. Then the action is what produces results.

Then you have to believe in yourself and believe that the world is there to serve you. The world is just a big computer. We can program it for what we want. Then we have to take a step down the road. I know that very often people say, 'All you have to do is think it and you don't even have to know how it's going to happen.' I would say this, 'You don't have to know every step on the road to having the car you want or the house of your dreams or the millions of people in your audience. You don't have to know every hundred steps along the way. You have to know a couple of steps so you can take the first two.'

When you take the first two steps, the next two reveal themselves. So many times I've had a great idea and thought, 'I'm going to go for this.' I don't know how to do it. I start asking people, 'If I wanted this in my life, how would I get it?' Well, do this and do this. Then I do those two things and then I ask the next person who shows up, 'Okay, what's the next step?' They give me another step. Then I do that one. That's why I read books and listen to CDs all the time. I'm looking for the next steps. They will show up."

Marci Shimoff followed in suit by adding, "For me, taking action means taking the action that's in front of me right now and trusting that it's going to lead me to what's next. That's the action that's meant to be taken."

Sometimes the next indicated step might just be a small step that gets you going in the right direction. It is easy to get stuck due to the fear that what is necessary is too big of a jump for where you are at right now. Taking small but consistent steps can be very powerful in getting you into action. If you consistently take these small steps in the right direction it will reinforce your confidence and build your strength to take on larger actions. I call this process "baby-stepping your way to success" and it works. There's many a success story that began by taking one baby step after another.

CREATE MASSIVE MOMENTUM

My passion is teaching through public speaking and training. I had built a decent business doing so before 9/11. I say "decent," because I would make a list of the prospects I would call and think I was doing grand if I made ten cold calls a day.

Well, little action creates little results. After 9/11 things changed dramatically. I had to take a job and pursue a different career direction while the economy recovered and I could return to the business I loved predominantly training for hotels and resorts. My life was off-kilter for several years professionally, and then financial disaster struck.

After I had completed all of the work for a well-known telecommunications company, the executives decided that the person who signed my contract wasn't qualified to do so and they decided not to give me the $60,000 check I was expecting. It was going to be my cushion to launch back into my speaking business. I had no other prospects in the pipeline, so I was devastated. Due to the challenges of business, and going through a divorce, I only had enough money to cover a couple of month's worth of living expenses. It was a devastating time, and if you recall, freedom is one of my greatest values. In the face of many friends telling me I should go and get a job, I refused. I wanted to have the freedom that made me very happy.

Overnight, and I mean literally overnight, I woke up and began making 25 – 30 cold calls a day, working 12 hour days to make it happen! I took this action day after day, week after week, for approximately three months. I told all of my friends that my socializing would only be taking place evenings and on weekends. I created a powerful laser focus, knowing that nothing was going to stand in my way. I posted pictures of all the gorgeous hotels and resorts I wanted to speak at, and with amazing precision, they began hiring me. I felt like they were apples hanging on a tree and all I had to do was to reach up and pick them.

I placed my goals on index cards and kept them with me everywhere I went about my day, reviewing them like it was an addiction giving me my fix. It was a magical experience. My heart was filled with gratitude every day that I got to do what I loved and my income soared. Sometimes fear can be just as good of a motivator as it can be an obstacle. I used it to my advantage at that time.

Earlier, I shared with you that I had set a goal of staying in a castle. That was one of the things that inspired me during this time, because the invitation to go to France came during my time of rebuilding. I had no idea how I was going to be able to fit "castles in France" into my budget while I was still working on "bills in time" when the invitation came. But I accepted, and by the time the trip arrived less than nine months later, my money worries were over.

There were several things that occurred as a result of the amazing focus I had during this time:

1) I developed a love of cold calling. That's right. Now two of the things most people either hate or fear I love - public speaking and cold calling. I saw results so fast it was shocking, and I was very inspired by it.

2) I created a massive momentum that continues on to this day. I told you about my "decent" business before tragedy struck where I was calling ten prospects a day. I never, in a million

years, would have established enough momentum at that pace to be able to feel the level of success I feel today. There is a lot to be said for momentum. You put in the work once, and you reap the rewards forever.

3) I began tithing with joy for the first time in my life. The process of giving back brings me such great pleasure. Almost immediately when the check hits my mailbox I write out another one to the individuals and organizations that help me stay plugged in spiritually.

These were all gifts that I never would have received, had financial tragedy not struck. Didn't we discuss earlier how it's not always what you think it is? At the time, I had no idea the Divine plan behind it all. But it really was a brilliant one. I wouldn't trade that experience for anything in the world. I am a much better person and leader because of it. I truly know that there is no obstacle that could ever be set before me that I could not overcome.

And by the way, I eventually collected most of the money from the company that had refused to pay me.

Whatever it is that you want to do or be good at, give yourself permission to begin it now, and get better at it as you grow and develop your skills. If you wait until you think you are perfect it just won't happen.

IT'S ALL ABOUT PRACTICE

After devastation hit and reality sunk in, I didn't just wake up that next day all excited about cold calling. I had to practice a lot before I felt like I was really good at it. My daily rule of thumb was, "Just suit up and show up." This was a way of giving myself permission to simply do the best I could do. So whatever it is that you want to do or be good at, give yourself permission to begin it now, and get better at it as you grow and develop your skills. If you wait until you think you are perfect, it just won't happen.

Rev. Jim Turrell put it this way:

"How do you get to Carnegie Hall? The answer is 'Practice.' You've got to practice. You've got to practice getting up every morning and focusing on what you want and taking action. Then you've got to practice gratitude. The transformation can be instantaneous, and for many people it is instantaneous. It happens right away. For others, the amount of time that it takes is only the amount of time it takes you to put your attention on what you want and not to be distracted by the negative. So if somebody said, 'I tried using the Law of Attraction and it didn't work,' they probably tried focusing on it like it was magic and they didn't understand that they have to change their mind and keep it changed."

Your key to success is in realizing that much of what you'll learn in *THE AWAKENING* is about taking small steps and looking at them all as practice as opposed to having it all be perfect in the beginning.

Mastering the focus required to "change your mind and keep it changed" is something you'll get better at over time.

ACT IN SPITE OF FEAR

Fear is an energy bandit. It can take your good energy, intentions, and action from you faster than you can regenerate the desire to go for it! David Koons shared his experience with dispelling fear:

"From my experience, the things that prevent people from taking action the most are the direct result of their ego, whose job it is to keep them safe. What it does is manifest, or make real, to this person the possibility of fear, or some injury occurring to them if they act.

For example, they're scared to take a single step or to write a sentence down on a piece of paper about what they want because it might be wrong. Through conditioning, teachers, friends, family members, and past history, they have this fear of being wrong. 'What if it's not right? What if it's not perfect? What if I'm not sure?' They have this rigidity to an idea versus going with the flow of life.

I want people to think about the last time they drove in their car. Think about, if you held the wheel perfectly straight with your fingers turning white from gripping it so tightly and not moving the wheel and refusing to move the wheel, what would happen? Very quickly you would crash. You need to constantly correct your course.

Imagine where you live, you want to get in your car and go to the grocery store. What you don't do is don't get into the car, draw a straight line, point your car directly to the grocery store six miles across town, or wherever it is, and drive a straight, perfect line from your house to the grocery store. There might be a few fences, trees, and houses you drove through in attempting to do that.

Your fear shrinks the closer you get to it.

As silly as that sounds, isn't that what a lot of people try to do in their lives? They go perfectly straight without any course correction. Why? Because this ego is assigning a negative message to that course correction, 'See, I told you, you did it wrong. See, you screwed up.'

When Thomas Edison was asked if he felt bad about failing to create a light bulb in 9,999 times he said, 'I never failed. I just found 9,999 ways of how not to create the light bulb.' On the ten thousandth time he succeeded.

This fear and doubt the ego is housing in our mind creates uncertainty under the auspices of keeping us safe. Recognize you are not your ego. It's there. It's been conditioned for years. The quickest way to get through it is to take action. Your fear shrinks the closer you get to it. It usually goes away as soon as you take the action or it's greatly minimized.

Learn how to act in spite of your fear. The best way to do this is to start small and take little steps. If you're in network marketing or some kind of sales or prospecting business, and you're worried about talking to people about your product, to go out there and say, 'I'm going to do an hour or three hours of prospecting today' sets you up for failure. Instead say, 'I'm going to spend five minutes a day talking to people about my product. I'm not even going to ask them for a sale.' You do that for a week, five minutes a day. Then the next week you say, 'I'm going to talk to people for five minutes a day and at the end I'm going to tell them about how they can buy my product' and you keep adding onto that.

The ego convinces you to go out there in a way that has you fail in order to justify going back into the hole of safety and stagnation. The key is to go out there and succeed in little bite size steps. You take little bits of action. You feel the fear and you do it anyway. You face your fear and you take action. You acknowledge the fear, 'Thank you for being there' and you take action anyway."

CREATE PERMANENT AND LASTING CHANGE

Creating change in your life, discovering your deepest desire, renewing your beliefs, and defining your goals are what your AWAKENING is all about. However, change is only productive and worthwhile if it's change that is done consistently and usually that means on a daily basis.

You can change your health habits by exercising in order to flatten your stomach, trim your overall physique, and sculpt your abs. You can get out of bed, put on your workout clothes, feel the adrenaline rush of your new outlook on your health and become very excited about bathing suit season for the first time in years.

But exercising once or twice a week won't work your muscles and make a change in your body or your health in general. It's consistent, daily workouts that will bring your desired results.

When asked about taking action and making it a permanent fixture in our lives, David Koons gave this advice:

"We know from accelerated learning and from research that there are three fundamental elements to creating permanent and lasting change. How I characterize them is this:

1. The first one is passion. Passion is that intense desire to change their results. That could look like being sick and tired of being sick and tired. It could be really inspired by a certain mission. It could be either positive or negative, it doesn't matter. It's just an intense amount of energy and desire to change the results.

2. The second one is purging the old information, the old thoughts, feelings, and beliefs they've had to get them to where they are. If they want different results, they need to take different actions. To get different actions they have to have a different skill set, a different knowledge base and a different belief base. They have to purge the old files, that old information, and replace it with new information.

That process takes time. It requires reviewing new material frequently. Reviewing this new material to fill in that vacuum of those purged old files. Reading a book several times, reviewing a home study course several times, multiple times or every day for a month, whatever it is. It has to be frequently occurring until it's permanent. Watch out for the ego, it is always looking to bring you back to where you are right now until you can create enough momentum to expand and grow permanently.

3. The third, most critical step here is the ongoing support. Again, another asterisk, we must receive ongoing support from like-minded people. If left to our own devices, our mind is a dangerous place to be sometimes, isn't it? We might surround ourselves with non-supportive people who tell us we can't do that or you're not good enough. We want to surround ourselves in an environment of support. That ongoing support helps keep us on track.

Watch out for the ego, it is always looking to bring you back to where you are right now until you can create enough momentum to expand and grow permanently.

The path between where you are and where you want to go is rarely ever a straight line. You zig, you zag, you have course corrections and you make mistakes. It comes back to what is a mistake versus what is failure? To me, when you trip and fall down, that's a mistake. Failure is when you choose not to get back up again. I can say quite frankly I haven't failed at anything in my life. I've made hundreds and thousands of mistakes. I believe it's only a failure when you throw in the towel.

PUT A DIFFERENT TWIST ON IT

Chellie Campbell said the following about how you can do anything if you put a different twist on it:

"The Law of Attraction is wonderful, and you have to follow it with the Law of Action, or it doesn't work. People want to do affirmations about how they're making so much money in their business, but they have a business plan where they're losing money.

If they're charging a dollar and it costs them $2 to make the item, there's a faulty piece in their business plan. All the affirmations in the world aren't going to fix that. You can't affirm your way into a talent you don't possess. You can't affirm that you're a fabulous singer if you can't carry a tune. You can't affirm that you're a star basketball player if you're four foot nine. I mean you can do it but you'd have to get a group of short people to play basketball with you. There would be a different twist on the picture.

You can do anything but not in the standard mode. You have to be open to twisting the picture so that it looks a little different. You can still have the value of what it is you think being a basketball player or being a singer is going to do for you. There's an underlying value and that's the truth that everybody's going for. Where's the fun? Where's the joy? Where's the goody? Where's the good feeling?"

GET LUCKY!

I've heard it said "Luck is when opportunity meets preparation." And I agree whole heartedly. Rarely is what appears to be luck just a random coincidence or chance happening. I believe that every step we take when we listen to our inner awareness will lead us to a meaningful end.

You could say that I got lucky to write this book. I was lucky enough to have a great idea. I was lucky enough to have met a great publisher. I was lucky enough to be able to write it in the 30 days he suggested I complete it within, and voila, here we are together making our dreams a reality.

But I would have to say that each of these steps was my previous preparation meeting the opportunity presented to me at the time, and then taking action on it! The preparation goes back two decades when I began running marathons. The reality is I'm not an athlete whatsoever. A friend recruited me and I had no idea what I was getting into so I went. We walked the whole thing and had a great time doing so. But the magic happened when we crossed the finish line. WOW! Rarely have I had an experience that instantly made me a changed woman. But the first time I crossed the finish line of a 26.2 mile marathon and they put the medal around my neck I was changed.

One friend told me he didn't like to drive that far, much less walk it. But walking all those miles, which took me around six hours in the Los Angeles heat, was treacherous and awe inspiring. When they placed the medal around my neck, I never felt like I deserved anything more! I don't know the man who gave it to me, but I hugged him and I began to cry tears of joy. That medal represented a huge reward for the effort I had just made. I was so exhilarated by it that I went on to earn ten more.

I share that story with you now because I never knew how much every single one of those marathons, including the San Francisco marathon, would mean to me. It seemed like noble recreation at the time. It was exercise, it was fun, I got be with dear friends and make new ones and of course, I loved all the glory of the finish line.

But today, every single one of those marathons was important preparation for me in writing this book. When my publisher told me it was important for me to finish *THE AWAKENING* in 30 days, and then he paused and asked, "Can you do that?" without a moment's hesitation, I answered, "Yes, I can."

I realized the reality of my over zealous confidence on day 20. Around mile 20 in a marathon you hit what's called "the wall." It's the point at which your physical resources, all those carbs you loaded up on, have been spent and all that takes you to the finish line is your singular, laser-focused determination. There really are no words to describe it! Every inch of your body is aching, and you want to stop more than anything, but your sheer determination is what takes you all the way to the finish line. The last 6.2 miles are more difficult than all of the first 20 combined.

On day 20 of writing this book I was so grateful for every step of every 5K, 10K, and 26.2 mile marathon I had ever taken. Every one of them was preparation for that very moment. When I hit the wall, and there were actually several of them, after days of writing without human contact, days spent in just writing, eating, sleeping over and over again, I knew I could make it. I kept taking the action and putting one foot in front of the other. I kept moving forward in spite of wanting to quit. I had the determination, self-discipline and ability to reach the goal and I wasn't going to give up for anything. You are now holding the prized medal in your hand.

Luck is when opportunity meets preparation. Every meaningful action you take prepares you for something better. What steps are you taking today that will prepare you for a better tomorrow?

Focusing on your goal, determining that you can do it, no matter what it takes, and taking even the smallest, most painful steps on the journey are the actions that will AWAKEN your soul. Although the marathons are now memories and stories for me to pass on, I know that I did what I needed to do to get there. I now have eleven of those marathon medals and I hang them on my Christmas tree every year as a reminder to myself that no matter how far away the finish line may seem, in whatever new task I take on, I have the strength, determination, and self-discipline to press onward and upward, no matter what obstacles may stand in the way.

When opportunity meets preparation and the door opens YOU are the one who has to be ready to walk through it.

WATCH FOR PATTERNS OF SABOTAGE

You can create a life of harmony and happiness, fulfilling your dreams and cheering your way to success, or you can become your greatest obstacle on the road to your AWAKENING. Are you the homerun hitter who suddenly chokes at the bat? Do you move in for the catch and miss the ball by a mile? How do you take yourself out of the game?

Look back over some of the projects you've been involved with and see what you do to sabotage yourself. Do you have so many talents that you don't know which one to focus on and monetize? Do you jump from job to job or project to project? Do you quit just when you're getting started? When success is around the corner, do you choke up and run for the hills? Are you "your own worst enemy?"

"You don't say, 'Make me rich, God,' said Stephen Lewis. "What you do is focus on not destroying your opportunity of success. You need to focus on being willing to be successful. You are still responsible. You must do the work. You just don't sit back and turn on the television and wait for God to make you wealthy. You focus on what you want and you focus on not short circuiting it."

Remember, whatever you focus on you will attract? By focusing on your failures, by waiting for the next shoe to drop, and by becoming paralyzed with the fear of not getting it right, you create a lack of self-confidence, self-esteem and you provide a breeding ground for negative thoughts and self-doubt.

Become your own cheerleader, not your judge and jury. We ALL make mistakes. There isn't a single person who is perfect. We don't always get it right the first time. It's okay. Keep going. It's when you're in the lowest valley and you can't see the horizon that you will learn, grow, and live. If we all made it to the mountaintop on our first attempt, the journey wouldn't be as special. Relish in your journey. Find strength in knowing that your life will unfold before you in its time. Keep focused on positive action and bring forth your AWAKENING and your renewed spirit. Let the journey mold you into who you are to become.

DON'T JUST STAND THERE, DO SOMETHING!

Leo Buscaglia, a tireless advocate for the power of love, once said, "The person who risks nothing, does nothing, and becomes nothing. He may avoid suffering and sorrow, but he simply cannot learn, feel, change, grow, live and love."

"If you keep doing what you're doing, you will keep getting what you're getting!"

Taking action and experiencing something new is a necessary step in making a positive change in your life. Whether you are looking for changes in your relationships, career, income, health, living environment or other area you must take action. I love the saying, "If you keep doing what you're doing, you will keep getting what you're getting!"

Many people become paralyzed when they reach this step in their process of AWAKENING because they 1) are afraid of change, 2) can't find the right time to make a move, or 3) they overanalyze each move until they find themselves confused, fearful, and full of self-doubt and worry.

More great ideas and success stories have been thwarted due to this form of "paralysis of analysis" than anything else. It doesn't matter the cause, it's difficult to be successful in life if you aren't a pro at taking action and making things happen.

You may not be a pro at it today, but when you put the great ideas in this chapter behind you, you'll be propelled to take action and you'll see amazing results. Results that you'll be proud of!

In spite of all the great business and success advice available today, when I first started training, I found that owning a business and relying on myself to create an income was very intimidating. But above all, I just had to DO something! I had to step out of my comfort zone and step into a world that was new to me. I worked through the fear and self-doubt and charged forward, knowing that my AWAKENING had begun and the world was my oyster. This wasn't easy for me to do, considering I had never fully realized what it took until that point to be the sole provider.

Alex Mandossian confessed that one of his greatest obstacles was lazy thinking. Well at one point, my greatest obstacle was just plain old being lazy! I found out you don't get very far that way.

The steps and advice you will absorb through reading *THE AWAKENING* and from reading other great books and listening to a lot of great leaders can be overwhelming. I remember feeling like

I couldn't do it as perfectly as the plan was that they had all suggested. So I just jumped in and got into action. I think that is affectionately referred to as the "READY! FIRE! AIM!" model of success! I am not recommending it, but if you are sitting at a standstill in your life it may be the best place to begin. Implement now, perfect later. It's better to do SOMETHING than NOTHING at all, even if you don't get it right the first time. Believe me, you and I won't be the last great success stories who used this plan.

DO something! Kick your fear right out the door and get busy now!

The bottom line is this, DO something! Kick your fear right out the door and get busy now! Right, wrong, or indifferent, sometimes you've just got to get started. I know. I'm going against what some of my own revered experts have said on the pages of this very book. But some of us are acute at not taking action. DO something, and then you can refine your technique later.

I know what you're capable of, no matter your current circumstances, and it's far more than you've ever dreamed.

In Chapter 9, we're going to talk about the most exciting part of it all, receiving your good. Life is about enjoying the journey, but receiving your good is the icing on top of the cake.

CHAPTER 9

Recieve Your Good

*"The enlightened give thanks for what most people take for granted.
As you begin to be grateful for what most people take for granted that
vibration of gratitude makes you more receptive to good in your life."*

—Dr. Rev. Michael Beckwith

The Seven Steps to AWAKENING are:

1. Discover Your Deepest Desires

2. Declare What You Desire

3. Believe It Is Yours Now

4. Raise Your Frequency

5. Eliminate Any Obstacles

6. Take Meaningful Action

7. *Receive Your Good*

GRATITUDE IS THE DOOR TO RECEIVING

Open your arms and receive your good! How exciting it is to experience the AWAKENING, knowing you can truly live the life of your dreams. The journey inward is an exhilarating journey and it makes all of the rest of life more rewarding and meaningful. As you own your power and get into the flow of attraction, you'll see more and more good coming into your life. Let your constant thought be a joyful "Thank you, thank you, thank you!" to your Higher Power for bringing all the good into your life. The more grateful you are for what you already have, the more you will receive!

Write a gratitude list of 101 things you are grateful for and review it daily. Start this before you put your head on the pillow tonight! You should ooze gratitude!

Don't keep your gratitude inside of you, show it! Show your gratitude by giving lots of P&A – Praise and Appreciation – to the people around you. Make them wonder what happened to you!

RECEIVING YOUR GOOD WITH OPEN ARMS

For some people it's been a very long time since they've had wonderful feelings of receiving even a tiny bit of good, much less receiving all of their good. What this can create is a pessimistic attitude and limiting approach to receiving more good and lots of it. In order for more good to come to you, you have to welcome it and believe it and be grateful for it! You cannot be pessimistic or cynical about it.

Repeat to yourself, "I'm now joyfully receiving my good. I now welcome everything wonderful into my life. I'm open to receiving all of the abundance of life."

One of the exercises I've found that works over the years is to stand someplace where you're comfortable, you don't have to be alone, but you might feel most comfortable if you were at first, until you get used to it.

As you do the suggested movements below, breathe deeply in through your nose taking in as much air as your body can possibly hold. Releasing your breath, place your hands on your heart. Repeat to yourself, "I'm now joyfully receiving my good. I now welcome everything wonderful into my life. I'm open to receiving all of the abundance of life." You may also choose any other Power Statement you're working with in addition to these.

Raise your arms out to your sides, palms facing upwards, and raise them all the way over your head and then bring them down placing them over your heart.

Extend your arms out to your sides, palms facing forward. Extend your arms in front of you and toward your heart like you are embracing your good and bringing it to you.

Do any combination of these movements ten times each day and you'll be opening yourself to receive your good. After you get comfortable with these exercises, you can incorporate them into other areas of your life. I like to do this when I do my power walk or when I am deepening my spirituality in nature. I will stand at the beach and look out at the beauty of the ocean and welcome my good in abundance, imaging each and every thing I want to receive.

GRATEFULLY TRAVELING IN BLISS

The benefits of practicing gratitude to receive your good are a well-kept secret. Many people think of gratitude as something you would put on a religious to-do list. However, gratitude far exceeds religious tenets.

My friend Rick talks about the surprising benefits gratitude has brought his marriage.

"Travel has been less than a pleasant experience for me for many years. I am a retired airline pilot who traveled all over the world for nearly forty years. After retiring, traveling just wasn't something I wanted to do. I like to stay at home, be up on my mountaintop, and in my cave, so to speak.

My wife, on the other hand, is thrilled with the prospect of traveling to distant lands at the drop of a hat. She enjoys traveling both with friends and by herself, and I always know that she's in good company and safe. However, our diverging tastes kept us miles apart, frequently, because she would venture off and I would stay in the comfort of our home.

Many people think of gratitude as something you would put on a religious to-do list. However, gratitude far exceeds religious tenets.

During one of our numerous conversations about gratitude and thanksgiving, I discussed my own desire to be with her more often. She agreed that she, too, would love to continue to create a world where we could experience all that life has to offer; specifically, whereby we were both comfortable with each other's travel choices.

So we set about looking for a solution to the challenges of traveling together. We discovered a form of travel that suits both our needs! We have become 'cruise hounds' – sniffing out the best destinations, at the best prices at the best times of the year. It's a method of travel that meets my wife's needs for adventure and my needs for staying in one place (on board!). And what joy we're now experiencing with this new addition to our individual happiness, becoming our joint happiness.

When I choose to be grateful for all that I experience in my life, I find that life provides solutions where there were former dilemmas. I believe anyone can find simple solutions to potentially difficult situations when consideration and gratitude are focused upon. There are often conflicts in relationships, and at times these conflicts can be the root cause of arguments. However, in our marriage, we do not choose to create problems - we choose to create solutions. It has been of great service to our relationship to communicate our needs in this manner – and to always be grateful for the gift of expression to fulfill our desires.

I once read something by Meister Eckhart, the medieval mystic – it said, "If the only prayer you say in your whole life is 'thank you,' that would suffice."

IT'S NOT JUST ABOUT RECEIVING, IT'S ABOUT GIVING BACK

To stay in the flow of attraction, create a Victorious Circle of receiving and giving back, receiving and giving back, over and over again.

"Giving is very important in using the Law of Attraction," mentioned Hale Dwoskin. He continued:

"Most of us are not very giving. We're more taking than we are giving. It's important to allow the flow. We breathe in and out. If we just simply breathed in, that wouldn't last more than a minute and then life would be over. It's important to allow the flow of giving and receiving to flow through our lives. An incredibly important step that a lot of people miss is giving without wanting anything back in return. Most of us live life as barter. I give you this and I expect this in return. That's not really giving. You still have strings attached.

Most of us live life as barter. I give you this and I expect this in return. That's not really giving. You still have strings attached.

If you're not really letting go of the gift, it doesn't come back to you. When you give without wanting anything back in return, that naturally produces the energy of givingness in your life. If you believe in the Law of Attraction, do you want to attract lack or neediness or do you want to attract the energy of giving and love? By giving without wanting anything back in return, you produce amazing results in your life.

In the beginning you give with strings. It's better to give with strings than not give at all, much better. What happens is if you notice there are still strings, when you let go you can just cut the strings and allow the flow more and more until you get to a point where you're not trying to get anything back in return. When you give without wanting something back in return, that's amazingly powerful.

Honestly, in my experience, giving without wanting anything back in return is even more powerful than what most people do with the Law of Attraction. If you're trying to attract what you want it's all self-centered. It's all about me, me, me, and me. We don't live in a vacuum. We live as part of a whole. When you acknowledge that and you give towards the affairs of others and you give to support the planet, the Universe takes care of you in far better ways than you could ever imagine you could through your very limited attempts at attracting into your life what you want.

I recommend people find ways to give without wanting anything back in return. It could be volunteer work, it could be actually giving money, or it could be just living life with compassion and doing kind things to the people around you. There are so many ways to give. If you make your life about giving, by the way not instead of receiving, just in addition to receiving. It's a flow. You need to be open to receive in order to give and you need to be open to give in order to receive. Most people get stuck with the Law of Attraction when they think it's all about getting and not about giving. You need both.

If you're in an environment where there is someone who you can help who's a friend, who's a relative, it doesn't matter who you give to. It's just that attitude of giving without wanting anything back in return. If you give without expectation, you find ways to do things that are going to be the most helpful to the whole and to the parent individual.

It's not based on a percentage. It's based upon your heart. Some days you might give 100% of your income. Some days you might give none as far as money is concerned. Remember giving is not just in the money. You do the best you can in life. Sometimes giving is saying a kind word to somebody else. Sometimes giving is letting someone in front of you in line. Sometimes giving is not trying to prove you're right. Sometimes giving is doing what someone else wants for a change as opposed to having it always go your way. Giving can take many, many forms.

You need to be open to receive in order to give and you need to be open to give in order to receive.

For the Law of Attraction to work in improving your life, remember first of all it's not all about you. We're all part of a whole. In addition to doing things to get what you want, do things to support others in having more too, or in feeling better, being happier, or having less suffering. Just allow the energy to flow in your life."

GRATEFUL FOR HER LIFE!

What's the next indicated step in your life? How do you know which step is the right step to move you forward and to create your AWAKENING? My good friend, Khatia, grew up with the Law of Attraction, and was taught from an early age that what she thought she would attract. Her AWAKENING came later in life. This was her process:

"So often I hear how fortunate I would have been to have had the advantage of understanding the Law of Attraction from childhood. I was introduced to these at the age of seven; I will be 60 this year. And yes, it has definitely had its advantages—when I used these principles!

I was raised in California on a chicken ranch that had affirmations above the chicken coups. This was nothing short of odd in the 1950s. Nevertheless, my parents believed in visualization, affirmation, and the power of positive thinking because I was raised in the Church of Religious Science. It was founded by Ernest Holmes, a charismatic leader that taught the Law of Attraction to thousands in the early to mid 1900s.

I married a man when I was 20, who turned out to be all of the things that I did not deserve in my life. He beat me in front of our two children and he went out with other women and spent my inheritance from my grandfather on his girlfriends.

I finally filed for divorce after 11 years of marriage. The next month I went into the hospital to have a very minor surgery for a health problem I was experiencing. While I was under sedation, the doctors found ovarian cancer and immediately gave me a radical hysterectomy.

When I came out from under the sedation and heard I had cancer and what they did, I was stunned. It was right then that I understood all I had learned and how it would save my life. All I had to do was apply those principles to my life now. My good fortune was knowing what to do. I had the arrows in my quiver; I simply had to use them to eradicate all that did not work in my life.

I came home from the hospital a revived person. I was determined to live cancer-free and have a long and meaningful life. Nothing could prevent me from living an amazing life. I was a single mother to a three-year-old and a seven-year-old – they needed me and I needed them.

One month later, I met the love of my life, the complete opposite of my former husband. As you can well imagine, I was doing a great deal of visualizing, creating meditations for complete health, and allowing myself the gift of a loving relationship. These principles work – when you work them. They're not merely words; they require a deep understanding of the energy of life. However, when you study these principles and apply them – miracles happen.

I know, because the love of my life and I are celebrating our 25th wedding anniversary this year. He is a caring, loving, intelligent, and compassionate man who has been an amazing father to my two children. I don't say "my" children casually; my former husband has not called, written, or contacted my children in 21 years. Life still has obstacles for me – I simply choose to handle them very differently than most people do.

It is true, when you, 'Change your thinking, you change your life.' You simply use The Law of Attraction to your benefit!"

THE GREATEST MIRACLE IN THE WORLD

I read the late Og Mandino's book, "The Greatest Miracle in the World"[1] on the beaches of Acapulco one summer when I was 18 years old. It was the first personal growth book I ever read. I highly suggest it. It's a small book that made a huge impact on my life. I remember reaching Chapter 9, which included "The God Memorandum." The entire book was leading up to this chapter and as I read it my heart was filled with more and more gratitude. I would like to share a section of the God Memorandum with you here.

"Are you blind? Does the sun rise and fall without your witness? No. you can see, and the one hundred million receptors I have placed in your eyes enable you to enjoy the magic of

---

1. Mandino, Og. The Greatest Miracle in the World. New York: Bantam Books, 1981.

a leaf, a snowflake, a pond, an eagle, a child, a cloud, a star, a rose, a rainbow, and the look of love. Count one blessing.

Are you deaf? No you can hear and the twenty-four thousand fibers I have built in each of your ears vibrate to the wind in the trees, the tides on the rocks, the majesty of an opera, a robin's plea, children at play, and the words I love you. Count another blessing.

Are you mute? Do your lips move and bring forth only spittle? No. you can speak as can no other of my creatures, and your words can calm the angry, uplift the despondent, goad the quitter, cheer the unhappy, warm the lonely, praise the worthy, encourage the defeated, teach the ignorant, and say I love you. Count another blessing.

Are you paralyzed? Does your helpless form despoil the land? No. you can move. You are not a tree condemned to a small plot while the wind and world abuses you. You can stretch and run and dance and work, for within you I have designed five hundred muscles, two hundred bones, and seven miles of nerve fiber all synchronized by me to do your bidding. Count another blessing.

Are you unloved and unloving? Does loneliness engulf you, night and day? No. No more. For now you know love's secret that to receive love it must be given with no thought of its return. To love for fulfillment, satisfaction or pride is no love. Love is a gift on which no return is demanded. Now you know that to love unselfishly is its own reward. And even should love not be returned it is not lost, for love not reciprocated will flow back to you and soften and purify your heart. Count another blessing. Count twice.

Is your heart stricken? Does it lead and strain to maintain your life? No. your heart is strong. Touch your chest and feel its rhythm, pulsating, hour after hour, day and night thirty-six million beats each year, year after year, asleep or awake, pumping your blood through more than sixty thousand mile of veins, arteries, and tubing, pumping more than six hundred thousand gallons each year. Man has never created such a machine. Count another blessing.

Are you diseased of skin? Do people turn in horror when you approach? No. Your skin is clear and a marvel of creation, needing only that you tend it with soap and oil and brush and care. In time all steels will tarnish and rust, but not your skin. Eventually the strongest of all metals will wear, with use, but not that layer that I have constructed around you. Constantly it renews itself, old cells replaced by new; just as the old you is now replaced by the new. Count another blessing.

Are your lungs befouled? Does the breath of life struggle to enter your body? No. Your portholes to life support you even in the vilest of environments of our own making, and they labor always to filter life-giving oxygen through six hundred million pockets of folded flesh while they rid your body of gaseous wastes. Count another blessing.

Is your blood poisoned? Is it diluted with water and pus? No. Within your five quarts of blood are twenty-two trillion blood cells and within each cell are millions of molecules and within each molecule is an atom oscillating at more than ten million times each second. Each second, two million of your blood cells die to be replaced by two million more in a resurrection that has continued since your first birth. As it has always been inside, so now it is on your outside. Count another blessing.

Are you feeble of mind? Can you no longer think for yourself? No. Your brain is the most complex structure in the universe. I know. Within its three pounds are thirteen billion nerve cells, more than three times as many cells as there are people on your earth. To help you file away every perception, every sound, every taste, every smell, every action you have experienced since the day of your birth, I have implanted, within your cells more than one thousand billion protein molecules. Every incident in your life is there waiting only your recall. And to assist your brain in the control of your body I have dispersed, throughout your form, four million pain-sensitive structures, five hundred thousand touch detectors, and more than two hundred thousand temperature detectors. No nation's gold is better protected than you. None of your ancient wonders are greater than you.

You are my finest creation."

TO INCREASE YOUR ATTRACTION QUOTIENT

1. Write a list of 101 things you're grateful for and review it daily. Start this list before you put your head on the pillow tonight! Aim to ooze gratitude everyday!

2. Give P&A – Praise and Appreciation – to at least five other people everyday. Make them wonder what happened to you!

This is the final step of *The Seven Steps to AWAKENING*. These are the basic principles to making the Law of Attraction work in your life. Embrace them, memorize them, practice them, and you'll be able to raise your frequency and keep it there so that you magnetize all that you desire. The next section will present to you *The Five Keys to Accelerating Your Power of Attraction*. Master these and you will turbo charge your ability to attract your desires and live in abundance, freedom and joy.

The Five Keys to Accelerate Your Power of Attraction

The following five chapters address *The Five Keys to Accelerate Your Power of Attraction*. They are five areas that I encourage you to spend extra time focusing on. They address some of the most common obstacles that prevent people from getting in the flow of using the Law of Attraction to create the life of their dreams. As your awareness and focus on these keys grows, your AWAKENING will begin. You're an amazing miracle. Tapping into the Law of Attraction will allow you to fully realize the perfection that you already are. Feel it. Believe it. Live it.

CHAPTER 10

Renew Your Beliefs

"You create your life with your consciousness. It is that simple."

—Stephen Lewis

THE SUBCONSCIOUS MIND

Do you feel like you're spinning your wheels, setting goals and never achieving them? Do you make headway, but always slip back to your old way of being? Have you tried reaching your goal so many times that you've given up hope and decided it's a futile struggle?

Don't worry, there is hope. Your subconscious mind is usually in charge, unless you make a special effort to move it out of the way. Unbeknownst to you, your subconscious mind controls your actions more than anything else.

Most people are unaware of the powerful role their subconscious mind plays in their success. They repeat self-sabotaging and self-destructive behavior over and over again and don't know why. They keep attracting the same kind of man or woman who isn't good for them. They have a pattern of making a decent living, but spending all of their money before the end of the month. They never seem to make enough money and live lives of lack and limitation.

When you see a constant pattern of failure to change, then you know to look within. A significant portion of the time the secret to creating your success is hidden in your subconscious mind.

With thorough investigation, you will be able to identify your Overriding Background Beliefs. These beliefs are originally generated around the age of five, sometimes earlier, and evolve as we mature. Over the years we gather additional information to support these beliefs, usually without even knowing it.

The neutral and positive beliefs aren't the ones that give us trouble. It's on the accumulation of negative Overriding Background Beliefs that we'll focus. It's time to renew your beliefs! Our goal is to bring them to the forefront of our conscious minds and disengage their power. They are called "Overriding Background Beliefs" for three reasons: they override your conscious goals and desires, they originate in your background, usually as a child, and they remain constantly in the background of your mind sabotaging your success, unless you work to make them conscious.

Reclaiming your power and beginning your AWAKENING isn't about the people around you changing, it's about you changing.

If you're not living the life you want to be living, most of the time it's due to one or more of these beliefs. They run our lives and we don't even realize it. Because these beliefs are subconscious, it takes focused effort to investigate and find out what is at the core of our unfulfilled goals and dreams.

Overriding Background Beliefs play an invisible game of tug-of-war in your soul. You make headway and think you are winning the game and then with a giant tug from an ugly, old, subconscious Overriding Background Belief you're back in the mud and you don't have a clue why. Overriding Background Beliefs are at the root of low self-worth, and without doing some powerful inner work, and renewing these beliefs, these beliefs will always win.

HOW OVERRIDING BACKGROUND BELIEFS ARE FORMED

Usually, it's well-meaning parents, relatives, teachers, members of the clergy, and others who originally contribute to our Overriding Background Belief(s) through their words or actions. They say things like, "You should be ashamed of yourself," "Rich people are greedy and dishonest," "You are never going to amount to anything," "You need to lose weight," and a variety of other hurtful things. Oftentimes we are too young to disagree with our parents, relatives, and teachers, or others and don't know what to say to put them in their place. Since we don't know any better, we believe them.

The bottom line is this, they tell us lies about who they think we are and we subconsciously agree with their lies. Now, our jobs are to consciously disagree, break those old agreements, and reclaim our power. Reclaiming your power and beginning your AWAKENING isn't about the people around you changing, it's about you changing. In some cases, the people who did the damage aren't even alive anymore.

You are far greater than any lie anyone has ever told you about yourself. You're bigger and better than any negative story, event, or situation that ever took place in your past. It's what happened to you, it's not who you are. Don't let such negativity define you another minute. Anytime you let someone else define you in a negative manner you lose your sense of personal power. You shrink a little bit more into the dark shadows of low self-worth and fear.

Fear then takes over, because you begin to worry more about what other people think about you than what you think about you. With low self-worth you have to spend a lot of time pleasing others and being "nice" so that they're not upset with you. When you renew your beliefs, you'll live in the present, not in the past. You'll be able to finally focus on what makes YOU happy, and eventually create the life of your dreams.

Hale Dwoskin said it this way:

"Recognize that any belief is just a memory based on what <u>was</u>, rather than what <u>is</u>. Decide to drop the belief and look into your own direct experience. This will liberate you to be open to totally new perspectives filled with unlimited possibilities, right action, success, ease, and joy.

The best way to do this is to simply remember your thoughts and feelings are not you and they're not facts. Then you can let them go. As you let go of the thoughts and feelings that are getting in your way of living the Law of Attraction, you'll find that it happens naturally. You don't have to force it. You don't have to use effort. You don't have to make things happen. They happen naturally."

LETTING GO OF THE PAST

Letting go of the past and breaking these agreements are not easy tasks. I'm stunned when people talk about "letting go" as if it were easy, simple, and fast. It's not an easy road to your AWAKENING. It's not easy, simple, or fast, but it's without a doubt worth every bit of the effort it takes to be able to live a life of freedom, love, abundance, and joy.

Chellie Campbell discussed it like this:

"What we have to do is take a close look at our beliefs. Where did they come from? I once had a friend who would address my beliefs every time he would hear me say things such as, 'You can't have everything.' He would just look at me and say, 'Yeah? Who told you that?' I would say, 'Well, who did tell me that? Where did I first hear that? Do I believe that's true? Is there ever a case where that's not true? This is called self-examination. It is really important to pick apart those 60,000 thoughts in your head and ask, 'Are they true, aren't they true? Where did this come from? What do I really think about that? Maybe I'd like to change that belief.'"

You have the power to make significant changes in your life right now. Many of the most amazing changes will evolve out of identifying and removing your Overriding Background Beliefs.

You have the power to make significant changes in your life right now. Many of the most amazing changes will evolve out of identifying and removing your Overriding Background Beliefs.

Until you discover your Overriding Background Beliefs, you'll stay stuck. Identifying, healing and letting them go are the keys to moving beyond them.

BARRIERS THAT BLOCK YOU FROM IDENTIFYING YOUR OVERRIDING BACKGROUND BELIEFS

Fear, judging and perfectionism are three thoughts and feelings that prevent us from identifying our Overriding Background Beliefs. During my years of practice as a therapist I became aware that most of us have some degree of each of these. Let's look at each of them closer.

FEAR

Fear is a very normal and natural feeling when it comes to looking into our hearts and souls. This is especially true if we've spent years trying not to look inside because of the pain and sadness there. Here are some of the most common fears that prevent us from looking within:

- Fear of what you will uncover
- Fear that you have to do something about what you uncover
- Fear that you have to change
- Fear that you have to say something to someone you aren't ready to say
- Fear that you aren't going to do it right
- Fear that it won't be good enough
- Fear of opening up a can of worms
- Fear of making a mistake
- Fear of making a fool of yourself in some way
- Fear of going crazy

JUDGING

This is a process where you must suspend judging yourself in order to proceed effectively. Once you begin judging yourself, the most powerful thoughts and feelings you need to heal will subside and you won't be able to reach them.

You can detect if you're judging yourself by a knot you may get in your gut that feels bad. You may get a headache. You may even notice feeling a sense of impending doom. Or you may have thoughts like, "I can't believe I did that." "Why did I do that?" "I must be a loser if I feel this way." "I'm never going to be all I want to be," and other self-defeating thoughts like these.

PERFECTIONISM

There is no way to go through this process thinking you're going to do it perfectly. It can be rather messy, uncontrollable, and random. The approach you want to take is one that allows you to make mistakes and to make progress at your own pace. You'll want to proceed in any manner that is acceptable to you at the time, even if it's not ideal.

DISCOVERY QUESTIONS TO UNCOVER OVERRIDING BACKGROUND BELIEFS

You may be feeling like you don't have any idea what your Overriding Background Beliefs are right now. Rev. Jim Turrell addresses this, he said:

"You have to take some time to sit in silence and ask yourself, 'What are my core beliefs? What do I really think about how life is working for me?'

If you ask yourself that question in silence over a period of time, it will reveal itself. Simply state, 'I want to see my core beliefs and I want to see them now,' then the Universe will start to reveal those core beliefs to you. They won't come to you like a dissertation, or a book. They'll come to you as feelings and you'll suddenly say, 'That's a strange feeling, an odd feeling' I want to look at that a little closer."

One of the most important tasks we must face, if we want to truly become enlightened human beings, is to uncover our Overriding Background Beliefs. People who do not take that step into AWAKENING are much like the walking dead, unaware of who they really are, what makes them the way they are, and what they can actually do to change. Most people don't want to dig that deep or do that much inner work.

Well, that's fine, but they'll never get the results they desire either. They'll never fulfill their true potential or be able to live a life of deep joy. We have to identify what happened to us and what was said to build these Overriding Background Beliefs. These beliefs don't just suddenly appear one day. Events, situations, circumstances, and words are said that develop and continue to feed them. Unless you take action to identify and acknowledge that these beliefs aren't true and break your agreement with them, they'll hold power over you forever.

As you go through this process you'll possibly feel some resistance. It takes a lot of courage to look these Overiding Background Beliefs straight in the eye and own them. But as you go into the pain, instead of avoiding it, you'll find tremendous joy. Uncovering your Overriding Background Beliefs will possibly be the greatest AWAKENING of your life!

THE AWAKENING PROCESS
DISCOVERING OVERRIDING BACKGROUND BELIEFS

As you read the list of Overiding Background Beliefs below, ask yourself these questions:

1. Could I possibly believe this?

2. Was there anytime in my life when someone communicated this to me, or made me feel this way, either obviously, subtly, or both?

3. Was there ever an event or situation in my life that made me feel this way, either obviously, subtly, or both?

4. Is there anything in my life's experiences today that would indicate I believe this, even if I think I don't believe it?

Overriding Background Beliefs

- I am not worthy.

- I am not good enough.

- I am no good.

- I don't matter.

- It is not OK to be rich.

- It is not OK to be slim.

- It is not OK to be happy.

- It is not OK to be assertive.

- It is not spiritual to be rich.

- It is not spiritual to be sexy.

- I am not pretty enough.

- I am not smart enough.

- You are greedy if you are rich.

- You are dishonest if you are rich.

- It is too much effort to be successful.

- You have to work hard to be successful.

- I am ugly.

- I am fat.

- I am unlovable.

- I am dumb.

- It is not safe to be thin.

- It is not safe to be in love.

- The world is not safe.

- Men are not safe.

- Women are not safe.

- People will expect a lot from me if I am successful.

- People will take advantage of me if I am successful.

- People will take advantage of me if I am thin.

- I must struggle to succeed.

- I must struggle to be OK.

- I must please others instead of myself.

- It is better to give than to receive.

- I should be ashamed of myself.

Let's examine each of these further:

1. **Could I possibly believe this?** Try each one on for size. Does it resonate with you? Notice your feelings as you read each one and pay particular attention to the beliefs that make you feel like crying, eating, drinking, going shopping, biting your nails, or anything else that could serve as a distraction. That's an indicator you're getting close to one of your Overriding Background Beliefs.

   You may relate on some level to many of them. But actually try each one on and say it about yourself like you mean it. If it's not one of your Overriding Background Beliefs, it won't evoke any emotion or discomfort. If it hits home, you'll feel it. When you feel it, press into the feelings deeper. Don't run from them. You must do the work to overcome these beliefs.

   Your healing in these areas is not dependant on anyone else. This process is about you claiming your right to live a powerful, abundant life.

2. **Was there anytime in my life when someone communicated this to me or made me feel this way, either obviously, subtly, or both?** Sometimes there is so much negativity in our backgrounds that we become numb to it and don't realize the damage it has done. People are capable of saying and doing some very cruel things that have a long-lasting effect on our minds.

Our backgrounds may have influenced who we are, but we're the one responsible for who we become.

3. **Was there ever an event or situation in my life that made me feel this way, either obviously, subtly, or both?** Sometimes there can be an event or situation that triggers these Overriding Background Beliefs, and we aren't clearly aware of it.

4. **Is there anything in my life's experiences today that would indicate I believe this, even if I think I don't believe it?** If you've never been able to get ahead financially, in spite of your many talents and abilities, this could point to any of the beliefs that have to do with worthiness or wealth. If you've struggled with being overweight much of your life, it could be a reflection of several different beliefs mentioned, a lack of worthiness, safety, or fear. If you've had issues with any kind of addiction, you're sure to find several of the beliefs you can identify with since the substance or behavior serves as a way to numb the pain of the feelings these beliefs create.

5. **Does this occur for me occasionally or often?** You may be able to identify with numerous Overriding Background Beliefs. Don't worry, you can take them one at a time and work through them. But asking yourself this question will help you to determine which ones you should begin with today.

Once you find one or more that you can identify with, I recommend you write about them in a journal. It has been said that talking is a head trip and writing is a heart trip. To get to the core of the issue and begin healing, writing about it can be very helpful. Don't worry about grammar and punctuation; this is for your eyes only. Its sole purpose is to help you acknowledge the Overriding Background Beliefs that may be holding you back and heal them.

Knowing these beliefs is not the whole process. Some people know this and still do nothing about it. Knowing why is not the magic. Breaking the agreement you made with the past is. Also, you don't do this once; you have to do it repeatedly! Chances are you've had these Overriding Background Beliefs for a very long time. How long have you believed this B.S. (Belief System!) 20, 30, 40 years? You don't deal with it once and then it's done any more than you ask once and receive. You have to find the truth and keep affirming it.

FOUR STEPS TO REMOVING YOUR OVERRIDING BACKGROUND BELIEFS

You can certainly go through this process alone, and some will prefer it that way. However, if you are comfortable with it, I encourage you to go through this process with a trusted friend with whom you can share some or all of your feelings. Sometimes our secrets can be our greatest anchors, holding us down forever. Bringing things out in the open and sharing them frees us from the dark impact they've had on us.

You'll get the most out of this exercise if you stop and get a pen and paper and do it in writing. You could possibly not experience the breakthrough you're capable of having by simply doing it in your head.

It's also important to know that this process can take one hour, one day, one week, or one month. There is no right or wrong way to do it. All that matters is that you do it. Most likely you will do these exercises more than once, because many of us have more than one Overriding Background Belief. Take charge of overcoming one at a time, and work through each by following these steps. First identify two to three areas that aren't working as you would like for them to in your life. Then take them one at a time and work through the following steps:

1. DISCOVER

You will discover the hidden beliefs that may be holding you back through self-examination. Ask yourself what beliefs you have that could be holding you back.

Look for patterns in areas where you consistently don't get what you want. Review the list of Overriding Background Beliefs you read earlier in this chapter frequently, and use writing as a tool to help you process your thoughts and feelings.

Ask yourself these questions:

- What areas of my life are not working and are filled with struggle or pain? What Overriding Background Beliefs are these struggles indicative of? For example, you may work long hours and feel resentful that you are working your life away. As you reflect on this, you may find that you were made to feel you weren't good enough so you are constantly trying to prove your worth by doing more and more.

- Did anyone make you feel like you weren't good enough and would never measure up to their standards?

- Whose attention or love did you want but were never able to get?

2. DISSECT

What events or situations happened that could have influenced you in feeling this way? It could have been something you heard. It doesn't have to be something that was said directly to you or about you. Examine carefully the full range of emotions you have regarding these background beliefs. This step can involve a lot of emotional pain. These Overriding Background Beliefs cause us a lot of heartache and prevent us from living our lives fully. The more you feel your feelings, as uncomfortable as they may be, the more you can heal them.

Go into the emotion, don't side skirt it. This will create a true healing. Make certain that you identify any guilt, shame, resentment, and anger. These have a tremendously low vibration and block you from being as successful as you're potentially capable of being.

3. DISCARD

This is the step where you break the agreement with the negativity that you've subconsciously felt for years and take back your power. It's time to acknowledge the truth about who you are as a person and disconnect from the lies others may have told you about yourself.

Write a letter (that you're not going to send). Begin it with one of the following phrases:

1. I am done thinking…
2. I am done feeling…
3. I am done believing…
4. I am done acting…
5. How dare you treat me that way…
6. How dare you say those words to me…

I now cut the cords and break the ties that have bound me to these old, inaccurate ways of thinking, feeling, believing and acting. I celebrate all that I am and my new life.

7. How dare you touch me that way…

8. How dare you even look at me that way…

9. I can't believe you ever…

10. I'm shocked to think that you…

11. Do not ever…to me again.

And close it with -

> *"I now cut the cords and break the ties that have bound me to these old, inaccurate ways of thinking, feeling, believing, and acting. I celebrate all that I am and my new life."*

Determine any additional actions you may need to take in order to break free, heal, and renew your beliefs. Some examples may include writing a letter telling a person or institution your feelings, feelings that you have possibly avoided or stuffed away for years. You may or may not need to send the letter; just writing it can break the chains and bring you the freedom you deserve.

Write Power Statements that declare who you are, what you want, and how you want to feel in the present tense.

You may need to confront someone face-to-face with their lies or the way they treated you. As long as you don't compromise your safety, then this is a very powerful step to take. Do not confront others face-to-face who are known to be abusive, have a temper, or could become violent. Regardless of what you've been told by well-meaning others, know that you can heal, whether you confront or not.

This is not about playing a blame game where you blame everyone else but yourself. This is about giving valid responsibility to those who made an impact on your life in the past through their words or action. And it's about you're now taking responsibility for your present and your future by acknowledging it, dissecting it, and disconnecting it.

These final two steps are where you begin to let go of your past.

4. DECLARE

Declare the new beliefs you want to embrace. The best way to do this is by writing Power Statements that declare who you are, what you want, and how you want to feel in the present tense. Here are some examples, and you'll find more in the appendix.

• I now love and accept myself just as I am.

• I am good enough now.

• It is OK for me to want to be wealthy, really wealthy.

• It is OK, wonderful and great for me to have all of the love, money and fun I want.

• I now give myself permission to be all that I want to be and have all that I want to have.

• In this very moment, I am whole, perfect, and complete.

In the Appendix located at the end of this book, you'll find several examples of declarations from people who have gone through these four steps and were able to renew their spirits, their beliefs, and find hope in the fact that they were well on their way to their own AWAKENING.

THE AWAKENING PROCESS
PAYOFF vs. PRICE

1. Choose three things you would like to change in your life.

2. List the payoff you get for continuing each of these behaviors or situations.

3. List the price you have to pay for each of these.

4. List the prize you would get if you eliminated these behaviors or situations.

5. Ask yourself, "Is the price I pay for this worth giving up the prizes I would gain if I gave it up?"

THE PAYOFF vs. THE PRICE

For everything we do in life, we get some kind of payoff. It seems odd that we would do things to defeat ourselves and call it a payoff, doesn't it?

Usually these payoffs are connected to one of our Overriding Background Beliefs.

It might go like this, "I keep extra weight on because one of my Overriding Background Beliefs is - "It's not safe to be thin." If I'm overweight, I have a greater sense of safety since I don't get as much attention as when I'm thin." So the payoff this person gets is that they get to continue feeling safe. The key word there is "feeling." Are they really any safer overweight than thin? No, but they do avoid attention.

I would then ask this person to "press into the feeling" further and ask, "What is the payoff of avoiding attention?" They might say that it's predictable, and they don't have to deal with the opposite sex, with which they might not have a level of comfort. So in their minds, the best thing to do is to stay overweight, because that's now their comfort zone.

However, when the price of being overweight is greater than the payoff, they'll do what it takes to eat healthy, exercise regularly, and release the need to be overweight. As long as there is a perceived payoff, they have the need to keep the negative behavior going.

We neglect to look at the price we pay for continuing to nurture these old beliefs. There is a huge price we pay, over and over again, that must be recognized before we can change.

The payoffs that I hear most frequently are:

1. I get to stay safe.

2. I don't have to take any risks.

3. I get to stay in my comfort zone.

CONGRATULATIONS!

It's time to celebrate you, the incredible and amazing man or woman that you really are. All of that inaccurate information led to a lot of inaccurate beliefs. Now you have a deeper and clearer understanding of what has been standing in the way of you applying the Law of Attraction in your life. Now you're on the way to claiming power like you've never dreamed you could have. It's surprising that nine times out of ten what we think is stopping us, is never what really is!

After you do these exercises, you may still wonder why things aren't falling into place for you. You might try and fool yourself by saying, "I don't know why?" Well, once you've discovered these, you can no longer say you don't know why. Continue to explore and delve even deeper into any Overriding Background Beliefs that you might not have discovered. Don't stop at just one sitting. Keep exploring.

Also, continue to focus on your Discard and Declare steps. Write four or five key phrases from each of these on an index card, and review them three times each day until they really sink into your core.

Rebecca's index card might read like this:

> I AM DONE hiding in shame; I AM DONE cowering in the corner! I WILL NEVER, never, never allow you to destroy my spirit again.

> I AM GOOD ENOUGH NOW! I always have been and always will be good enough! I absolutely deserve all my good NOW! I AM a precious and loveable child of God!

You can read her entire process in Appendix 2 at the back of the book.

If you weren't able to identify with either of the key processes in this chapter, don't give up. Come back and revisit this chapter again until you're able to renew your beliefs, move toward your AWAKENING, and feel confident that you've broken any negative agreements that you may have made before you even knew the negative impact these agreements would have on your life.

As a result of doing these processes, you have begun to create a new reality for your life; a new beginning. You're now in the flow of clearing away the past issues that bogged you down and decreased your vibration. You're no longer going to be the person you were last year, last month, last week, or yesterday. You're starting anew as you awaken the person you were born to be. Be courageous in facing these issues and share your success with those you trust. Be proud of the new you! Love who you are today and who you're going to be tomorrow. Your AWAKENING will be the most powerful experience you've known to date. Be prepared! Once your eyes are open to the possibilities of your renewed life, you'll create many more amazing and exciting experiences to come.

Next, in Chapter 11, we will discuss how you can expand your thoughts. Your thoughts are incredibly powerful! They can be your greatest asset or your greatest liability. Continue reading so that you can make certain your thoughts are consistently working in your favor.

CHAPTER 11

Expand Your Thoughts

"Carefully watch your thoughts, for they become your words. Manage and watch your words, for they will become your actions. Consider and judge your actions, for they have become your habits. Acknowledge and watch your habits, for they shall become your values. Understand and embrace your values, for they become your destiny."
—Mahatma Gandhi

The Law of Attraction is impartial and works, whether you're focused on something positive or negative. Therefore, if you want good things to happen in your life, but you're being negative or focused on negative situations, you'll continue attracting what you don't want.

You must expand your thoughts beyond the current boundaries that are present within our society. Our world today thrives on negativity. You see it in the newspapers, television, magazines, movies, books, video games, and in most every conversation. Negativity is so rampant that people expose their children to killing and violence before they're out of kindergarten through video games and movies, without giving it a second thought.

Negativity is the #1 way we repel our good on a daily basis. Much of the time we're not aware we're holding ourselves back by entertaining it. Some of the most positive people you know still engage in negative, nonsensical conversations.

If you want good things to happen in your life, but you're being negative or focused on negative situations, you'll continue attracting what you don't want.

This is also a way we repel people, both strangers and loved ones. Some people have negativity so intense that it feels toxic to be around them. They seem to find the negative, sarcastic bent on everything, no matter how positive it is. A young single woman might say to a friend "I just signed up with an online dating site and I'm excited to start dating again." Her toxic friend might respond, "Good luck finding a decent man out there. The good ones are all taken." An executive might say to a colleague, "Looks like I'm up for a great promotion soon, my boss is moving to another division." His colleague replies, "Ha, that'll never happen. They'll probably bring someone in from the outside."

There is also the gossipfest that happens frequently when two or more people get together and dish it out on another person. They say anything and everything to put down, judge, or humiliate someone else to make themselves feel better. Gossip is terrible and sends out energy that is so low you certainly don't want it coming back to you!

Negativity and thoughts of fear and limitation prevent us from powerfully attracting all that we want into our lives.

Just like it's difficult for us to admit if we're bad drivers or bad communicators, we can't admit we're negative. Have you ever heard anyone say, "Yes, I'm a bad driver. I sure am. I cut people off, never use my turn signals, and I brake for no apparent reason. I'm just a downright bad driver"? Or have you ever heard someone say, "I'm a bad communicator. When I don't know how to say what I need to say, I get passive aggressive and make people pay for not doing things my way. I expect people to read my mind and I never come right out and say what I want. And then I manipulate people with my anger or oversensitivity. Yes, I'm a terrible communicator"?

No, people don't admit they are bad drivers, bad communicators, or that they have bad attitudes that are predominantly negative. They will dress it up and say they're "realistic," or just offering the ever helpful "devil's advocate" point of view, but they'll never say they're just plain old negative.

Negativity and thoughts of fear and limitation prevent us from powerfully attracting all that we want into our lives. Since there are many different ways negativity seeps into our lives, I will describe negativity in all of its many forms in the next section.

NEGATIVITY IN ALL OF ITS MANY FORMS

To begin expanding your thoughts to all of the positive things in your life and in the world, you'll want to be very conscious of the following forms of negativity. Because so many people engage in these, they're considered normal, acceptable, everyday conversations. You may want to establish a "new normal" that is positive, powerful, and uplifting.

1. Negative Self-Talk

Others might never hear the way we talk to ourselves, because we do so within the privacy of our own minds, but it's very powerful and destructive. It's through negative self-talk that we undermine ourselves before we ever have a chance to make progress.

We say things like:

- I can't do that.
- I'm not good enough.
- I'm too fat.
- Why did I do that again?
- I'm such a klutz.
- Nobody cares about me.
- I'll never get it right.
- I can't believe I'm so stupid.
- I always lose my keys.
- I'll never get married.
- You idiot!

Establish a "new normal" that is positive, powerful, and uplifting.

Hale Dwoskin says:

"We have fifty or sixty-thousand thoughts a day. If you wake up on the wrong side of the bed and stub your toe or have one disaster happen to you after another, it's not because you're thinking badly. It has more to do with how you feel. Say you do stub your toe. If you stop for a second and let go of the pain, let go of your anger at yourself, and let go of any judgments or self-talk you're having in that moment, then so what? You stubbed your toe, now what's the next thing you do. What you are is always present in the here and now. It has nothing to do with what was. You can discover this directly, as you let go, by allowing yourself to simply let go of whatever is happening in the moment, you allow the flow. Life is flow, it's not stagnant."

Remember what Marci Shimoff said in Chapter 7, "This idea that being hard on ourselves is going to motivate us is backwards. The more we are able to love ourselves and others, the better the Law of Attraction works in our lives." We must replace this negative self-talk with positive self-talk. The Power Statements in Appendix 3 will help you do this.

2. Negative Emotions Toward Self

This is where the reservoir of emotions begins to overflow. Negativity builds and builds over the years and these emotions are like a steel plate that prevents you from truly believing you'll ever receive all that you desire. We gather these emotions and collect them as if they are something to be treasured and we hold on to them with a very tight fist, defending our need to keep them.

The negative emotions you may have toward yourself include:

1. **Shame**

   A feeling of disgrace and humiliation for something you did. This is the most toxic and damaging feeling you can have. And the worst part about it is that we usually carry it around all our lives and never process it out by forgiving ourselves and going on. Instead, it festers in our bodies causing us all kinds of heartache and disease.

2. **Guilt**

   A feeling of responsibility, deserved or undeserved. Feeling guilt is a sign that you're living in the past.

3. **Fear**

   A sense of impending danger or pain. Feeling fear is a sign that you're living in the future. When you're living in either the past, by experiencing guilt, or in the future with fear, you miss out on the joy in your life today.

4. **Low Self-esteem**

   Having an unfavorable opinion of yourself. Children are born with high self-esteem. It's parents and the rest of the world that teach them to feel bad about themselves. It's natural and very important to feel good about who you are.

5. **Unworthiness**

   Giving yourself little worth or value. As with self-esteem, we're all born worthy. Someone has to tell us a lie to give us the feeling that we're not worthy of having good in our lives.

6. **Worry**

   To torment yourself with disturbing thoughts and scenarios that may or may not occur. The worst part about worry is that it's absolutely wasted time because 90% of what you worry about never happens.

7. **Regret**

   A sense of loss, disappointment, or dissatisfaction. This is wasted time as well, because you cannot go back and change what has happened. You have to come to terms with it and move on as best you can.

8. **Uncertainty**

   Hesitation and indecision about what to do in a situation. Frequently, we're not taught to trust our intuition and are told that we don't make good decisions. As a result, we develop a debilitating case of uncertainty and doubt about ourselves and our ability to make decisions.

9. **Being a Victim**

Repeatedly acting like someone else did something to you, when in reality, you volunteered. There is a payoff in acting this way and it's an ugly one. People who do this think they don't have to take responsibility for their lives. They get to blame everyone else for their misfortunes and failures.

10. **Perfectionism**

Being displeased with anything that's not perfect or doesn't meet extremely high and usually unrealistic standards. I call this a cancer that eats away at your joy in living. When you're a perfectionist, you place a very demanding and heavy burden on yourself and others. It's important to have standards and pride in your work, but you have to know when good enough is just that.

11. **Being Critical**

Finding fault and knit-picking with severity, too often and too quickly. Being critical is hereditary and contagious! You have to inherit it or catch it from someone, because it's not natural for us to be critical and fault-finding. But if you had a parent or other significant person in your life that was, it's likely you are too.

12. **Comparing Yourself to Others**

Examining yourself and others in order to determine similarities and differences. This causes you to constantly feel either better or worse than others, neither of which is necessarily reality.

13. **Superiority**

Feeling better than others. When you have a healthy sense of self-worth, you don't need to build yourself up by putting other people down. These last three items are usually a result of feeling bad about yourself, so you have to unnecessarily put other people down.

14. **Self-righteous**

Believing in your own righteousness and being smugly moralistic or intolerant of the opinions and behavior of others. We often call this having an attitude of "holier than thou."

15. **Judging**

Relentlessly forming a critical opinion about yourself or something you did. When you have an internal judge and jury that always finds you guilty, it's difficult to ever be happy.

3. Negative Talking To or About Others

1. **Reporting**

Reporting is an innocent way that even positive people can get pulled into negativity without knowing it. Reporting is repeating something negative that happened to you just to be telling the story.

Its purpose is usually for one of the following:

- To create a feeling of connection with others.

- To get attention from others.

- To gain the sympathy of others.

- To have something to talk about to add to a conversation.

- To have something to talk about to pass time.

Reporting negative trivialities is like spending $1,000 worth of emotion on a ten cent aggravation. It just isn't worth it.

Here is an example of reporting: "On the way here I was almost in an accident. The car in front of me was cut off and I had to slam on my brakes and so did the guy behind me. It was almost a four car collision." You can see the search for attention, sympathy, and possibly connection. There is absolutely no other reason to share this story again.

When I made the commitment to raise my vibration and eliminate all negative thinking and speaking, this was the most challenging arena for me. As I would go through any given day, negative things would happen. As I would talk to my friends I would repeat the story and go through the whole negative event again just to "catch them up on my life." When I noticed I was doing this, it was a painful realization how I was perpetuating negativity in my life and innocently calling it "catching up." I realized it was my way of connecting to my friends and they all did it too.

I put an end to it immediately, but I must say it was not an easy task. For a few weeks I didn't have much to talk about. I had to learn that my life was about way more than the negative events of my day. And I certainly did not want to give one ounce of energy to a negative event by repeating it over and over again. If it was something that I needed help in processing through with another person to decide my course of action or to release the negative sting of it, I gave myself permission to talk about it briefly one time with one other person and that was it. Before I would open my mouth with a negative story I would ask myself, "Is this reporting or processing?"

Ask yourself, "Why do I want to repeat this story? Do I want a connection, attention, sympathy, to have something to talk about or to just fill the time with idle chatter?" None of these are good reasons to report a negative story.

When there's something negative to share, preface the conversation with, "I have something to share that you might think is negative, but it turned out positive and I want to focus on the positive aspects. I want to tell you this and then move on to the question I have regarding it." I think this is important, because unless your listener is committed to keeping their vibration high, they could take you downhill with their response and exaggerate the negative aspects of your story that you didn't even mean to focus on.

2. Gossiping

Talking about others behind their back can be one of the most hurtful things we do to ourselves and others. Gossiping is usually done with the intent to put another person down and to build ourselves up. This gives the gossiper a superficial sense of superiority while the gossipfest is going on. To determine if it's gossip or not, ask yourself if it is something you would say to the person's face, or shouldn't say to their face? If you wouldn't or shouldn't say it to their face, then you shouldn't be saying it behind their back either.

3. Discouraging

One of the most common places I see discouraging going on today is in the dating world. There is a constant flow of "All the good men or women are taken." How discouraging is that? It implies that if you aren't already married, you're left with damaged goods. I don't think so. Because this attitude is so prevalent today, it gives people permission to say something very negative and get away with it. People are also very discouraging when they feel the need to point out all of the negative things that can happen in a situation. They call it being "realistic." If you're a discourager, bite your tongue until you want to scream, but stop spreading negativity around. What you put out comes back to you and puts a halt to your ability to attract your good.

If you're around people who are habitually discouraging, give them a short class on the Law of Attraction and how important their thoughts are creating the results they experience. Let them know that you're working on increasing your vibration so that you attract more of what you want in life and to do this you need to eliminate negative thinking and speaking. Give them a copy of this book and invite them to join you on the journey.

If these kinds of people don't join you on the journey and continue to be negative, then I would encourage you to limit your contact with them as much as possible. They're not bad people, it's just that it's difficult to get up and stay up as long as there are well-meaning friends or relatives around ready to give you a swift kick and knock you down again.

Oftentimes, people are discouraging because they're not ready to change, and the fact that you're growing and changing forces them to look at their life and that makes them feel uncomfortable. The only thing they know to do is to discourage you.

4. Complaining

When I was 17 years old my summer employer sent me to a Dale Carnegie training program. One of the foundations of their program is not to "Criticize, condemn or complain." I got the part about criticizing and condemning, those seem obviously harmful, but I didn't get the part about not complaining. The whole world does it, so it looks like it's okay to do. Well, no it's not. Some people have a terminal case of this type of negativity and they are called "complainaholics." Once you're on to them and how ridiculous idle complaining is, you'll spot it in a heartbeat and all you'll start to hear is "blah, blah, blah, blah, blah!" Next time you sit down to dinner with friends keep a tally of how many times someone at the table complains. You'll have a long list!

Complaining also comes along with a lot of heavy sighing and whining. It's really a downer.

If something negative happens in your life and you think it's important that others know what you're experiencing, then you need to be like a reporter and find a different spin on the same story. You need to find a way to tell the story from a positive perspective.

For example, my largest client asked me to fly to Chicago to teach presentation skills to a group of 25 managers from all over the Chicago area. Pinning down dates for these kinds of training programs is usually the most challenging step since so many people have to be included. Our date was set for a Monday in March.

I was supposed to leave the John Wayne Airport in Irvine, California on Sunday afternoon around 3:00. The flight was delayed several times, and when we finally boarded the plane two hours late, the pilot announced that the flight was cancelled because the crew had been flying too long and they didn't have a replacement crew in place. The airline was booking everyone on a flight that left the next morning at 8:30 arriving in Chicago around 1:00. I needed to be in Chicago the next morning before 11:00 to train these managers. I was not about to call the Eastern Regional V.P. of Operations who hired me and cancel this training without going to the ends of the earth to get to Chicago. In my mind I saw myself giving this training with gusto as though everything it took to get me there had been in perfect order.

Pandemonium took over the plane and people were irate. Getting angry creates a total plummet in your vibration and is a complete waste of precious energy. Instead, I stayed calm and focused. I got on the phone and was able to reserve a flight from Los Angeles to San Francisco and then a red-eye flight from San Francisco on to Chicago arriving at 5:55 a.m. I even got upgraded to first class! My fellow passenger told me I couldn't get on that flight because there were no seats left. I just smiled and said, "Well, I guess I must have gotten the last seat because I have a confirmed reservation." I had time to drive the hour from Irvine to Los Angeles and the sometimes daunting LA traffic flowed smoothly. I found the perfect safe parking place under a big street light near a parking toll-booth. I was set. Everything else flowed like clockwork. They replied, "No, I called before they made the announcement and they said there was no way to get a seat."

A limousine picked me up at 5:55 a.m. when I arrived in Chicago and took me to my hotel. I was able to get a couple of hours of sleep before my training. I gave an awesome training and had a ton of energy throughout the day, with never a slump.

What I went through was an amazing experience and a total breakthrough for me. I love my sleep and I always take measures to make certain I am in peak condition before any public speaking engagement. I would never take a red-eye flight for any reason, much less before a very important presentation.

The breakthrough was getting me past my own limited belief that I have to have the perfect amount of sleep and circumstances to deliver a great presentation. In this instance, next to nothing was perfect, I did fantastic, and I felt great, as well.

I also got to experience the exciting twists and turns of the Law of Attraction at work in my life. I was originally scheduled to return home after my training on Monday at 7:40 p.m. But since I arrived at 5:55 that morning, I decided to spend the night and leave the following day. I cancelled my flight and asked the hotel to cancel my limousine to the airport that evening and reschedule them both for the following morning at 9:00.

However, when I finished the training I felt great and reassessed the situation and decided I wanted to go home and sleep in my own bed that night. It was a few minutes before 6:00 and I knew there was a 7:40 flight because I was scheduled to be on it. I pulled my things together in the meeting room and was headed out the door to go pack when a woman entered and asked, "Are you Alicia Ashley?" I said, "Yes, why do you ask?" And she said, "Your limousine is waiting to take you to the airport." It still gives me chills to think about it! I told her to give me 10 minutes and I would be right there. I was at the airport in plenty of time and was at home asleep in my own bed, joyfully before 1:00 a.m. I spent a grand total of 13 ½ miraculous hours in Chicago.

Now, I could tell that story complaining about the airlines, complaining about having to wait in San Francisco for two hours, complaining about not getting enough sleep, complaining about how difficult it was to be a powerhouse speaker on so little sleep, complaining about what I "had" to go through to pull all of this off, pumping myself up about how awesome I am and how my client should really appreciate me because of what I did for them, and lots of other blah, blah, blah. And what would that get me? Nothing but a lot of negativity and a lower vibration. Every time I would tell the story it would once again lower my vibration. Every time I would tell that story people would be discouraged about air travel and how tough it is and that whole blah, blah, blah scenario.

No way! As I shared the story afterwards I focused on the breakthrough and all of the amazing miracles I experienced along the way. The predominant part of the story was positive – because I chose to look at it that way. I searched for the silver lining and I found it.

5. **Negative Emotions Regarding Others**

The list of negative emotions we may feel toward others is a long and painful one. Harboring these emotions can do us more damage than we realize. Research has shown that experiencing prolonged stress and negative emotions contribute substantially to diseases of all kinds. It's important to acknowledge these feelings and eventually move to a place of acceptance and forgiveness. We'll discuss these further in a moment.

- Resentment

- Anger

- Hatred

- Jealousy

- Envy

- Fear

- Criticism

- Judging

- Worry

6. **General Negativity**

General negativity includes:

- Being cynical.

- Being sarcastic.

- Talking negatively about the weather.

- Talking negatively about society.

- Talking negatively about the government.

- Regurgitating what is in the news.

These are often things we can't even do anything about! What good does complaining about the weather do? I'm not saying you can't make a difference in some of these other areas, because you can. But do something about it instead of just talking negatively about them.

Before we move on, I want to distinguish general negativity between people who want to talk about the negative events in their lives and those who have experienced something that might have been truly traumatic. It's very important for all of us to process, not deny, our feelings. So I'm not suggesting that you stuff, hide, ignore, or deny your true feelings. I'm suggesting that you be cautious of how much time you spend focusing on them, randomly talking about these situations to gain attention, sympathy, and to have something to add to conversations, etc.

THE "F" LETTER

Two of the frequent negative emotions we have towards other people are resentment and anger. These emotions block us from receiving our good. It is critical that you release all resentment and anger because it hurts you way more than it does the person toward whom you are angry and resentful.

Tom Justin, who is the author of *How to Take No for an Answer and Still Succeed,* shares this touching story about forgiveness.

"My brother stood behind me as I unlocked the door to our father's office. The funeral had been yesterday, yet it seemed like only moments ago.

I entered the room softly as if not wanting to awaken any thing or memory. I had flushed the tears and sadness so thoroughly these past days, I was sure there was none left. At first, we opened each file and desk drawer and folder slowly, partially out of reverence and partly out of guilt for invading our father's privacy.

Then, in its own file, there was a solitary letter. The linen paper was still bright white, showing its recent vintage. Thank God for this letter, I thought. The 'F' Letter.

As a youngster, my earliest memories are of a loving family. But that all changed one night when dad's drinking made him angry instead of sleepy.

He slammed the front door and yelled my name. I was twelve. Slowly I edged down the stairs, filled with fear and dread of this familiar, yet unknown father/beast. While still three steps up, he grabbed me by the corner of my pajama top. 'I thought I told you to empty the garbage tonight!' he said. He pushed me down in front of the garbage can, now overflowing, on the kitchen floor. Those few moments in front of that hellish altar of trash would be ingrained in my mind for years to come.

As time went on, I was to be the focus of his occasional drunken rages. I was the oldest and usually the one who hadn't followed some order or had done a chore too late. The events were significant enough so that long into adulthood, the slamming of a car door at night would again bring me, normally a deep sleeper, straight up off my pillow. We carried an uneasy yet cordial relationship into my adulthood.

Then one evening, on a plane, I read an article about the power of forgiveness. I suddenly felt the darkness of all the anger and rage I'd stuffed down about dad all these years. It was past midnight when I got home that night and sat down to write the most important letter of my life. Now, as I stood at his desk, reading it again, I smiled through more tears, recalling what happened next.

In the letter, I'd recalled the many wonderful events of my childhood with him and reminded him (and myself) of his generosity and of his teaching, the love and esteem he showed me throughout my life, exclusive of those horrible events. I concluded it with this:

'We've all made our share of mistakes in life, and that's a part of life. But I know the biggest mistake would be to not acknowledge the love and special times we shared together, both as father and son and as a family. I owe you a thank you for each time when I look back and remember. Thank you, Dad. I love you.'

As a boy he warned me never to use the 'F word.' I told him that it had taken me all these years to realize there was another 'F word' that I also hadn't used. Forgiveness. This would be my 'F Letter.'

The last time we spoke was on the phone. Dad sounded strained, his powerful voice subdued. He'd been having chest pains but wouldn't see a doctor. He assured me that he would go in the morning if he didn't feel better. Finally, he said he was going to bed and I said, 'I love you. Good night, daddy.'

He said, 'I love you too, son.'

Act like your life depends on you being positive, because it does!

When we hung up, I was surprised at the word 'daddy.' I hadn't called him that since I was a little boy.

Twenty minutes later he died. A fatal heart attack, while sitting in the same chair he'd been sitting in during our final conversation, the phone still in his lap.

The clean up, cataloging, packing and moving out of dad's office was complete. I peered into the now barren space for the final time, holding my breath as I softly closed the door, locking it behind me. *I love you daddy*, I whispered."

WORDS CREATE WORLDS

All of the above examples revolve around words; words that are spoken and words that are thought. Words you say to yourself, words you say to others, words others have said to you.

Never underestimate the power of words!

Words that you say or think are very powerful. Your words can either be weapons that wound, or a balm that heals.

Words are in every arena of our lives, whether we're listening, reading, or speaking; whether it's business or pleasure, words are present everywhere.

When you think or say any word, it carries a vibration much like a tuning fork activates the vibration of another tuning fork - so does the vibration of your words activate the power of the Law of Attraction.

Now, we'll examine the ways you can use words to help you stay positive and attract your good.

THE PATH TO POSITIVE THINKING AND SPEAKING

Act like your life depends on you being positive, because it does! It's the difference in struggling and getting by, or thriving in abundance and joy.

Monitor your thoughts and conversations for just one day and you'll see how prevalent negativity is. You have to make it a major priority to abstain from ALL negativity. The more you abstain from negativity, the higher your vibration will be and the more likely you are to attract your good. When you are aware that you're talking negatively about yourself, say, "Cancel! Cancel!" immediately. It's best if you say it out loud with conviction in your voice. Saying "Cancel! Cancel!" alerts your subconscious mind and lets it know that you don't want to create the statement you just spoke. But there are clearly situations where this would not be appropriate, like when you're sitting in a business meeting, church, or on a first date, silently would really be better at these times.

When you are aware that you're talking negatively about yourself, say, "Cancel! Cancel!" immediately. It's best if you say it out loud with conviction in your voice.

These are all the type of phrases I hear people say that should be followed with "Cancel! Cancel!"

- I can't afford that.
- I'm too fat to wear that.
- I don't do very well on tests.
- I'm always late.
- I'm going to be single forever.

Over the years I've had friends that were at varying stages of enlightenment. I recall one friend who beat herself up mercilessly with the words and phrases she would say about herself. I casually encouraged her to be more positive and she would try, but she never saw how vile she talked about herself. Finally, at the end of one of her verbally abusive monologues, I kindly but firmly asked, "Would you please stop talking about yourself with such disdain? It's very painful to listen to you do this. I love you so much and you are such a wonderful friend that it really hurts to hear this. I know you would not talk to anyone else that way, so why would you talk to yourself that way?" She got it and changed dramatically. After our conversation she would catch herself and say "Cancel! Cancel!"

We all must awaken to the fact that we cannot habitually engage in negativity of any kind and be a powerful magnet for positive attraction. Being negative and attracting your good are in direct opposition to each other. You are always a magnet. You will just attract more negative things into your life.

There are a couple of things some people do that makes it difficult for them to be positive. It's a pattern of reading the newspaper in the morning, listening to news on the radio in the car, and then watching the news at night. It's difficult to stay positive when you're beginning and ending the day with such negativity. Also, we must look at the books and magazines we're reading. We have to ask ourselves if what we are watching and reading is helping us or possibly hindering us.

In one of my darkest hours, when I felt overwhelmed by life being a single Mom with an infant, I was desperately trying not to completely derail into the negativity of it all and I coined the phrase "It is a beautiful day, life is good and we are blessed." I would say it to myself and to my son everyday, sometimes on several occasions, no matter what was going on. I remember wondering why I was saying it because everything around me seemed to be tumbling at my feet. But I clung to the fact that as long as I was alive I had the opportunity to turn things around. I knew nothing was so bad that, with time and with faith, I couldn't overcome it. I was tremendously grateful for that.

LIZARD BRAIN

Have you ever noticed that one minute you'll be on the right path and suddenly the next minute you're way off track, possibly seething with anger, flooded with fear, or paralyzed by the unknown? This is when your lizard brain slithers in and takes over! Just like a lizard shoots out his tongue, catches a fly, and eats it, your lizard brain shoots out thoughts, nails a positive one, and then tries to destroy it and you, by taking you down a negative self-defeating path.

Rev. Jim Turrell discusses the lizard brain as a real part of the brain that has three responses: 1) Fight, 2) Flee, or 3) Freeze. He goes on to explain:

"It's pretty simple because the lizard brain is not a complex organism. So, you get angry and want to fight, you start to get scared and you run, or you just don't know what to do so you freeze. It's the default which your mind goes to when you haven't taught your mind other ways to think.

The best way to calm the lizard brain down is to focus on gratitude, so that you can displace the emotional reaction. When you focus on what you are thankful for, you've started to calm that lizard brain down, because you started to focus on something other than your knee-jerk reactions to life.

When you do this, you've got the ability to monitor the emotional energy you have inside of you. This emotional energy can be an obstacle to creating powerful results using the Law of Attraction because it relates to your fears, reactions, resentments, limitations, or the sense of unworthiness you may have.

The lizard brain has a lot to do with with your feelings of worthiness. Do you feel worthy of having what you want? If you don't feel worthy of having what you want, then you really need to start creating a consciousness, an awareness that trumps the lizard brain. The lizard brain is the default mechanism – that's where you go when you get scared."

I've recognized that my lizard brain is a real saboteur. Its goal is for me to stay safe at all costs. Take a risk, break out of the mold, and make a change for the better? No way! My response is, "Okay lizard brain, go back into your hole or under a rock and stay there. You're not welcome here anymore."

HOW TO DEAL WITH THE NEGATIVITY OF OTHERS

Give yourself permission to change and really be the best you can be and live the best life you can. To really do that and get in the flow with the Law of Attraction, you must limit the amount of negativity in your life.

I mentioned previously, that oftentimes those around you are not ready to change. They may resent the fact that suddenly you're trying to be a positive person. They may make fun of you or try to belittle you because of their insecurities.

Misery loves company and negativity loves a party!

You've heard the phrase, misery loves company. Well, misery loves company and negativity loves a party! If you're taking your name off the party list, it may surprise and disappoint some of your friends and relatives. It's easy for people to get together and start criticizing a person, institution, or situation. Negativity is a way people bond. If you're really going to get on a positive path and stay on it in spite of others, you need to become acutely aware and keep in mind the following:

1. **Be Prepared**

    Honestly assess the person with whom you'll be talking. Think to yourself, does this person tend to be positive or negative? Depending on your answer, you need to go in aware of what could happen and be prepared. You may have to initiate a "conversation intervention" to shift things in a positive direction.

2. **Remember the Reality**

    The reality is that it doesn't help the negative person to continue to rant with no end in sight. When you allow this, you're contributing to the negative person attracting more bad things into his or her life. You don't have to be the recipient of negativity. It can be very difficult for you to sit and listen to it and stay positive yourself, even if it's not directed toward you at all.

3. **Be Respectful of the other Person's Current Reality**

    I recall being in the middle of a financial disaster and talking to a woman I respect and admire tremendously. She was a mentor, and I was telling her the sad state of affairs in my financial life at that time. It was shortly after 9/11, and I was in the middle of a very upsetting and difficult divorce. So there was a lot going on, to say the least, and I had unfortunately derailed and spiraled into a pathetic state of negativity.

When I finished, she began telling me how she had more business than she'd had in years, how she was making $7,000 per speech, how great her husband was, and on and on and on. In the end, I was very happy for her and not envious an ounce. But it felt like she had no emotional intelligence or sensitivity to my current reality. It was just very poor timing. It felt like she was more invested in stroking her ego than in giving me any comfort whatsoever.

Here are some things you can say to show empathy:

- I'm very sorry to hear that. I have all due respect for the challenges you're facing.

- I know you'll pull out of this.

- What are you doing to start pulling out of this?

- You've gone through tough times before and come out on the other side a better person, and I know you will this time, too.

- How are you taking care of yourself in the middle of this?

- What can I do to support you in getting through this?

- You're a very strong and positive person and I know this will not get you down for long.

- I know there is a silver lining to this that you will be able to see at some point.

4. Set a Time Limit for Negativity

If you're new to being assertive, this might be challenging, but it's a must if you know someone who tends to be negative, or has a negative situation going on in his or her life.

You can say something like, "I really want to hear what's been going on since we last spoke. However, I'm aware of the magnitude of negativity that's going on in your life (or in this situation), and I think it would be best for all of us if we set a time limit for discussing this."

If they're talking and have been doing so for what seems like an eternity, you can interrupt and say, "I'm sorry to interrupt you, but I'm aware of our time and there are some things I would like to have time to talk with you about as well. So is it okay if we spend five more minutes maybe summarizing this topic and then move on to something else?"

Then, set a time limit in your mind, and when that time has elapsed, excuse yourself to the bathroom. This can break the momentum and gives you a chance to change the subject more graciously.

5. **Change the Subject**

   You may need to initiate a "conversation intervention" to shift things in a positive direction if you feel them spiraling into a permanent state of negativity.

   - You can do the innocent interruption: "I'm sorry to interrupt you, but before I forget I want to ask you…." This may work for some people and others will get right back on their soapbox.

   - You can take a detour on something they say: "That reminds me of …"

6. **Find the Good in the Situation**

   Timing is the key to this one. If you aren't careful, it can seem insensitive and inconsiderate. If there is a recent upset and it's still fresh, it may be too soon to take this step.

   Know that no matter what you or others are going through, there will always be some good in it. It may not seem to warrant the events that took place, but continue to search for the good relentlessly.

7. **Take Care of Yourself**

   It's self-defeating to hinder yourself while you're trying to take care of someone else. In the end, you'll help the negative person more when you set positive boundaries.

8. **Don't Try to "Fix It"**

   Remind yourself that it's not your responsibility to "fix" another person or the problems he or she may face. It's helpful if you can point out a solution. However, many times individuals get stuck in the negativity of their lives and even when the perfect solution is presented, they ignore it.

FORGIVENESS

I would like to close this chapter by discussing forgiveness. When we address expanding our thoughts, I don't believe there is any greater expansion than forgiveness. When we have been wronged, or feel as though we have, our hearts close up and our minds tighten around judgments and resentments blocking our flow of energy and lowering our vibration. The energy of resentment attracts the low energy of further negative feelings and things to you. You cannot be in tune with the Law of Attraction while harboring anger and resentment toward yourself or others.

As much as we all know forgiveness is important and beneficial to us, it's nevertheless very difficult to do. Our ego resists everything about it. It tells us "they" were the ones who wronged us, why do we have to forgive them?

---

2. Ferrini, Paul. *The 12 Steps of Forgiveness*. Greenfield, MA: Heartways Press, 1991.

Paul Ferrini, in his book, *The 12 Steps of Forgiveness*[2] talks about the Four Axioms of Forgiveness. They are:

1. Forgiveness starts in our own hearts. Only when we have forgiven ourselves can we give forgiveness to or receive it from others.

2. Forgiveness is not conditional, even though our practice of it often is.

3. Forgiveness is an ongoing process. It continues in response to every judgment we make about ourselves and others.

4. Every gesture of forgiveness is sufficient. Whatever we're able to do now is enough. This understanding enables us to practice forgiveness with forgiveness.

Before we talk about forgiving others, we need to discuss forgiving yourself. This is part of clearing the muddy water we talked about earlier. To move beyond many of these negative thoughts and feelings, you must forgive yourself and learn to love and accept yourself just as you are. The unrealistic expectations we place on ourselves are defeating. Lighten up and don't be so hard on yourself. Have mercy on and approach yourself with a spirit of gentleness and kindness.

Write a letter of forgiveness and love to yourself for only you to see. You have always been doing the best you could with the awareness you had at the time. You are becoming more aware and able to do better, but you must forgive yourself first.

A STORY OF FORGIVENESS

Janet shared the following process of how she was able to overcome debilitating guilt, freeing her to live her life to the fullest.

"Within a time span of about a year I got pregnant three times. I had gone off of the pill because I was having problems with it and I had been celibate for almost a year, and had not found a suitable birth control replacement.

My divorce was not final, finances were challenging, and I had a three-year-old daughter. Plus, I was on my own, for the first time in my life. All three times I let my boyfriend talk me into the 'easy way out,' even though I don't really believe in abortion, and definitely don't see it as a legitimate means of birth control.

Having a beautiful, precious three-year-old daughter, I knew the value of those dear beings I did not give a chance to come into this world, and I knew they were all just as special as my daughter.

My self-esteem plummeted and I became depressed and guilt-ridden. I beat myself up pretty badly over the mistakes I had made. I had no self-confidence, and went through my days on auto pilot. I felt I was a worthless, horrible person. I lost my desire to be a part of life. I felt like I was a coward, that I didn't have the strength and courage to do what I believed was right. It was painful caving into pressure from my boyfriend, instead of standing strong for what I believed in. I let fear get the best of me.

I also gained 30 or more pounds after each abortion, resulting in a total weight gain of more than 100 pounds in one year. The emotional weight of the guilt and shame were painful enough to deal with, and then the physical weight made it even worse.

It was really difficult for me, knowing I had taken three lives of my own children. That's a pretty hard fact to face. Especially since being a mom is the greatest joy in my life.

I lived with this guilt for years, until I finally confided in my minister. He suggested that I write the aborted children a letter, and then read it to him if I wanted to, or not. He urged me to forgive myself and let it go.

I wrote the letter and read it to him and the tears of grief and healing flowed. I told the children how sorry I was that I didn't give them a chance to come into this world, that I cheated the world of what they would have brought to it, how I regretted that I would not get to see them grow up, and how I would never have the experience of being their mommy. I told them that I hoped they would forgive me and that I would see them in Heaven someday.

Afterwards, I felt tremendous love, peace, and great relief. I felt that I could be free to go on and to live my life. I felt compassion, for myself, and the children. I felt hope in the future. I could have a new beginning.

I faced my feelings, and shared them in a safe, loving, non-judgmental environment, the weight of the guilt was lifted, and my self-esteem and confidence were restored. I understood that I wasn't a terrible person, but simply, a person who had made some serious mistakes. I believe in a God who loves me no matter what. Realizing this, I felt that in spite of what I had done I too must be worth loving and being forgiven.

I will always regret taking the easy way out and not giving those precious children a chance. But I'm no longer bogged down by the terrible load of the guilt and shame. I've learned to forgive myself and let it go. I can never undo what I did. But as I grow closer to God in my search for healing and meaning, I'm able to live my life to the fullest, and I know that I can use my experience to help bring encouragement and healing to others."

Forgiving yourself, as Janet's story demonstrates, is a key factor in being able to access the Law of Attraction to your greatest ability. Guilt and shame have extremely low vibrations. The weight of these negative emotions attracts negativity in many forms. On the other end of the spectrum, love and acceptance both have extremely high vibrations and attract more positive things and experiences into your life.

FORGIVING OTHERS

Yes, you must also forgive others. Not necessarily because they deserve it, but because you do. Resentment, judgment, and anger hurt you; they do not hurt the person you're holding them against. Each of these inhibits your energy, blocks your spirit, and damages your health. Holding on to grudges is like allowing a terrible tenant to live rent-free in your most prized real estate space, your mind. This is baggage you want to move out and let go of as fast as possible.

You want to replace these resentments, judgments, and anger with acceptance. It doesn't mean you're going to be best friends with the person who harmed you and invite them over to dinner tomorrow night. It just means you're cutting the cords that choke the life out of you, not them. Our world is so filled with judgments and criticism that acceptance isn't something you frequently hear about. It's one of the most important ways to expand your thoughts in order to increase your Attraction Quotient.

One of the best passages I've ever read on acceptance is found in the *Big Book of Alcoholics Anonymous*.[3] It reads:

"Acceptance is the answer to all my problems today. When I am disturbed, it is because I find some person, place, thing, or situation – some fact of my life – unacceptable to me, and I can find no serenity until I accept that person, place, thing, or situation as being exactly the way it is supposed to be at this moment. Nothing, absolutely nothing happens in God's world by mistake. Until I could accept my alcoholism, I could not stay sober; unless I accept life completely on life's terms, I cannot be happy. I need to concentrate not so much on what needs to be changed in the world as on what needs to be changed in me and in my attitudes."

Keep your thoughts on a higher plane through positive thinking, forgiveness and acceptance, as these will support you in deepening your spirituality, which is the topic of our next chapter. As I mentioned in Chapter 2, the Law of Attraction is not secular, it is spiritual.

---

3. Alcoholics Anonymous World Services, Inc. Alcoholics Anonymous. New York, 2002.

CHAPTER 12

Deepen Your Spirituality

"God is the Ultimate Source. God is the Ultimate Light of Love. When people are tapped into the prevailing force that binds all of us in humanity together it's all a part of God." —Chellie Campbell

SPIRITUALITY IS A GOOD THING

It saddens me how some organized religions give God a bad name. They turn people off to the power behind the Law of Attraction that can change their life for the good more than anything else.

I remember sitting in church when the minister said, "Look around you, these are the people you'll be with for eternity in heaven." I was 15 or 16 years old at the time, and I was mortified. These were people I didn't want to sit in church with, much less spend eternity with! Where's the love, where's the joy, where's the fun in these people's lives? Call it blasphemy if you wish, but I didn't want to go to heaven at all. It sounded like a miserable destination if that was the company I was going to keep throughout eternity!

Today almost all of my friends and associates closest to me have a deep level of spirituality. Their current connection to the Higher Power of their understanding is alive and strong. They are happy, joy-filled people who know that the power behind the Law of Attraction is God, and they stay connected to that power on a daily basis.

Don't let any challenges you've had with organized religion delay you from making a conscious contact with the God of your understanding today.

SPIRITUALITY AND RELIGION

It's important to recognize that spirituality and religion are two very different things.

1. Spirituality

A person may be considered spiritual if their beliefs about a Higher Power are more universal, broad, and open. They may see and appreciate the presence of a Higher Power within all religions. They may feel that there are many paths that lead to the same destination of connecting to this Higher Power.

2. Religious

A person may be considered religious if they have a particular belief system about a Higher Power. They may follow a specific set of boundaries and rules that are set up around a specific religion. They may feel that there is one way to approach this Higher Power or that only one certain path leads to the Higher Power.

Your Higher Power, or whatever you choose to call it, is trans-denominational.

It's not unusual for a person to be both religious and spiritual. They may enjoy following the specific guidelines presented by a specific religion but appreciate and respect other approaches to connecting to a Higher Power.

Dr. James Golden elaborated on the powerful role your intention plays in finding the path that's right for you. He said:

"The true spiritual path is the enfoldment inside a person. It's not about the religion, the book, or the teacher. It's what happens inside of somebody, it's their own personal transformation. I would say if a person is sincere about wanting to know the truth, or to know about God, in one sense it doesn't even matter what spiritual path or religion they follow. It's going to work for them, because they have the intention, they have the desire. As a result, they'll get what they need. They'll experience their own personal transformation."

CREATE A FRESH, CLEAN SLATE

I was raised in a religion that focused on all of the rules, restrictions, and regulations you had to follow to get to a Higher Power that they called God. From what I recall, they didn't really focus on the love, grace, or goodness of God. The list of things you couldn't do was miles longer than the list of things you could do. There was no joy in the kind of God I was taught to worship, just a lot of fear. I walked away from that religion the minute I was old enough to do so. I realize there are millions of people who are content in these kinds of religions, including members of my own family, it just didn't work for me.

If you find yourself having trouble with this facet of the Law of Attraction, then I encourage you to start with a fresh, clean slate. Erase from your mind everything you've learned about God and religion up to this point. If it was really good, then I promise, it will most certainly come back to you. But begin to define your Higher Power in a manner that moves and inspires you.

I realize some will want to toss this book in the trash right now, but I stand firm on the fact that your Higher Power, or whatever you choose to call it, is trans-denominational. Your Higher Power does not care how you choose to acknowledge it or connect to it.

The rules, restrictions, and regulations that each denomination around the world has created helps that group of people to honor and deepen their connection to the Higher Power of their understanding.

If none of those rules, restrictions, and regulations works for you, you can still have an incredibly meaningful and rich relationship with the Higher Power of your understanding.

That's exactly what I did. While I did not continue to attend a specific church, I continued to deepen my spirituality and my connection to my Higher Power in many meaningful and touching ways. I continued my spiritual practices of prayer, meditation, journaling, reading spiritual books, and mindfulness in seeing my Higher Power in everything that I did. I finally found joy in my Higher Power, more joy than I ever could have found before.

After about ten years of deepening my spirituality and never attending a church, I decided I wanted to return. And then I attended several churches that focused on the joy, goodness, and grace of a loving and kind God.

You can have a great connection to the Higher Power of your choice and never walk through the doors of a church. You can find a Higher Power in many other wonderful places and ways. You can also connect to your Higher Power on any and every day of the week, not just Saturday or Sunday.

Dr. James Golden stated it very well, "There are many paths to the same destination. It has more to do with what a person takes from their religion or from their spiritual path. Does it actually do something inside of them to change them so that the Spirit can be more understood and revealed?"

Spiritual practices are the things you do to establish and keep your connection to your Higher Power strong and alive.

GET PLUGGED IN

Spiritual practices are the things you do to establish and keep your connection to your Higher Power strong and alive. If you don't have a daily spiritual practice your current connection becomes weaker and weaker until it's nonexistent.

I travel a lot with my work so I'm in hotels two to three weeks a month sometimes. I love to read every night before I go to sleep. Sometimes I'll reach over to turn on the bedside lamp and it won't turn on. I'll jimmy with the switch, and jimmy with the bulb, and if nothing happens I'll look to see if the lamp is plugged in.

Sometimes the lamp is unplugged. The connection clearly isn't there, so no wonder the light won't turn on. Or, I recall one occasion looking at the socket and it looked like the lamp was plugged in, but it wasn't the right cord.

Other times the lamp still won't work after I've verified that the correct plug is indeed plugged in. That's when I'll call the engineering department and they'll come bring me a new bulb and voila! Let there be light!

Your spirituality is quite the same as the lamp being plugged in, or not. Are you plugged in to your Higher Power? If not, you may not be seeing any results from trying to use the Law of Attraction. You've got to stay plugged in so that you keep your current connection strong. And just like a light bulb burns out, sometimes you outgrow a certain kind of spiritual practice and need to establish a new one that will help your connection burn bright again.

SPIRITUAL PRACTICES

The spiritual practices you choose are personal and will vary as you develop and grow in your own spirituality. Get connected and stay connected to your Higher Power in a manner that suits you.

The practice you choose will have two functions: to help you create a deeper level of self-awareness, and to help you create a deeper connection to your Higher Power.

Below you'll find some examples of spiritual practices that you may want to try. This list is not meant to be comprehensive in its discussion, as there are many excellent books, tapes, teachers, and resources for each. I hope that you'll seek them out and begin your journey to inner peace today. This list is meant to give you examples of ways you can begin and deepen your connection to your Higher Power.

1. **Contemplation**

   Contemplation is one of the best spiritual practices to begin with. There are many books available now that have daily readings. They are short and can be very helpful. Find a page or passage that touches you and spend time contemplating the meaning it has in your life. Or, you may find an inspirational poem, verse, or song and reflect on how it connects to your daily life. With both contemplation and meditation you create a very sacred kind of stillness and silence that deepens your spirituality more and more with regular practice.

2. **Meditation**

   There are many different forms of meditation. Overall, the goal is to quiet your mind and slow down the constant and rapid pace of thoughts at any given moment. To do this it's recommended that you focus your mind on one word, thought, or object. There are many books, tapes, and CDs that can guide you in making this a spiritual practice you enjoy. With practice, the stillness you experience will feel as if you're in perfect union with your Higher Power.

   One form of meditation is to focus on your breathing. Notice the rise and fall of your chest as you inhale and exhale. As other thoughts creep in, simply return your focus to your breath. Notice the peace you feel even if it's only for a few minutes. Continue to focus on your breathing, aiming to sustain your focus for ten minutes or more.

In his book, *A New Earth: Awakening to Your Life's Purpose,* Eckhart Tolle speaks of the powerful transformation you can experience if you will simply focus on your breathing. He uses this story to illustrate:

> "Someone recently showed me the annual prospectus of a large spiritual organization. When I looked through it, I was impressed by the wide choice of interesting seminars and workshops. It reminded me of a smorgasbord, one of those Scandinavian buffets where you can take your pick from a huge variety of enticing dishes. The person asked me if I could recommend one or two courses. "I don't know," I said. "They all look so interesting. But I do know this," I added. "Be aware of your breathing as often as you are able, whenever you remember. Do this for one year, and it will be more powerfully transformative than attending all of these courses. And it's free."

3. Prayer

I've heard it said that prayer is talking to your Higher Power and that meditation is listening to your Higher Power. Dr. Golden describes prayer like this:

> "It doesn't matter the style that you pray in. It doesn't matter whether it's a lot of words or only a few words. It doesn't matter where you do it or when you do it. If you ask for help there is help. If you ask to have God be more experiential, to know God more or to be aligned with God, then God is always there. What really matters is that when you pray, you're sincere. Many times people pray and what they're really asking for is some kind of material gain. That's not all that prayer is for."

When you put your thoughts and feelings down on paper, it gets them out of your head and gives you more courage to actually face them.

From past church experience, you may think that prayer is something you need to get on your knees to do, or that you need to do it in the same kind of manner that a minister or priest does. This is not true at all. Prayer is any manner in which you choose to talk to your Higher Power.

4. Journaling

Since I embarked on my path of personal growth and transformation some 25 years ago, this has been my

favorite spiritual practice. Over time I've found it to be the most efficient tool to connect me to my Higher Power and alter my consciousness. I can pack a journal and take it with me wherever I go and find solace after writing only a few pages. I have filled numerous journals with all of the aspects of my multi-faceted life.

This is not the kind of writing that you would want anyone to read. This is for your eyes only, so spelling, punctuation, and grammar are not important. What is important is for you to express your thoughts and feelings, to write what is bothering you and what you can do about it, to focus on your Power Statements, to write what you are grateful for and why, and most important to find something, no matter how small it is that is positive.

Julia Cameron in her book, *The Artist's Way* recommends writing what she calls "Morning Pages." She suggests writing three pages of stream of consciousness thinking every morning. You just begin writing your thoughts and feelings without judgment until you've completed three pages. Whether you write in the morning or the evening, writing is a very powerful tool to connect you to your Higher Power. When you put your thoughts and feelings down on paper, it gets them out of your head and gives you more courage to actually face them and take the appropriate actions to handle them.

Over the years this is the tool I depend on frequently and have found to be the most powerful. Whether I spend 10 minutes or an hour writing I see amazing results fast. The benefits far supercede the amount of time it takes to do the writing. If you will take the time to incorporate this spiritual practice in your daily life you will see powerful changes.

5. Mindfulness

Mindfulness is the practice of focusing on the presence of a Higher Power in everything you do. You observe this while you're driving the car, doing the dishes, taking a shower, or at dinner with friends. When you enter into every situation with the spirit of mindfulness, it brings a calm, peace, and tranquility to your life. Dr. Golden addressed the topic of mindfulness as follows:

> "Mindfulness brings a different point of view, a different perspective on the world because you're not getting caught up on the surface of things going on in the world. You're able to bring your intention to be loving, to be kind, and to know the truth into every interaction as you're going about everyday life. Mindfulness is a state of consciousness that allows you to meditate on the go, so to speak."

6. Attending Meetings or Services

Participating in a group who has the same goal in mind is a wonderful step in supporting your daily practice of inner awareness and connection to your Higher Power. There are millions of people around the world who attend meetings for the various 12 Step programs that have evolved from the original Alcoholics Anonymous program. All of these programs are based on a spiritual foundation and will aid those who have addictions to overcome them. If there are church services you enjoy attending, this can also be a meaningful part of your spiritual practices. But don't feel like you must attend any church in order to enrich your spiritual life. You may also want to seek out groups that study the book, "*A Course in Miracles.*" You will find these groups support your work in applying the Law of Attraction in your life.

7. Connecting to Your Higher Power through Nature

This is one of the easiest and fastest ways to connect to the Source. When you look at a breathtaking vista, walk across a sandy beach, or follow a meandering trail, you can't help but observe the hand of a Higher Power everywhere you turn. Just being in nature slows you down, but you can still be there and be thinking about your to-do list and that isn't the point. For this to be a spiritual practice, you must focus your attention on your inner awareness and contemplate your current connection to your Higher Power. Many individuals choose to do their daily walk or run in nature and find it a way of both connecting to their Higher Power, and benefiting their health.

8. Yoga

The practice of yoga helps to promote a deeper awareness of your body and soul. Getting your body involved through stretching and postures, as they are called, has a very grounding effect. It helps to calm your mind, which in turn slows down your emotions so that you feel more relaxed and at peace. You'll also notice a higher level of mental clarity and inner well-being.

9. Chanting

Many people are initially uncomfortable with the silence of contemplation or meditation. Chanting gives them the opportunity to use their voice in singing or speaking a sentence or phrase repeatedly. Focusing on one sentence or phrase helps to shift your consciousness and deepen your spiritual awareness of your Higher Power.

10. Seva

Seva comes out of an Eastern meditation tradition. It means "selfless service to God." It's the act of giving to, or serving your Higher Power, through giving to or serving others. It's helping others without any desire for personal gain. It's offering your time and energy without any strings attached. When you participate in Seva, you set your ego aside and think of others more than yourself. When you give freely and openly on a regular basis, you're a changed person. Your ego subsides and your connection to your Higher Power deepens exponentially. Seva can be as simple as picking up a piece of trash on the street and placing it in the trash can or it can be volunteering for your favorite charity. It's the manner in which you give of yourself without expecting anything in return.

How you establish your daily spiritual practices will determine the results you create using the Law of Attraction. Remember, the power behind the Law of Attraction is your Higher Power. The more you stay connected to your Higher Power, the more you'll believe, and the more you'll receive.

Your aim would be to experience one or more spiritual practices each day. It doesn't have to be the same one, but use self-discipline to keep your practice consistent. It will always work to help you deepen your connection.

Remember back in Chapter 6 when we talked about doing three things for yourself each day that make you feel good? Any of these spiritual practices would be great to include on your list of three.

THE FOUR STAGES OF CONNECTING AND INNER AWARENESS

1. Careless Connection

2. Casual Connection

3. Committed Connection

4. Constant Connection

1. Careless Connection

Look at the word "careless" carefully. You'll see the word "care" and the word "less." This approach indicates one could "care less" about creating inner awareness or a strong connection with their Higher Power. If your goal is to create amazing results using the Law of Attraction, you won't get far using the "care less" approach.

2. Casual Connection

This is the stage in which you'll find most people. They casually approach self-examination and creating a connection to their Higher Power. They give these things priority every now and then. They have busy lives, and busy lives aren't conducive to introspection and connection. The Thesaurus compares casual with "informal," "relaxed," and "laid-back." If you approach your Higher Power casually, then you'll receive casual results.

3. Committed Connection

When you are committed, you take the necessary time for daily personal examination so that you can discover an inner awareness of your thoughts and feelings. You also take the time to participate in daily spiritual practices that deepen your current connection to your Higher Power. It's sad, but true, that most people want something for nothing. They want all the miracles contained within the Law of Attraction, but they don't want to do the work. Consequently, they'll not create the results. The people who know that anything worth having is worth taking time for will gradually work up to this stage of commitment, and they'll live a life of miracles - one right after the other!

4. Constant Connection

This is the most exciting and exhilarating stage of all. You'll feel divinely connected to your Higher Power, no matter where you are or what you're doing most of the time. Your life is a moment-to-moment experience of peace, love, joy, and abundance. You're able to see and feel your Higher Power in everything you do. When you have a constant connection, you're able to see that everything works in divine order. You know unequivocally that your good is on its way to you because you have a constant connection to the Source.

These are the four stages of connecting to your Higher Power and establishing inner awareness. Please be patient with yourself as you move from one stage to the next. If this is all new to you, please know that each stage takes time. This is not something that can be rushed. If you move steadily and consistently, you'll create the results you want in your life. I must also underscore that the more gratitude you give, the faster you'll transition from one stage to the next.

A note of caution: Don't think once you're at a specific stage you'll stay there automatically. There is nothing automatic about deepening your connection to your Higher Power. Yes, the daily practices can become so habitual they'll seem automatic and they'll keep you plugged in. But you don't arrive at Stage 4 and think you're going to stay there just because you achieved that level while vacationing in the Caribbean!

OMNIPOTENCE

I invite you to plug into this omnipotent power and call it whatever you wish. It doesn't care what you call it. It only wants you to keep your connection current and your life to soar!

There are miracles happening in your life right now, you're just too busy to notice them. When you learn to slow down and live a soul-filled life, you'll begin to see, hear, and feel differently. And you'll begin to notice miracle after miracle all around you; funny miracles, shocking miracles, joyful miracles, amazing miracle, miracles of all kinds, all the time. Nothing is impossible!

LISTEN TO THE STILL, SMALL VOICE

One of the things that most prevents us from deepening our spirituality is the stress and pressure of our busy lives. Most of us are stressed to the max! We run around going from one thing to the next, getting the kids to school, getting ourselves to work, meeting deadlines, going on business trips, going grocery shopping, fixing meals, doing laundry, cleaning the house, going to dinner with friends, going to the movies, buying gifts for birthdays and holidays, washing the car, washing the dog, watching TV, reading the paper, going shopping, and going on a vacation. That keeps us going, going, and going!

All of this "going" is exhausting! And it all adds up to a lot of stress. We never stop going long enough to slow down and connect to our heart and soul. This kind of stress-filled lifestyle is a significant obstacle on the path to creating results using the Law of Attraction.

Dreams rarely come true in a mess of stress. I'm not saying they never do, but what happiness and joy can they bring when born out of chaos? Most people are running on empty all the time. We all need to slow down to hear the inspiration, to do the necessary soul-searching, and to stay current in our connection to our Higher Power.

Our current connection to our Higher Power is critical to having the Law of Attraction work in our lives. Believing is a key step in receiving our good. For us to believe 100% there is an element of faith involved. For us to have adequate faith, we must believe in a power greater than ourselves.

Create a life where you can hear the still, small voice within telling you the hunch or inspiration that points you toward your greatest good.

This requires us to slow down, way down. Stress and the demands the world places on us are Big, Loud, and Busy. The longings of our souls do not yell at us in the midst of Big, Loud, and Busy to try and get our attention. Our souls don't cry out, "Hey you, pay attention to me!" Instead, the voices of our souls are usually Small, Quiet, and Still. You can't hear it in the noise and bustle of a stress-filled life.

THE EQUATION LOOKS LIKE THIS:

Stress = Big, Loud, and Busy

vs.

Our Soul = Small, Quiet, and Still.

To really get the Law of Attraction working in your favor, you need to deepen your spirituality; create a life where you can hear the still, small voice within telling you the hunch or inspiration that points you toward your greatest good.

But if you race through your days from the minute you open your eyes in the morning to the time you land in your bed exhausted at night, there isn't much room for inspiration, and there is too much noise to hear the longings of your soul. Your spirituality shrinks more and more everyday until it's non-existent.

Slowing down gives you the opportunity to create an inner awareness, and establish a connection to your Higher Power. It helps you to keep your focus on all that's good in your life. Therefore, you create more and more good.

Marci Shimoff added these comments:

"I believe deepening our spirituality is where it is at. The whole principal in the Law of Attraction is that feeling good is what draws things to us. We manifest on the basis of feeling good. We can manifest on the basis of feeling bad, and then we manifest things that are not what we want. The way to get to that expanded feeling, or feeling good, is by living a soul-filled life, rather than a stressed-filled life.

A stressed-filled life is based on the small mind and the ego. A soul-filled life is based on surrender and peace. I've interviewed over one hundred people for my book, *Happy for No Reason*, and they all live an expanded soul-filled life."

ESTABLISH INNER AWARENESS THROUGH SELF-EXAMINATION

Most of us have a tendency to look outside of ourselves for answers. We think it takes something outside of ourselves to make us happy. Once we have achieved our basic needs of food, shelter, and clothing, the hunt is on for something to make us happy. We think it's going to be a bigger house, a better car, finer clothes, exotic vacations, expensive watches, and jewelry, and so on.

The search for happiness and fulfillment can go on all of your life and you'll never find it as long as you're looking outside of yourself. The answers you're looking for are nestled within your heart and soul right now. You don't have to look any further than within yourself. I'm not saying you're so great and powerful that you personally have the answer to everything in the world, but I'm saying that you have all of the answers that are important to you for living a great life – right now. You're the only one who knows what's best for you, and looking outside yourself will always point you in the wrong direction.

Why don't you feel like you have all of the answers within you? Possibly because you were taught that others know what's best for you, therefore you learned to discount what you thought to be true for you. Or, you may have received disapproval for following your heart at some point and made a decision to never do that again.

Also, it's human nature to look outside of ourselves for happiness. Advertisers know we all long for happiness and fulfillment, and they play into this perpetual search. What they show us in magazines and on TV promote that happiness is found when we buy a certain new car, shopping at a certain store, buy the current fashions, own expensive jewelry, and so on.

Owning great things and going fun places can be wonderful. But in the end it's not what we own or what we do that creates fulfillment in our lives. It's our inner awareness through self-examination and our current connection to our Higher Power that brings us the most joy.

If you're just beginning on the path of enlightenment and spirituality, this may sound absurd to you now. That's okay. If you'll do all of the exercises contained within this book thoroughly, you'll begin to point your thoughts in the right direction – and that's within. It will be the most exciting journey of your life!

Socrates said, "An unexamined life is not worth living." Without self-examination, it's impossible to create an inner awareness. Without an inner awareness, our lives are random, haphazard, and we're buffeted around from one thing to the next without rhyme or reason.

With regular self-examination you'll gain a powerful focus in your life and learn how to fill the longings of your soul.

THE PARADE OF LIFE

Here's a great quote that captures the essence of inner awareness perfectly:

"There are three kinds of people in the parade of life: the people who make the parade, the people who watch the parade, and the people who don't even know there's a parade going on."

Let's dissect this quote further.

"There are three kinds of people in the parade of life":

1. **"The people who make the parade."**

   These are the people who have a heightened sense of inner awareness. They're firmly rooted in their spirituality. They practice daily self-examination and soul-searching. They know who they are and what it takes to truly make them happy and satisfied. They know the greatest gifts and talents they were born with, and they're fulfilled sharing them with the world. They keep their current connection to their Higher Power strong, and therefore create amazing results in their lives using the Law of Attraction. They know the importance of making a difference in the lives of others, and they give back generously their time, money, and other things. They love their life and they make the parade of life more enjoyable for everyone around them.

There are three kinds of people in the parade of life: the people who make the parade, the people who watch the parade, and the people who don't even know there's a parade going on.

2. **"The people who watch the parade."**

   These are the people who are occasionally soul-searching. They're conveniently spiritual. They see the vision of joy in front of them, but have yet to really reach out and fully grasp it for themselves. They have a moderate amount of inner awareness, but are distracted with the details and trivialities of their lives to stay consistent with developing it. They'll occasionally get on the path with a focused intensity and create amazing results, but then they get derailed back into self-defeating habits that keep them on the sidelines of life. They're aware enough to know the greatest gifts and talents they were born with, but fear holds them back from sharing them with the world to their fullest capacity.

   For example, someone who is a great dancer rarely dances, someone who is a great artist rarely paints, someone who is a great teacher rarely teaches. Sometimes they're connected to their Higher Power, but frequently they're not. Therefore, they'll occasionally be filled with joy as a result of creating something exciting in their lives using the Law of Attraction. But then they get discouraged, because they attract an adequate amount of negative things as well.

3. **"And the people who don't even know there's a parade going on."**

These are the people who have no idea about the amazing life they could be living right now! They may claim to be spiritual, but really have no idea what that really means. They're unfortunately in the dark and don't even know it. They don't have any inner awareness and have never practiced self-examination. They live in a state of feeling fearful about their lives and blaming others for all of their problems. Depending on the severity of their problems, they may have a sense of hopelessness about their lives. They have huge expectations and place demands on others, because they count on others to make them happy. They may have great wealth and many possessions, but still feel empty on the inside because they don't know that their soul has a deeper longing. They're frequently negative and complain a lot; therefore they attract a lot of negative things into their lives. They frequently feel average and ordinary because they're not aware of the special gifts and talents they were born with.

Are you ready to join the parade of life? If you're watching the parade, or don't even know there is a parade going on, you can harness the Law of Attraction by creating a powerful sense of inner awareness. You can create the kind of life that's abundant in all of the feelings and things you want to attract.

To make the parade will be different for each individual. It doesn't mean being on stage or being the center of attention. It means following your heart and living the life you desire.

It's impossible to join the parade of life when you live in a mess of stress!

It's impossible to join the parade of life when you live in a mess of stress!

CREATE WHITE SPACE IN YOUR LIFE

To join the people who are making the parade, you'll want to make some very important changes in your life. Of all the obstacles presented in this book, this may be the most difficult obstacle for many to overcome because our society doesn't support slowing down and creating an inner awareness. You have to go against the grain of our society and possibly your close-knit circle of family and friends.

To be successful in deepening your spirituality, you must open up your life and make room for some white space. You may be wondering, "What on earth is white space?" "White space" is an advertising term used when writing copy. You've seen flyers and advertisements that were jammed with so many words you just ignored them because you didn't want to read that much. On the other hand, you've seen flyers and advertisements that have fewer words on them. They have space between the words, paragraphs, and borders. They're well-spaced and easy to read. This is called "white space."

How do you create white space in your life? When your life is constantly non-stop, fast-lane-living you need to take action and put a halt to the frenetic energy. In the rapid pace we lose our ability to focus on what's really important in our lives. Here are four steps that will save your life from burnout, and from being sick and tired all the time. It's time to take the "S" off of your chest and stop trying to play Superman or Superwoman!

1. Wait

First, stop taking on additional responsibilities, projects, volunteer work, socializing, etc! That means accept invitations for one or two nights out a week instead of four or five. You can also decline additional requests by saying, "I'm sorry, right now I'm overcommitted. I need to WAIT until I have more time before I take on any additional commitments." Some of you are gasping for air at the thought of saying "no" for possibly the first time in your life. That's okay, just say it. Your life is worth it! And your health is worth it. The Law of Attraction cannot work to your benefit if you are worn out, exhausted, and have no current connection to your Higher Power. It's just not possible. This describes a life on a very low vibration and you'll attract people, things, and situations on a low vibration. To attract your good you must feel good and start loving your life now! That means you need to take care of yourself, relax, get plenty of rest, and have fun, too.

To attract your good you must feel good and start loving your life now!

2. Eliminate

Second, see what demands you can ELIMINATE from your plate immediately. Ask yourself what responsibilities you have accepted that you can remove from your list. You have the right to change your mind. You have permission to call the person back and say, "I'm sorry, I'm seriously overcommitted right now, and I'm unable to fulfill these responsibilities as I thought I could." Everything will be just fine if you take these kinds of actions. People won't write you off, they understand, and will respect you even more for being honest. And you give them permission to do the same thing when they need to. Also, you can eliminate low-payoff, high-stress activities. Turn off the TV and get to bed earlier. Getting more sleep is more important than watching the news.

3. Delegate

Third, ask for help. There are possibly several things on your list of responsibilities that you can DELEGATE to someone else's list. If you have children, and they aren't taking on responsibilities appropriate for their age, you aren't doing them any favors. Teach them how to help you and you'll all be better for it. Or, if it is a $10 an hour job, chances are it would be better for you to pay someone to do it so that you can focus on higher priority tasks or just have some quiet time for yourself.

4. Initiate

Fourth, turn a new leaf and INITIATE a new way of living that supports you in deepening your spirituality. Take a walk after dinner. Nap on the weekends. Go to a special location and watch the sunset. Take ten minutes, sit down, and just focus on your breathing. Ask yourself, "What are the top three things I could do to enjoy every day of my life more?" People think about enjoying their vacations, but don't frequently think about what they can do to really enjoy each and every day. Once you've made this list, do the things you've listed. Don't just think about them, do them. Initiate and take action on at least one of them within 24 hours of reading this paragraph.

Some of these things may be challenging for you to do; however, you must take this very seriously. If you're overworked and unhappy, you're not going to attract all of the good you deserve. When you run around in a panic most of the time, it's difficult to hear the Small, Quiet and Still voice of your soul. It's drowned out by the Big, Loud, and Busy voice of the world swirling around you. You must slow down to stay in the flow of the Law of Attraction.

YOUR CURRENT CONNECTION

In order to deepen your spirituality, you want to create what I call a "current connection." I call it that for several reasons. When you have a "current connection" to your Higher Power, you are:

1. Connected to a powerful current, as in electricity, frequency, or vibration. To live plugged in to this current gives you the power to attract what you want, and to eliminate what you don't want.

2. Flowing with the current and going smoothly along with all that is good in life, just as you would flow with the current of a river. Removing the obstacles or debris opens you up to riding a current that takes you to your good.

3. Current in connecting with your Higher Power. This means you've connected yesterday, today, and you plan to tomorrow. You are in the flow of receiving your good when your connection is current. If you checked in with your Higher Power a couple of weeks or months ago it may not be helping you to believe and receive today. It needs to be a "current connection."

A shallow connection to your Higher Power will yield shallow results using the Law of Attraction.

The goal of creating a strong current connection to your Higher Power is threefold: 1) to tap into the highest vibration possible, 2) to eventually have a deep and meaningful connection, one that makes you feel like you're in the flow and that all things are possible, no matter what the circumstances may look like at the time, and 3) to eventually feel a connection every day and every night.

DON'T MISS THIS EXPERIENCE FOR ANYTHING

At first I had a very difficult time with creating a current connection with my Higher Power. If you're having a difficult time with it, I hope you'll keep an open mind and listen to what happened to me.

Here's my example: I was vehemently against having children until I was in my early thirties. This was solely because I did not have a happy childhood myself, and I would never want to treat a child the way my mother treated me. She was very angry and mean. She had no joy in parenting.

She never came right out and said, "I wish I never had you," but her attitude and actions screamed it louder than words ever could have.

I had friends who frequently told me the joys of parenting, and they encouraged me regularly to have a child. They told me I would be an amazing mom. I have friends who have wonderful mothers, so I understood that not all mothers were like mine.

I also had three nieces and two nephews that I loved dearly, and I enjoyed being around children any time I had the opportunity.

On the morning of April 19, 1995 at 8:30 a.m. Pacific Time, a friend in California, where I lived, called me and said that daycare centers in Oklahoma City were being bombed. All of my nieces and nephews lived in or near Oklahoma City. My heart raced and the fear that one of them was injured, or possibly dead, horrified me. I immediately got on the phone to my family in Oklahoma and found out that no one in my family had been harmed and that it wasn't daycare facilities that were being bombed it was the Oklahoma State Federal Building, which housed a daycare center on the bottom floor.

The information had been presented to me incorrectly, but it served as a huge AWAKENING for me. I realized that I had an immense love for my nieces and nephews, more than I ever knew. I couldn't imagine harming them or saying anything unkind to them. I was able to see that I had the love in my heart that it took to be a good parent, and it helped me to see how much joy I would have in being a mom. I knew that if the love I had in my heart for them was that significant, then it would be even more so for my own child.

I made a decision that day that I wanted to have a child. And three years later my son, Kenneth, was born.

Today, I love being a parent so much that I cringe at the thought of not having a child. When my son was born, the most amazing, unconditional love filled my heart. Having a child has been one of the greatest gifts and most healing processes I could ever have experienced. I'm eternally grateful for the gift of Kenneth in my life.

I feel exactly the same way about the connection I have with my Higher Power. At first I was completely resistant to the idea, and today I can't imagine living my life without the powerful connection I have. There are days where I feel so much love, care, protection, and guidance that I think I have my own personal Higher Power hotline. It's an overwhelmingly sacred and joyful experience that I relish in daily. I certainly have, and remember my first introductions to God were not positive ones. So it took time but I am glad I kept the door open.

Please don't miss this opportunity because of misguided messages from past negative experiences or people. There are so many paths of spirituality that I'm certain you'll find one that you can begin on and then continue to grow in. Just open the door and more will be revealed to you, if you'll simply be open to it. When you deepen your spirituality, you'll awaken to a happier and more meaningful life.

ATTRACTION QUOTIENT QUESTIONS

1. When you know what's right for you, do you honor it, or do you discount it and think others know better than you do?

2. I believe God is beyond definition, but to begin to use this power and to connect to it, it helps if we have some kind of definition. How do you define your Higher Power?

3. What does your Higher Power do for you?

4. What does your Higher Power not do for you?

5. How do you prefer to stay in current contact with your Higher Power?

6. When was the last time you thought about your Higher Power?

7. How frequently do you think about your Higher Power?

8. How do you create white space in your life?

9. What are the top five things you could do to enjoy each and every day more?

10. What are your values?

11. Does the way you live match your values, or are you too busy for that?

12. Do you lead a stress-filled life?

What are the top five things you could do to enjoy each and every day more?

13. Are you ready to make the parade? What's your first step to join in on the parade of your life?

A compelling result of deepening your spirituality is that it will help you overcome any fears that may block your ability to attract what you desire. In the next chapter, we are going to focus on how you can face your fears, the fourth key to accelerating your power of attraction.

CHAPTER 13

Face Your Fears

❧

"What you fear the most controls your life the most because you spend your life trying to avoid it." —Anonymous

FEAR VS. POSSIBILITY

Fear is perhaps the greatest obstacle to utilizing the Law of Attraction for your greatest good. Fear thoughts are lower, ego-based energy and will only bring you more of what you don't want. Fears keep you stuck in old habits and negative thinking that defeat you on a daily basis. They creep in when you least expect them and appear to take over your entire being.

Hale Dwoskin discusses how fear can block the Law of Attraction in your life:

"Fear is a major factor in obstructing the Law of Attraction. Fear is just a feeling, it isn't who you are. You can let it go. Fear colors your behavior and holds you back. It also prevents you from enjoying whatever it is you do accomplish because you're afraid of losing it. Rather than seeing new possibilities and taking on opportunities that help you grow, fear holds you back. There are no limitations except the ones you impose on yourself. You are already perfection."

Fear is at the core of all negative feelings and behaviors.

When you overcome your fears, you'll see that nothing can hold you back. You'll be able to see the perfection that you are as Hale mentioned.

Living in fear prevents you from imagining all that's good in your life by keeping you focused on all that's potentially bad. Fear is at the core of all negative feelings and behaviors. It's at the root of hopelessness, depression, addictions, under-performing, over-performing, low-self esteem, anger, and even arrogance. At its worst, fear is at the root of every war that has ever been fought. Fear-based thinking causes your vibration to plummet fast. You'll attract negative people, situations, and things to you in a hurry when you're focused on fear.

David Koons added the following on the topic of fear:

"Focus on supportive thoughts and realize that everyday we all face fear and doubt. The ego is working overtime to point out all the things that could go wrong to protect us. Recognize, like we say in our programs that everyday you're at the crossroads of your life; you get to decide whether you're going to move in a supportive direction or non-supportive direction, whether you're going to move more into your passion, or more into your fear. Let's be clear, if you're not living your passion, you're living your fear. Which direction do you want to go today?"

Yes, fear is natural and normal, but it's impossible to live in fear and to live in possibility at the same time! Possibility is what AWAKENING to the magnificence of your life is all about.

Fear is limiting. It's constricting, restricting, and paralyzing.

Possibility is freedom. It's openness, expansiveness, and liberating.

If you're not living your passion, you're living your fear.

In order to get out from under your current circumstances, you need to face your fears and Awaken to the possibility of a better life. You need to imagine all of the good that awaits you! Every successful person you know has felt fear at one time or another; they just didn't let it stop them from taking action and moving forward.

When you're able to contemplate all of the wonderful possibilities in your life and realize that fear is really only an illusion, you feel inspired, uplifted, and motivated to move forward. You can see endless opportunities to be more of who you want to be and do more of what you want to do. This kind of thinking raises your vibration up, up, up! And because your vibration goes up, so does your ability to attract more of what you really want.

To create powerful results using the Law of Attraction you must overcome your fears! You're so much more than your fears will ever allow you to believe!

SEVEN PRIMARY FEARS

Dr. John Demartini has identified Seven Primary Fears we all face. They specifically relate to seven key arenas of your life; Spiritual, Mental, Career, Financial, Family, Social, and Physical. Each of these fears can immobilize you in your ability to meet your needs and fulfill all of your desires. As you read through these, identify areas where you tend to have the most fear. The Seven Primary Fears are:

1. **Spiritual Fear**

   The fear of violating the morals and values of some spiritual authority to which we've given power.

2. **Mental Fear**

   The fear of not being intelligent enough, smart enough, articulate enough, or creative enough.

3. **Career Fear**

   The fear of out right failure. The fear you won't get the outcome you want, that it won't work, and you'll fail miserably.

4. **Financial Fear**

   The fear of not making money or losing money that causes hardship.

5. **Family Fear**

   The fear of not being able to manage a relationship, resulting in the fear of the loss of loved ones, or the loss of respect from loved ones.

6. **Social Fear**

   The fear of rejection by somebody you respect, have given power or authority to in society, or within your social circle.

7. **Physical Fear**

   The fear of not being healthy enough, good looking enough, tall enough, or strong enough. The fear of ill health, death, disease, or anything that negatively affects you physically.

Dr. Demartini elaborated on how these fears have operated in his life:

"All of these fears have periodically affected me in one way or another. There are many different situations where each of them has surfaced in my life. Speaking and having a concern about what people will think, what kind of reactions will I have, whether or not I said my point clearly, whether or not the group will understand it, or if I'll be intimidating or intimidated? Any of those fears can surface and have periodically all the way through the journey. What helped me to overcome my fears was to always remember something my dad used to say, 'You have to walk through the dark, go where fear lurks, and turn on the light.'"

WHAT IF?

How often do you use these two little words at the beginning of a fear thought? "What if...?" What if I lose my job? What if I get a divorce? What if I can't pay my mortgage? And on and on...

These are only two little words, but they carry a heavy burden of dread, fear, and anxiety. "What if?" thinking with a negative twist, is some of the most destructive thinking you can do. It's a destructive way to use your imagination. You begin to entertain and make up in your mind all of the worst case scenarios and options, blocking yourself from imagining all of the wonderful opportunities that are available to you. Most of the scenarios you think of are nothing more than remote chances, and they don't even come true. You waste your valuable time and energy thinking about them and causing yourself needless suffering.

When you worry, it's just a way of dressing up the word "fear." People who worry all the time live with fear as their status quo, their normal mode of operation.

When you worry, it's just a way of dressing up the word "fear." People who worry all the time live with fear as their status quo, their normal mode of operation. They have become used to the negative payoff derived from living in fear and worry all the time. But fear and worry are very low on the vibration scale and will only attract negative things into your life. The only way out of this hole of constant fear and worry is to focus on the positive opportunities and possibilities before you.

Being in the military, fighting against an enemy, and experiencing what it must be like to face your fear head on is something that few of us even dream about. David Koons faced his fear and led a group of men through the cover of darkness as he tells in the following story:

"I don't really love to talk about it. It makes me uncomfortable to tell this story. I joined the Marines after years of dreaming of being in the Marines Special Forces. I was in the Marines for several months and they came around to offer the test to join Special Forces. I was told that I had only one shot at this test for infantry school because it only came around once per class. That was it. That was my only chance. Now you would think I've dreamed about this for years and that I would be there. A funny thing happened the weeks leading up to the test. I started hearing all this fear. I started hearing all this doubt. I started hearing all this uncertainty, 'What if I fail, what if I don't make it? What if I don't like it? What if I'm not good enough? What if they don't want me? What if, what if, what if?'

Mark Twain has a great saying. He says, 'I had thousands of tragedies in my life, most of which never occurred.' I love that saying because we create all these scary, scary concepts most of which never take form. The day of the test came around on a Saturday morning. Dozens of my friends came to take the test. It's an all day test, starts at 7 in the morning and goes late into the evening. At any time if you fail any of the many events, you're out. You don't make it into Special Forces.

Guess where I was that day? I found something else to do. I gave into my fear. I didn't go. I can tell you I felt that regret of what could have been. I felt horrible. I felt sad. I felt so many negative, non-supportive thoughts it was terrible. It was horrendous to be in my own body. I had that bittersweet regret. Now here's the amazing thing. I don't believe in coincidences, but a couple of weeks later they announced to our class that they were coming by again. Special Forces would come back by again and administer the test. No reason was given, they were just doing it. This time, having such a big regret, such a big decision before me, I acted in spite of my fear, in spite of the doubt. I went and took the test. I was one of two people out of fifty that passed the test. I was fortunate that they came by again, that I had that opportunity over time, learning how to act in spite of my fear.

Acting in spite of your fear is like clarity. It's a practice. It takes practice to get good at. You don't start with these big huge fears, you grow into it. For me my fear at the time was taking this day-long test. As I was in that unit and dealing with more and more of this rigorous training, my tolerance increased. My ability to face greater and greater fears grew. Because of the intense training and practice, the fear eventually began to diminish and focus replaced it. I can tell you when we're jumping in that water under the cover of darkness, whether it's out of an airplane, out of a helicopter or just slipping into the shoreline, there's not a lot of fear. There's a lot of focus. The fear doesn't serve us. It actually creates more problems. There's a lot of focus on the work at hand. There's a focus on the mission.

Facing our fears, and acting in spite of fear and doubt is a practice. Start small.

Facing our fears, and acting in spite of fear and doubt is a practice. Start small. There's a riddle about how do you eat an elephant. The answer is one bite at a time. Financial freedom, an ideal life, all these things are like a big elephant. If you try to eat it in one bite you'll fail. By following a simple process each and every day, you're taking small bites each and every day. It's the same with fear. Swimming miles in the ocean under cover of darkness is a big huge elephant. Try to do that, get anybody off the street and do that, they'll freak out on you. Go through the long progressive training that I experienced all those years and it's fun. It's enjoyable and there's minimal fear. There's still fear but I still act in spite of my fear. There's still exhilaration when I jump out of an airplane at 25,000 feet at three o'clock in the morning and it's minus twenty six up at altitude. There's still some fear but I've learned how to act in spite of that fear.

In the Marines it was easy. Life or death, it's a clear choice. What about you in your everyday life? Everyday at that crossroads you're living a little bit more fully or you're dying a little bit each day. When you're living your passion, you're expanding, you're growing and you're excited. When you're living your fear, you're contracting, you're dying and you're depressed. Every day you come up against a choice to live your passion or your fear ask yourself, 'Is this serving me or not serving me? Am I catering to my fear or am I being reasonable?' That's the practice.

CATASTROPHIZING

When you get into fear-based thinking, you begin to entertain some of the most bazaar circumstances, and you're so deep in fear that you don't realize how absurd your thinking really is at the time. These thoughts and feelings can stop you in your tracks and prevent you from taking action and following your dreams.

When you're engaging in fearful thinking, you blow it out of proportion, which I like to call "catastrophizing!" If something bad is going to happen, it won't be just a little deal, it will be a huge deal! Once we begin catastrophizing on one topic, it snowballs into many others and spirals downward to a painful oblivion of hopelessness.

When you take a single fear thought and keep building on it until you get to the very worst case scenario, that's catastrophizing. For example, you may have the thought, "I'm afraid I'll get fired," which leads to "Then I won't be able to pay my mortgage," which leads to "Then I'll lose my house," which leads to "Then I'll live on the street," which leads to "Then I'll die."

Acknowledge your fears, but don't cling to them.

You may be catastrophizing without being conscious of exactly what your thoughts are. You're only aware of the intense dread you're feeling in the moment. When you feel this intense dread or when you realize the destructive path your drastic thoughts are taking you down, you can STOP, write them down, and identify what's really going on in your mind.

Are you really afraid you're going to lose your job? Is there a situation at work that needs to be addressed? The key is to look deeper than the surface fear thoughts and get clear on what's really happening. When you have the clarity of how the fear relates to the real situation, you can take the necessary action to remedy the situation.

TAKE A CLOSER LOOK

Acknowledge your fears, but don't cling to them. I love the following acronym for fear:

False

Evidence

Appearing

Real

When you take a closer look at your fears, you'll realize that most of them are completely false and a tragic waste of your mental energy. You want to spend your time thinking about and visualizing all the wonderful things and experiences you'll enjoy having in your life. You don't want to waste your time on thinking about and visualizing negative situations.

Most of your fears didn't develop overnight and they won't disappear overnight either. Stop and take a closer look at them to see how they developed and what you need to do to dissolve them.

Also, as you examine your fears further, get a clear picture what your future will be like if you never face your fears. If you continue to let certain fears paralyze you, what are some of the things you'll miss out on? Over time, the more you let your fears control you in one area, the more it spreads to other areas. Many people live lives in which fear runs rampant and has complete control.

Here are some common fears. Many people face, the fear of:

- ☐ Failing
- ☐ Succeeding
- ☐ Being criticized
- ☐ Being hurt
- ☐ Being rejected
- ☐ Being fired
- ☐ Being hired
- ☐ Taking on too much responsibility
- ☐ Taking on too little responsibility
- ☐ Looking stupid
- ☐ Spending life alone
- ☐ Standing up for oneself
- ☐ Showing people one's authentic self
- ☐ Never reaching one's full potential
- ☐ Putting one's needs first
- ☐ Not making enough money
- ☐ Losing money
- ☐ Being spontaneous
- ☐ Being too sexual
- ☐ Not being sexual enough
- ☐ Being taken advantage of
- ☐ Being taken for granted
- ☐ Not being good enough
- ☐ Not being liked by others

- ❑ Being homeless
- ❑ Pain and suffering

This list could go on and on for pages. We aren't even looking at fears that have progressed to the level of phobias, such as the fear of flying, the fear of heights, the fear of spiders, and the fear of snakes, all of which can wreak havoc in people's lives as well.

INSPIRING MUSIC

My dear friend Merilee tells about her experience overcoming her fear to sing.

"I didn't believe I could ever be a singer. I was afraid I wasn't good enough and that my voice wasn't good enough. I studied voice and took voice classes for many years. I'd marvel and thrill at the students who could stand up with complete calm and confidence and belt out a song. I could not do that. But I stayed with it.

Then after about eight years, I got a chance to sing lead at a local church. That meant I had to stand up in front of the room and lead a couple of the songs as the congregation sang along with me. I was terrified, but I wanted to try it. I did that for about a year, all the while, watching and listening intently each Sunday as the soloists thrilled me with their songs and their confidence.

A few years later, I decided I wanted to try to sing a solo. I picked a song that was much too difficult and also too high of a key. But my passion and love of singing only kept growing. It would not go away. I tried another solo, then another. Each was excruciating. I'd feel sick. I'd shake. I couldn't eat. Then after it was all over, I'd feel exhilarated to have at least tried and gotten through the song.

One day, someone asked me if I wanted to record a CD and said they knew of a local recording studio and would introduce me to the owner. I went to check it out. I decided I would just record one song to hear how I sounded. I liked it. I chose 12 of my favorite songs and recorded a CD. It was done in four months.

People are now buying my CD and they are being moved, inspired, and uplifted by my voice. I am being asked now on a weekly basis to sing at churches, weddings, retirement centers, concerts, fundraisers, etc. I am enjoying it more and more and have actually experienced some performances with absolutely no fear.

Singing is one of the most fulfilling things I have ever done. I delight in the joy and comfort it brings others. I have never known anyone who has had to walk through a greater fear of singing in public as I have. I am now starting to live my dreams as a professional vocalist and recording artist. I am now being paid well to do what I love to do.

I used the Law of Attraction to heal myself of my inadequacies and fears and to now stand in my power and grace as a singer who has the power to move, inspire, and uplift her audience.

Oh, and did I tell you that I am 51 years young and began singing at 38? It is never too late to live your dream. I continued to listen to that still, small voice within that wanted to sing, through all the fear, false beliefs, and inadequacies that I carried from my childhood and adult life. I have triumphed and am thrilled to be beginning a new career!

My new CD was released in March of 2007, just in time for my 51st birthday! It is called 'Inspired!' If I can do it, so can you!"

THE CLIFF DIVERS CLUB

It was a beautiful summer morning when my cell phone rang. I was carpool Mom for the day and I tried to quiet the crew before I answered the phone. In the midst of the noise the assertive voice on the other end of the line came through loud and clear, "You might as well ask me to go to Acapulco and jump off the cliff with the cliff divers!" I recognized the voice, it was my dear friend Celeste, and without any other information I knew exactly what she was talking about.

Celeste had been at a pivotal point in her personal growth. She could stay in a rut or take a leap into a whole new realm of living. I knew she was ready for more. I suggested she take a step that was totally out of her comfort zone and she had just taken it and called me saying, "You might as well ask me to go to Acapulco and jump off the cliff with the cliff divers!" At that moment she was in the space between the top of the cliff, which she had just left, and splashing into the water below. She was experiencing the in-between, the free floating space of "What on earth have I done and what am I going to do now?"

Beware; the voice of fear speaks the loudest through justification and resignation.

That's when you know you are doing it right! Complacency is comfortable. Too much comfort and pretty soon you're stuck in a rut. Stepping out of your comfort zone is truly a leap of faith.

I had suggested for Celeste to keep her heart open to a friend by calling her in spite of the fact that the friend had not been particularly kind to her. It was a relationship that she wanted to nurture, but the wounds were causing her more pain than she knew what to do with. She was teetering on shutting down and closing off from this treasured relationship. Beware; the voice of fear speaks the loudest through justification and resignation. And yes, Celeste had plenty of reason to justify and resign herself, but that would close her off from receiving all her good via the Law of Attraction. Her friend was clearly unskillful, but I knew Celeste was capable of being a bigger person and bridging the gap.

That day when Celeste stepped into the unknown and compared it to Acapulco's famous cliff divers we formed The Cliff Divers Club and I appointed her president! This comparison is absolutely perfect. Here's why -- several brave young men swim across a narrow channel and scale the sheer cliff on the other side. Once they are at the top of the steep cliff they say a prayer, because they really do risk their life each time they judge the tides, and then they make the 120 foot dive into the narrow channel below. They do so with the utmost elegance and grace. I can't even fathom how each of them must have felt the first time they made the leap. I've seen this amazing feat several times and it is an unbelievable site to see.

So when the comparison popped out of Celeste's mouth that fateful summer morning it was brilliant. Would you like to be an honored member of the Cliff Divers Club? The only requirement for membership is the desire to break through your fears and create a more abundant life than you ever dreamed of. Membership is not for the faint of heart however. You have to be able to leap into the unknown and give up your comfort in the moment for something much bigger in the future. This might feel like terror at times, but unless you take the leap you will stay in the exact same situation you are in forever. Face your fears and take the leap!

Face your deepest fears and overcome them! Begin taking steps to break down the wall of fear today!

Throughout this book are examples of men and women who are clearly members of the Cliff Divers Club. In this chapter, David Koons was so riddled with fear of the test to join the Special Forces that he avoided it altogether. He finally overcame his fear, took the test, passed it and had the experience of a lifetime as a member of this elite group. Also in this chapter, Merilee said at first she was terrified singing in front of the church, even with others singing along. But she kept practicing and now sings beautifully in front of audiences and on her own CD. In chapter 4, Barbara spoke of the fear she had when she initially turned down smaller weddings. Now her calendar is filled with planning the full service weddings she desires. In chapter 11, John spoke candidly about the financial fear he lived with daily, and how he took the leap into action and lives an abundant life today. And there are many more examples throughout the book where men and women just like you faced their fears and jumped off of the cliff into the unknown only to find a new and better life.

I'm certain The Cliff Divers Club will grow and THE AWAKENING Mastery Community will be taking pilgrimages to Acapulco to watch our namesake together and discuss the proverbial cliffs we're all diving off in our own lives. What cliff will you be jumping off in order to face your fears?

TAKE ACTION

Face your deepest fears and overcome them! Begin taking steps to break down the wall of fear today! If you are living behind your fears, you're hiding out, not showing the world your authentic self. Begin to take risks that help you build the courage to remove your fears completely. You'll find that courage and confidence will soon replace fear and doubt.

Here are some exercises to help you move through your fears:

1. Fear as a brick wall.

When you feel fearful, visualize your fear as a brick wall that's between you and your greatest good. Picture the words for your fear painted on the brick wall - "I'm afraid of failing," "I'm afraid of getting hurt," etc. Then imagine yourself standing tall and strong, putting on a pair of boxing gloves, flexing your muscles, and confidently busting through the brick wall of your fears to the other side and receiving all of your good!

2. Replace the fearful thought.

When you take action in spite of fearful thoughts that may arise, you're building belief in yourself, belief that you can and will achieve your dreams. When faced with a fearful thought, you have a choice: give into the fear and do nothing, or counteract it with opposing positive and powerful thoughts.

First you have the fearful thought – "I'm going to blow this interview" and then the negative feelings come flooding in. Counteract this fear with "I feel great! I can do this!" Say these declarations out loud with energy and conviction for as long as it takes to make a mental shift and relieve your fear.

3. Focus on your breathing.

Focus on getting yourself into a more confident, calm state of mind. To do this, one technique is to concentrate on your breathing. As you concentrate on your breathing, notice the rise and fall of your chest. As you inhale, think about breathing in the feeling of confidence and all that it would mean to you. As you exhale, think about letting go of all your fears, just release them. You can also think about breathing in the feeling of courage and all the positive feelings courage would bring you, and then releasing all doubt and uncertainty. Contemplate breathing in abundance and prosperity, and exhaling lack and limitations.

4. Use visualization.

Through visualization you use your imagination to your greatest advantage. Athletes have used this technique to help them succeed for decades. First you need to have a clear picture in your mind of how a confident person would act and feel doing the thing you are presently afraid of doing. To get a clear picture of this, close your eyes and breathe deeply. Visualize filling your body with the calm, cool, confidence and poise necessary to take the action you want to take. Imagine your mentor, role model or someone you admire – what would they think about, how would they feel, and how would they act when they're doing what you want to do. Continue to keep your eyes closed and visualize yourself thinking, feeling, and acting the same way for three to four minutes until you can clearly see yourself acting with confidence. When you open your eyes, write the thoughts and feelings you had during the exercise in your journal. Repeat this visualization and take the action as frequently as possible until your fear has subsided. Just doing the visualization will help, but for the fear to go away substantially you have to take action along with it.

Depending on their origin, some fears will never completely go away. But when you face them with courage, they can diminish to the point that you rarely realize they're there.

MAD, SAD, AND GLAD

Fears build up within us so much that they prevent us from taking in all of the positive things happening in our world. I like what the Rev. Jim Turrell suggests in monitoring what you're glad, sad, and mad about. With a little self-examination and a lot of honesty, these are fairly easy emotions to watch. He describes the process like this:

"Glad refers to what is happening in your life that's positive and how closely you are monitoring it with the intention of 'I want to create more of that. I really want more of that.' To do this, you need to be fully present in the here and now and being fully present is part of what activates the Law of Attraction."

Abundance is your birthright!

Fear prevents us from being fully present to all of the great things happening in our lives. They also cause us to be critical and have unrealistic expectations.

He goes on to say, "Sad is a sense of grief. The unexpressed grief in people's lives today is epidemic. I really mean that – epidemic – a lot of people get healed just simply when they have a good cry about something. Many times they can't even remember what they're crying about. They just need to go have a good, emotional, cathartic release."

Our fears prevent us from fully expressing our sadness and grief, causing us tremendous problems and stopping the flow of positive energy and emotions in our life.

Lastly, his thoughts on anger, "And then if you're mad about something say, 'Do I really want to live mad the rest of my day or possibly the rest of my life?' Obviously not! So then you have to say, 'I'm willing to let go of what I'm mad about.'"

We experience the most anger when we fear not getting something we want or losing something we want to keep. So you can see how fear is intertwined in all of these emotions - mad, sad, and glad.

He went on to say that to get out of negative emotions you need to take three steps:

1. Become aware of the fact that you're feeling the negative emotional energy in the moment.

2. Then focus on what you really want in your life, instead of the negative emotional energy. What do you want to replace it with? If you're feeling angry, you may want to replace it with peace of mind. If you're feeling fearful, you may want to replace it with courage. If you're feeling hurt, you may want to replace it with healing or wholeness.

3. And finally ask, "What am I grateful for?" once you shift your thinking to what you are grateful for, the negative emotional energy dissipates. If it creeps back in again, simply direct your attention to what you are grateful for as many times as necessary.

FEAR AROUND MONEY

There is possibly no greater fear prevailing on the planet than the fear around money. Money is just energy and as you raise your vibration overall, you'll be able to attract more and more money into your life.

During childhood, you may have received negative messages about money. When in truth, abundance is your birthright! No matter what your current circumstances, you were meant to have financial freedom. Don't get stuck in looking at your bank account now. See your financial future filled with joy and prosperity around money.

I was raised in an environment where there was a tremendous amount of fear and stress around money all of the time. Bill collectors were constantly calling and my parents would never answer the phone. I was in college before I realized that there were people around who actually answered the phone every time it rang! We had a code we were supposed to use if we needed to call home for any reason so my parents could avoid the bill collectors. We were supposed to let it ring twice and then hang up and call back. These were the days long before caller ID was around.

There was also a lot of wishful thinking around money. I'm a Native American Indian and my parents were always saying, "Maybe this year the Indians will pay off and we'll be set for life." That kind of talk was the norm. It wasn't until 40 years later that any of us ever received a check from the tribe, and that was for a couple thousand dollars after they built a casino in Oklahoma. My parents were always stressed about money and there was a lot of talk about getting out of debt. Facing your fears will greatly enhance your self-esteem, the final key to accelerating your power of attraction. The more

We are all so afraid of failure that we do nothing and therefore end up a failure!

you truly love yourself and treat yourself with the same kindness and respect you give others you admire, you will become a magnet attracting all that you desire.

Chellie Campbell added her thoughts to fear of money as follows:

"People focus on their fears around money rather than on the money they want to attract. We spend a minute on the positive and the rest of the day we focus on our fears, whether we're conscious of it or not. We think 'Oh no, there is another bill. How am I going to pay this?' and 'Oh no, I have a client who doesn't want to pay my bill in full. What am I going to do about that?' 'Oh no, I can't afford that new outfit I want.' It's all money, money, money and fear, fear, fear. The people who don't have money are afraid they're never going to have any money and the people who have money are afraid they're going to lose their money."

To overcome these fears Chellie recommends the following exercise:

1. Make a list of all of your fears surrounding money.
2. Ask yourself "Where is this fear coming from?"

3. In order to really get a clear picture of your finances, write your financial autobiography. Answer these questions: How did your family handle money? Did they talk about it or didn't they? What were you told about money? Did you ever have any training around how to make or manage money?

A FINAL WORD ABOUT FAILURE

Out of that long list of fears you read earlier, the one that looms the largest in most people's minds is the fear of failure. We are all so afraid of failure that we <u>do nothing</u> and therefore end up a failure!

The fear of failure has a close cousin and it's perfectionism. We think we have to be perfect and that we're not allowed to make mistakes. We label anything less than perfect as a failure.

There is no such thing as failure as long as you keep on trying. Don't give up. You can be a powerful magnet of attraction when you focus on moving through your fears. The joy you'll feel when you break down that brick wall and take action will help you soar.

One of my favorite heroes is Abraham Lincoln. When I heard that Abraham Lincoln, one of the greatest presidents the United States has ever had, failed running for office SEVEN times, I was shocked! I don't know about you, but I think I would have given up after losing the third election. This and many other facts about his life continue to inspire me, especially when failure has once again made its way back to my list of fears. He never let failure stop him. I won't let failure or the fear of it stop me and I hope you won't let it stop you either.

ATTRACTION QUOTIENT QUESTIONS

Take a closer look at the fears you relate to. In your journal answer the following questions. First identify a specific fear. Work through the questions, and then move on to the next fear.

1. What is your fear preventing you from doing?

2. Who is your fear preventing you from being?

3. How is your fear preventing you from being the best you can be?

4. When did your fear first originate?

5. What do you do to continue feeding the fear?

6. How can you stop feeding the fear?

7. What steps can you take now to face the fear and break through the grip it has on your life?

8. Write a letter to your fears and share it with someone you trust.

Facing your fears will greatly enhance your self-esteem, the final key to accelerating your power of attraction. The more you truly love yourself and treat yourself with the same kindness and respect you give others you admire, you will become a magnet attracting all that you desire.

CHAPTER 14

Nurture Your Self-Esteem

⤜∞⤛

*"Our deepest fear is not that we are inadequate. Our deepest fear is
that we are powerful beyond measure. It is our light, not our darkness,
that frightens us most."* —Marianne Williamson

YOUR SELF-ESTEEM AND THE CONTINUUM OF BELIEF

What is self-esteem? It's quite simply the value you place upon yourself. If your self-esteem is low, then you don't feel like you're worth much, you don't feel very valuable. If your self-esteem is high, then you feel like you're valuable and have great worth.

Self-esteem also ties in with feeling worthy of, or deserving to, receive your goals and dreams. In order for the Law of Attraction to work, you have to have a firm belief. The correlation between belief and your self-esteem is significant. The greater your feelings of self-esteem, the higher you'll go on the Continuum of Belief, and the more of your goals and dreams you'll actually manifest.

If you have low self-esteem, then your main focus should first be on increasing that. As you work through each of the chapters presented here and take the suggested actions, your self-esteem will increase.

If your self-esteem is low, to imagine getting a $1.00 or $2.00 an hour raise might be as much as you can comprehend. But you must believe you can get it with all of your heart and soul. You must believe you deserve it and that you are 100% worthy of it in every way, shape, and form.

Then when you courageously go in and ask for a $2.00 an hour raise and get it, you go up on the Continuum of Belief scale. As you increase your self-esteem, your belief will continue to rise, and so will your Attraction Quotient.

That continuum is based on your self-esteem and what you think you deserve and are worthy of right now. Whether you choose to take baby steps or go great guns, the Law of Attraction will work for you!

WHAT ARE YOU WAITING FOR?

Have you ever heard of a bestseller called "How to Condemn Yourself to Success"? Have you ever seen any actor or actress win an Academy Award and in their acceptance speech say, "I owe this to my incredible ability to keep on criticizing myself, no matter what. I would sometimes practically crucify myself with sharp words"? No! Criticizing and hurting yourself does absolutely no good. There is no gain in it whatsoever. The world would be a perfect place by now if criticizing and condemning ourselves helped us.

Criticizing and hurting yourself does absolutely no good. There is no gain in it whatsoever. The world would be a perfect place by now if criticizing and condemning ourselves helped us.

From a very early age you were taught how to be critical of yourself. Now it's time to learn how to be loving and accepting of yourself. It will be a process, and the first step is awareness. Become aware of how often you say negative comments toward yourself. Commit to loving yourself wildly, 100% every single day, without exception.

Being good to yourself means not waiting for "Someday I'll" to arrive. You know what I mean. "Someday I'll love myself when I lose weight." "Someday I'll be good to myself when I have more money." What are you waiting for? Whatever your "Someday I'll" is, don't wait until "someday" to be happy or to be good to yourself. Don't deprive yourself one more minute of loving yourself and being good to yourself.

Rev. Jim Turrell commented on the abuse we tend to shower upon ourselves, he said:

"The biggest abuse that people have in their lives is typically self-abuse because we're so hard on ourselves. We're so unforgiving of the mistakes we make. Then, we keep paying for the same mistakes, over and over and over again, even to the point where our friends are saying, 'When are you going to finally give it up, and stop talking about, thinking about, acting as if that was important.'

Pay for it once and then move on. Self-esteem has a lot to do with the way you reinforce what it is that you're working at, what it is that you want. Are you gentle with yourself? Are you kind with yourself? Are you patient with yourself? Are you unkind? Or are you your own worst enemy? Because if you are, your measurement of self-esteem will directly affect the results you create using the Law of Attraction."

THE ABYSS

Steven Lewis spoke about the bottomless pit within each of us and how we need each other to fill it. He said:

"Each of us have our very own private abyss, a seemingly bottomless pit that we can never fill. It's a scary place, the abyss, and considerate beings that we are, we isolate it. First we try to hide it and, if that doesn't work, we protect others from it. We build walls, put up fences, post signs, "DANGER KEEP OUT" and "NO TRESPASSING."

Your abyss is what separates you from your soul, and from the personal and collective souls of everyone else. The good news is you can fill your abyss, just as you can heal your soul. The bad news is you cannot do it alone. You need the help of me and a few billion others who are ready, willing and able. All you need to provide is a little courage. The courage to face whatever fear keeps you in your abyss. Tear down your walls and fences. Remove your warning signs. Invite every curious creature in the universe to peek into your abyss and feed and pet the monster that lives there and put a ribbon around its neck. There are a lot of curious creatures out there, and you know what's going to happen? They're going to fill up that void and you'll have nothing left to hide from and no place to hide in. You will have healed your soul from its "original disease," and obviously, once that's gone, you can't have any new symptoms."

FROM SELF-DOUBT TO SELF-CONFIDENCE

Marci Shimoff is a perfect example of self-confidence. As you read her story, you'll see that self-confidence and self-esteem aren't something we're all born with, yet you can develop them over time. She told this story:

"I think that everybody has their own particular brand of obstacles. For me, my brand was self-doubt. I think that's a common obstacle. It relates to self-esteem.

I remember in the fifth grade going to Girl Scout camp, I was a drag. All of the girls used to point out to me that I was a drag because I was always so self-deprecating. I was putting my self down all the time. One of my girlfriends came to me and said, 'Marci you've got to stop this. This is just a bummer; you're always putting your self down.'"

Since I was 13 years old I wanted to be an inspirational speaker. I saw Zig Ziglar speak and I had an inner knowingness that speaking was what I was supposed to do. But I had a lot of self-doubt about it. It was an unusual goal for a 13 year old in 1971. Most teenagers wanted to be teachers or doctors.

I started teaching seminars when I was 22. I taught for a company called 'Yes to Success Seminars.' I didn't feel like I knew enough at the time to be able to speak. When I would get caught up in my own fears from my ego of wanting people's approval, that would really hang me up, but when I would come from getting in touch with what I felt was my soul's calling and how I could serve others, that's what would always move me forward.

This sort of self-concern of 'How will I look?' and 'Will people approve of me?' hangs people up all the time. Self-esteem is not based on what others think of you. Self-esteem is an internal feeling of being loveable, worthy, and capable, regardless of your circumstances, and regardless of what other people think or say. It's an inner knowingness. For me, the way I came to that was through focusing on the feeling that I'm here to serve, and asking myself 'How I can serve others?' rather than being absorbed in myself.

I came from an extraordinary loving and supportive family. My low self-esteem and self-doubt did not come from any of them. I think they are just prevalent in our culture. The only thing I really wasn't allowed to say was, 'I can't.' My parents deeply believed that I could do anything that I set my mind to do. That was the message I got and I know from the depths of their souls that they believed that. That was a saving grace for me. I think people come in with certain tendencies in life. I think that low self-esteem was one of my tendencies.

Ask yourself, "What does it take, to take care of me?"

It's great that Marci had friends who would be so candid with her. In Chapter 11 we discussed the importance of talking to yourself in a positive manner. An excellent guide to find out if you're talking to yourself with love and care is to ask yourself, "Would I talk to someone I loved this way?" "Would I talk to my best friend this way?" "Would I say these things in the same tone to my child?"

You can build your self-esteem, but it begins by talking kindly to yourself.

PRACTICE EXTREME SELF-CARE

How well do you take care of yourself? This includes your: health, nutrition, feelings, body, energy level, play time, learning time, and spiritual life, to name a few things. Learn to practice "Extreme Self-Care." Before you take an action like schedule one more thing to do, anything ask yourself, "Is this self-loving?" Sometimes the answer will be "Yes," and when you are exhausted and run down the answer will be, "No." Ask yourself, "What does it take, to take care of me?" If you aren't taking care of yourself, most likely no one is. That's called abandonment, you would never do that to someone you love. So don't abandon yourself either. If you aren't #1 on your own list, you can guarantee you aren't #1 on anyone's list. And if you are, it's probably a very unhealthy relationship.

There are three ways to relate to yourself and others, which will give you a better understanding of what it means to be self-loving:

1. **Self-Centered**
   Everything you do focuses on you and not others, at the loss of important relationships.

2. **Self-Less**

   Everything you do focuses on others at the loss of your own self-esteem and respect.

3. **Self-Loving**

   A balance of taking care of yourself and making a difference in the lives of those important to you, because that is self-loving.

Marci Shimoff elaborated on taking care of ourselves, "I actually believe that one of the most important things in the world for us to do is to take care of ourselves. I think that you have to absolutely take care of yourself and what that means, first and foremost, is listen to yourself. Listen to your inner voice, and your inner calling. Many people might think that's selfish, but it's not. It's honoring your own inner messages and your own voice inside."

WHAT DO YOU "DO" TO PROVE YOUR WORTHY?

Part of building our self-esteem is recognizing that when we feel good about ourselves, we treat ourselves with kindness and respect. That means not having to "do" anything to prove we are worthy. You're worthy just because you breathe. Some of the things people do to try and prove they are worthy include:

- Working all hours of the day and night.

- Staying in an unfulfilling career

- Staying in dead-end relationships

- Having to do things bigger and better than everyone else

- Having to make a lot of money and have a lot of things

In my private practice I dealt with a variety of different issues, and one of them was eating disorders. One day a very unassuming man came to me to talk about resolving his weight issues. He quickly stated that his wife had sent him. He was a very tall man, so his weight wasn't something that I noticed immediately, but he claimed that "his wife" wanted him to lose 50 lbs. He had tried to lose the weight over and over again, and was always unsuccessful.

Part of building our self-esteem is recognizing that when we feel good about ourselves, we treat ourselves with kindness and respect.

His story was a very poignant one to me because he was such a happy, jolly man. He had the rosy cheeks and all. While he was possibly 40-something, he had a youthful, boyish look and demeanor about him, and seemed to be an easy-going guy.

Overall, he was happy with his life. He thought he could possibly eat healthier, but he wasn't bothered by his weight in the slightest. He had achieved a very high level of affluence and had acquired more accoutrements than most ever do.

It quickly became clear to me that he was burdened by a wife he could not make happy. No matter their level of wealth, it was not enough for her.

After several sessions, it was evident that he had no motivation to lose weight, and I felt it was unproductive for him to continue to see me if that was his only issue. I tried to explore a host of other issues with him to no avail. It became clear that his biggest issue was why he didn't stand up to his wife.

To be most effective in working with him, I wanted to meet his wife. He agreed and she set up an appointment with me the following week.

To make this really clear, I need to describe these two people in dog terms. He was a big play-ful, fun-loving, St. Bernard. Yes, he might drool a lot and knock over a few things wagging his tail. And he was so warm and loveable that you wondered if he had teeth to eat, let alone bite. Love him, play with him, scratch his head, and he's yours forever.

His wife was a different story all together. When she walked into my office there was nothing warm, nice, soft, or feminine about her. There was tightness in her face, and her body was rigid from head to toe. She was a Doberman, growling with her lips pulled back and teeth showing so that you knew she would bite you if you made one wrong move.

She was very annoyed that I had requested to see her. "He" was the problem not "her," so why did "she" have to take time out of "her" very busy schedule to see "me," she asked.

She was in a real snit because her high school reunion was in a couple of days and her Mercedes Benz was in the shop being repaired. She told me which model and style it was like it really mattered to me. It was supposed to have been out the day before, and she was furious that it wasn't. "I am not about to drive Richard's truck to my reunion. I'm not going to drive anything but the Mercedes. I won't go to the reunion if the Mercedes is not done by then."

In 50 minutes I could see that she had tremendous insecurities, and a deep well of pain that she was covering up by her materialism and distraction with him. These are all signs of low self-esteem. If she could focus on his problem, needing to lose weight, then she didn't have to focus on hers. As the old adage goes, "When you point your finger at others, there are always three fingers pointing back at you." She was hell-bent on making her husband kowtow to please her. But since she had her own low self-esteem she wasn't facing there was no way he could ever make her happy.

Plus, no one else can ever make us happy. They can make us happier. But most importantly, that's not anyone else's job. It's our own job to build our self-esteem and create our own happiness.

Her need to drive her Mercedes, live in the biggest house on the hill, and "look" socially-sophisticated and nice, defined her. That's a pretty sad definition of oneself. In her opinion, with-out all that, she was nothing.

I couldn't tell Richard the sad news about his wife because he never returned. But if I could have, I would have told him that she was a self-centered perfectionist, who was materialistic and had no intention of ever looking at herself as long as he would let her focus on him. I wanted to work with him further and help him to own his power and not let her walk all over him.

What defines you? Do you have a list of things necessary to prove your worth? I hope not.

ALL WORK AND NO PLAY

Some people depend on their work to define their worth. If this sounds like you, that's a treadmill you may want to get off of fast, because there will never be an end in sight. When you're working to prove your worth, it indicates something missing inside. As you build your self-esteem, you'll naturally be drawn to creating a well-rounded life between work, rest, and social time.

When I spoke with Chellie Campbell about this, she addressed her previous habit of working too much. "One mentor of mine was an attorney. We were working late one night when he came by my desk saying he was going home. I said, 'Man, there's just so much to do. It's endless.' He nodded and said, 'Yes, it is endless. What you have to do is just do as much as you can until you think that's enough. Work will expand to fill the time you're willing to devote to it. At a certain point, you just have to say "That's enough and go home."'

"What I have done in my life is I've been making it a practice to say "That's enough" and go home earlier and earlier. One of my positive affirmations, which is a new belief I've chosen, is "The more time off I take, the more money I make."

A recent participant in THE AWAKENING seminar was Connie. She shared openly about the journey of self-discovery she was on. She had privately suffered from a host of past experiences that caused her to have low self-esteem and feelings of guilt and shame:

- She was let go from her job and was dumped by her boyfriend all in the same week

- She had attempted suicide and been admitted to a psychiatric hospital for ten days

- She carried over $20,000 in financial debt

- And she hadn't filed her taxes in 5 years

In spite of all these challenges, Connie landed the job of her dreams and was quickly gaining the respect of her family, friends, and business associates. She networked with the best in her field locally, and she flourished *on the outside,* but she was painfully withering on the inside.

The reality was that Connie put taking care of everyone else as her primary job, ahead of taking care of herself. After working numerous 14-16 hours days, weeks at a time, she would end up sick in bed for 7-10 days repeatedly.

In time and with the help of a life coach, Connie began to make big changes in her life and in her work hours. She graciously set the clear boundaries she needed to take care of herself and to create a more balanced life.

Connie learned to listen to her inner voice. She no longer betrayed herself and what she knew. She gave herself the credit she deserved for truly turning her life around. As a result, her health returned and she had more energy than she ever dreamed. Her self-esteem was finally aligned with the amazing woman she truly was.

In less than four years she was out of debt, and she had amassed a net worth of $160K. Her job is secure, but even if it wasn't, she now has an unshakable sense of self-confidence. She now lives the life she dreamed of having, and best of all, she now has her life and her self-esteem back!

COLLECT LOVE NOTES AND CHERISHED MEMORIES

We're all really good at finding reasons to delay our happiness, and put ourselves down. If you want to build your self-esteem and self-confidence, now is the time to look for, or collect, reasons to feel great about yourself.

If you want to build your self-esteem and self-confidence, now is the time to look for, or collect, reasons to feel great about yourself.

It wasn't until I was in my late twenties that I suffered from low self-esteem, because most of my youth and early adult years I suffered from NO self-esteem! One of the first action steps I took to begin feeling better about who I was as a person was to listen carefully to the positive statements and compliments people gave me and I would try to believe them.

In order to do that, I wrote them down and I collected them in a fabric covered box. I would review them from time to time. I still have the box and all of the notes in it. As I browsed through it, I found some of the positive feedback notes people gave me from my days of attending Toastmaster's. I found notes that I had written quoting someone who had given me a compliment that made me feel good. There were a couple of jokes that I liked and some quotes that were very touching. But I remember opening the box when I would have what I call a "tiny attack," where the world seemed huge and I seemed small and insignificant, unable to handle the problems of the day. I would take out my box of love notes and cherished memories and read the notes tucked inside of it and I would feel better.

The most important part about this is to begin listening to all of the positive things people tell you and to start believing them. Ask yourself, "How would I really feel if I believed what he/she just told me?" The words and letters that make you feel great are what you want to focus on and re-visit anytime you want or need to.

Here are some of the items to collect, but it can be anything that makes you feel good about yourself and your accomplishments:

- Positive feedback notes
- Compliments
- Love notes
- Cards
- Jokes

- Poems
- Verses
- Quotes

Here are some ways to collect these love notes and cherished memories:

- Jar
- Binder
- Scrapbook
- Shoe box
- Jewelry box
- Plastic storage box
- Fabric covered box
- Valentine candy heart box

How will you harness the power of your thoughts and create a new reality?

It took watching and listening diligently to collect all of the nice things people said and did that made me feel good. As I would take out the box and review them from time to time, it began to help me feel better about myself.

Recently, after we attended a business success summit, Pete Nelson, one of the marketing experts I work with, sent me the following note, which is a true testimony to the fact that my little fabric covered box worked.

"Dear Alicia,

I have to say you are absolutely the most impressive and dynamic woman I've worked with. The way you command attention, respect, and in many cases, awe, from those around you is to watch someone who is in total command of their space, fully confident, and projects nothing but success. I can only imagine how you are in your business arena. Bravo!"

That note definitely went into the box!

As you nurture your self-esteem, you'll find that you have more excitement about taking risks, trying new things, and making changes in your life.

CREATE A NEW REALITY

Now that you're aware of *The Seven Steps to AWAKENING* and *The Five Keys to Accelerate Your Power of Attraction*, how will you create your AWAKENING? How will you harness the power of your thoughts and create a new reality? Take it step-by-step and remember that anyone can eat an elephant one bite at a time. Your AWAKENING will soon come to you.

AWAKENING to your full potential is a process, and each step that you learned within the pages of this book are an important part of the process. Let's first review *The Seven Steps to AWAKENING*:

1. **Discover Your Deepest Desires**

   Forget what you've heard all your life that you "should" do. What is it that you desire? Discover what kind of life you desire to live.

2. **Declare What You Desire**

   Once you know what you want, it's time to shout it from the rooftops! Make a declaration that you know what you desire in your life and be ready to claim it as yours today.

3. **Believe It Is Yours Now**

   Don't allow 1% doubt to take you out of the flow of receiving your good. Believe you have what you want now!

4. **Raise Your Frequency**

   Like attracts like. Raise your vibration through positive thinking and feeling good and you will attract more of what you want.

5. **Eliminate Any Obstacles**

   Let go of the past. Don't let anything stop you from living a life of total and complete amazement. Keep going, failure is not an option.

6. **Take Meaningful Action**

   Your dreams will become a reality when action propels you forward. Decide to act and then do it!

7. **Receive Your Good**

   The Universe is ready to deliver your good today. You will receive your good in light speed when you have a thankful heart for all you have in your life now! When you give back you keep the flow of giving and receiving in constant motion.

Practice these steps daily and you'll see the floodgates open wide! Now, let's review *The Five Keys to Accelerate Your Power of Attraction*:

1. **Renew Your Beliefs**

   What do you believe you can do with your life? Create a powerful set of beliefs by discovering, dissecting and discarding those that no longer serve you. Then declare your new beliefs daily.

2. **Expand Your Thoughts**

   What do you focus on? Where your attention goes, energy flows and results show. Cultivate positive thinking by using Power Statements daily.

3. **Deepen Your Spirituality**

   The Law of Attraction is where science and spirituality meet. Deepen your connection to the Higher Power of your understanding by slowing down and establish daily spiritual practices.

4. **Face Your Fears**

Acknowledge your fears, but do not let them paralyze you. Breakthrough your fears by realizing they are usually False Evidence Appearing Real.

5. **Nurture Your Self-Esteem**

Build your self-esteem daily by practicing extreme self-care. Search for things in your daily life that encourage and support you. The more you love yourself the more you accelerate your power of attraction.

This is a summary of the main principles presented in THE AWAKENING. You have now learned what you need to make your hopes and dreams a reality. But just like many other things in life, knowing what to do and actually doing it are very different. Anytime you want learn something new, whether it is a musical instrument, a new language or how to create the life of your dreams, you need to practice certain steps regularly. As you apply the principles you've learned in this book with dedication and devotion, you will see results, and you will unlock the secret behind the Law of Attraction.

You are a magnificent creator. You create the reality of your life everyday through your consciousness. You possess the power to manifest the kind of life you would love to live. Now it's your turn to go and do it!

Appendix

1. THE AWAKENING in The Workplace

2. Examples of Overriding Background Belief Processes

3. 101 Power Statements to Increase Your Attraction Quotient

4. 101 Actions to Increase Your Attraction Quotient

5. THE AWAKENING Mastery Community

APPENDIX 1

The Awakening in the Workplace

"First comes thought; then organization of that thought into ideas and plans; then transformation of those plans into reality. The beginning, as you will observe, is in your imagination." —Napoleon Hill

THE WORKPLACE CULTURE

A significant factor in determining the ease of applying the Law of Attraction in the workplace is the culture of the organization. Culture has been described as the sum of attitudes, customs, and beliefs that distinguishes one group of people from another. In the workplace, it is the overall personality of the organization. This culture usually evolves over time. Each new leader brings his or her beliefs into the ever evolving organization making it either easier or more difficult to practice the Law of Attraction principles.

What is the culture of your workplace? Is it one of the following?

- Fun-loving

- Intense

- Committed to excellence

- Customer focused

- Honest

- Dishonest

- Employees work long hours

- Employees strive for work/life balance

- Positive

- Optimistic

- Negative

- Fear-based

Scott Hunter, a successful speaker and business coach, takes the Law of Attraction into the corporate arena regularly. Here he shares a dramatic shift in culture that one of his clients experienced and the impact it had on the organization:

"A large San Francisco law firm asked me to come in and work with them. The firm had grown rapidly and extensively from its beginnings in 1975 up to and through 1990. Then, something happened and the growth suddenly stopped. When I was contacted in 1996, it was on the verge of a decline.

The management team was leaving for a strategic planning retreat to plot a course to get them back on track, and they contacted me to facilitate the retreat. When I agreed, the first thing I insisted on doing was to interview as many of the partners as possible who were at the firm since the beginning so I could find out what the problem was.

What I learned was truly fascinating. Everyone told me that during the growth years, the firm's 'leader,' whom I'll call 'Larry,' was the most optimistic, the most positive, the most encouraging person you could ever imagine meeting. His philosophy was to have fun, do good work, take care of the clients, and let success take care of itself. The firm never did any marketing; they just did what Larry said to do. They had lots of fun, they did the best job they could for their clients, and most importantly, they never worried. Why? Because Larry told them not to.

One of the firm's partners, whom I'll call 'Paul,' shared with me a particularly telling story. The firm specialized in litigating very large cases, and it wasn't atypical for a team of lawyers to work on a single case full-time. Paul was part of a team of five lawyers who had worked for several years on one multi-million dollar case. One day the case settled, leaving the five lawyers with no work and with no obvious source of new work.

So Paul went to Larry and asked, 'What do we do now?' As was typical for Larry, his response was, 'Don't worry about it. You five have been working hard for a number of years. You've earned a break. Tell your team to take some time off and have fun. I guarantee you it won't take long before we'll be screaming to get you back here.'

That wasn't what Paul expected to hear because he was worried they'd all be laid off. But Paul was a young attorney, and if Larry said not to worry, who was he to do otherwise? So Paul and his team took off.

Less than thirty days later, a new case came in, and Paul and his team were back at it. I heard story after story that replicated Paul's. The energy of the firm was one of faith, trust, and optimism, because that's the kind of leader Larry was. As a result, the firm grew and grew and grew. It's a great example of the Law of Attraction operating in all its glory.

So what happened? Well, one day in 1990, Larry woke up and looked at what he had created. He had hundreds of people working in the firm, with a payroll in the tens of millions of dollars. Stated simply, he got scared. He related to the group and to me at this strategic planning retreat that up until that fateful day he was confident in their ability to thrive. But for some reason, on that day he awoke and said, 'Oh my God. We have most of our work coming from one client. They have been able to send us big cases for 15 years, but can it really continue?' He started to doubt. Fear set in. And the rest got ugly.

The day after that realization, Larry gathered his partners around the conference table and expressed his concerns. He said that they had to market, diversify, and look for new clients; it wasn't good that they had all their eggs in one basket. Unfortunately, Larry's partners didn't know what to make of this. They didn't want to market. They never had and didn't know how. Everyone had a different opinion about what they should do. They started to argue, bicker, and make each other wrong. The teamwork went out the window, taking all the wind out of their sails. In the face of their confusion, results suffered and took a downturn.

Happily, this story has a wonderful ending. We got what happened out on the table during the strategic planning retreat. We followed it up with several multi-day partner retreats to 'clean up' all the upsets, disappointments, and frustrations that occurred during those six rocky years. In the end, everyone committed to get back to what had created success for them in the first place: having fun, taking care of the clients, doing good work, and being optimistic about the future."

Imagine the changes that would take place in corporations around the world if employees were encouraged to embrace these four steps: have more fun, take exceptional care of all clients, do good work, and be optimistic.

It's very difficult to evaluate the toll that negativity, gossiping and bickering have on an organization. Organizational success depends on teamwork and each of these undermines teamwork, making it impossible for organizations to excel.

It's very difficult to evaluate the toll that negativity, gossiping and bickering have on an organization.

Scott went on to further discuss some of his observations on workplace culture:

"An organization is a collective group of thinking beings. As a result, it has a collective energy and that energy determines what's possible and what's not possible. If the energy is upbeat, enthusiastic, positive, and optimistic, and people are all pulling together, they're going to create great results.

But if people are fearful, negative, selfish, coming from scarcity, or not working together, then this is a formula for disaster.

After years of working with organizations of every type and size, I've noticed a common theme among the successful ones. They consist of a group of enthusiastic, confident, positive people who work together on behalf of a future they have all committed themselves to create."

COMMUNICATE THE MISSION, VISION AND OBJECTIVES

So, how do you establish this group of people who work together on behalf of a future they have all committed themselves to create? You need to identify and clearly communicate the mission, vision and objectives of the organization.

Many employees have no idea of the intended direction for their company or their role in taking the organization there. Just like individuals need to discover their deepest desires and then declare them as stated in steps one and two of *The Five Steps to AWAKENING*, the leaders of an organization need to do the same. The organization leaders must determine and clearly communicate their mission, vision, and objectives.

Once the mission has been communicated clearly, each employee must be held accountable for following through on the stated objectives within their scope of responsibility. This establishes the integrity of the organization and integrity is on a high frequency. It's out of integrity when an organization's leaders set objectives, employees don't meet them, and no one cares. That falls into the category of stagnation, complacency, and toleration. These are all of a low vibration and attract more negative than good.

Many leaders don't seek to hold their employees accountable because they don't want to be held accountable themselves. But a workplace that is positive, productive and successful doesn't happen without accountability.

TROUBLE IN THE WORKPLACE

I don't want to be cavalier in my discussion of bringing the Law of Attraction into the workplace. Many business environments are entrenched with challenges. Part of the training and consulting work I do involves working with teams who are in turmoil. I'll never forget the day when one busy executive called me requesting this kind of consulting. The message he left stated, "I received your message about presentation skills training, Alicia, but I'm not interested in that. Do you offer any training or facilitation for teams who are in turmoil?"

First of all, I thought it was very insightful for him to pinpoint his issue with such clarity, and then to take action to correct the situation. Both were exemplary. Most leaders think their problems will simply go away, or at least they hope they will. All that happens is that the problems fester and grow. As the problems are increasing, productivity and effectiveness are decreasing into a never-ending downward spiral.

This executive pointed out to me that his team had done the normal team-building fun-and-games kind of programs, and they made the situation worse. After two years of battling with the issues he inherited when he stepped into the position, it was time to get to the heart of the matter.

After having personal interviews with all 15 of his employees, it was clear that his perceptions were indeed correct. Most of the employees were so unhappy that they hated going to work. Out of my very candid discussion with them surfaced the following top ten issues troubling the team overall:

1. Gossiping
2. Negativity
3. Blaming
4. Disrespect
5. Lack of trust
6. Lack of appreciation
7. Lack of camaraderie
8. Poor communication
9. Little or no accountability
10. Lack of true problem resolution

> *The bend in the road is not the end of the road, unless you fail to make the turn.*

I met with this group for several different team retreats. Our initial goal was to give everyone the opportunity to share their thoughts in a constructive, non-judgmental environment. As the issues arose, we assigned a person who would be in charge of creating a plan to handle them. We instituted a P & A Plan, (Praise and Appreciation) so that people were being acknowledged for their contributions to the success of the team.

After our first session they all reported dramatic improvements. They focused on one of my favorite quotes, "The bend in the road is not the end of the road, unless you fail to make the turn." Making the turn was key.

Much of the magic was in giving each person an opportunity to be heard without being criticized or judged. It is difficult for most teams to create this kind of environment successfully without an outside facilitator. Be extremely cautious in attempting to create this setting without a facilitator or coach as it could have a very detrimental effect.

One look at the above top ten list and you can see many violations of the Law of Attraction. Any time you get people together in an organization you're going to have a few of these. But some teams, departments and organizations have these challenges more so than others.

How many of the top ten list of items are present in your organization?

One online services executive I spoke with presented her company in this manner:

"I work for a company that would like its employees to speak and feel positively about the culture and the environment they work in, but unfortunately, that's not the case. You won't find it written in any handbook, but many of our employees don't think they can even talk with each other, let alone with management.

Operating in silos is the norm, and while it's common for teams not to communicate, they don't even know what function the other performs. Our sales team is motivated with an element of fear; fear of making suggestions or sharing opinions and fear of retribution and labeling. The results are evident in erratic sales tied to weakened team morale and efficiencies. Our future is so uncertain, many of us wonder if we'll have a job six months from now.

I wish we'd use the Law of Attraction in our workplace. If we used the Law of Attraction as a company, with each employee applying the principles, we'd not only be a company favorably thought of, we'd be a company people would want to work for whose revenues would go through the roof.

If our environment were more open, less fear driven, with people focused on the good and positive attributes of all our employees, our individuals and teams would excel and we'd be telling a very different story today. Simple things could start the shift. A pat on the back more than once a year isn't too much to expect. Our company giving back to the community would help employees feel they are giving back. All in all, the results would be highly satisfied, higher performing teams resulting in lower employee and customer turnover and increased sales. Our culture would be inspiring and motivating instead of one where it appears that our leaders are simply out for the almighty buck."

Does this sound like your organization? Helping an organization like this example reposition itself is like getting a cruise ship to make a u-turn. It takes a tremendous amount of energy and doesn't happen as quickly as one might hope, but it can be done.

Scott Hunter shares some of the challenges companies experience when they begin to implement the principles of the Law of Attraction:

1. Getting the entire organization, including the management team, to take responsibility for the overall initiative.

2. Helping each member of the organization believe they have the power to create a company that works the way they want it to, regardless of anyone or anything.

3. Creating a powerful, attractive energy within the organization, instead of one that focuses on negative circumstances and situations.

4. Motivating employees to relinquish their role as victims of circumstances and situations and to claim their power to create results.

5. Taking the focus off of the competition, the economy, etc., and placing it on all of the positive opportunities that lie before them.

WHY BE AVERAGE?

I've been teaching the Law of Attraction in the workplace for years through my customer service and hospitality training program, "BE AWESOME, NOT AVERAGE!" Negativity is so average. Anyone can be negative, and anyone can be average. It doesn't take much effort to be either.

Sometimes negativity goes undercover in the workplace. Instead of calling it "negative," they dress it up and call it, "being realistic," "being the devil's advocate," "appropriately pessimistic," or just "honest."

When I was a little girl my aunt used to tell me, "It's easy to love loveable people, but it takes a lot more character to love unlovable people." As I talk about this in relation to customer service, I underscore the fact that it's easy to be nice and caring to nice and caring customers and coworkers. But it takes character to be nice and caring to inconsiderate or unkind customers and coworkers. When you're able to do that, that's when you step up from average to awesome! And that's when you put yourself in alignment with the Law of Attraction.

When it comes to the Law of Attraction, what you give out, you'll get back. When you send out negative thoughts towards your boss, your coworker or your customer, it isn't any different than sending them out towards the people in your personal life. For some reason people think once they walk through the doors of their workplace that the rules change. Well, they don't.

Many people are negative at work, and think they are so positive outside of work that you just don't know why they're not attracting their good like gangbusters!

Applying the Law of Attraction in your life is only as good as you apply it in your workplace. It's often the most difficult place, because you don't love, or even necessarily like, the people you have to be around all day long.

The Law of Attraction isn't something you only put into practice or think about during your evenings, weekends, and vacation time. All of the principles surrounding the application of the Law of Attraction are in effect at the office too.

A STEP IN A POSITIVE DIRECTION

In spite of the challenges, creating a powerful workplace where employees are using the Law of Attraction in all of their interactions is possible. Organizations that have done so are extremely successful.

Scott Hunter shares his observation of one company:

"If a company really understands and applies the Law of Attraction, then the sky's the limit. I worked with a company in 2005 whose sales were flat at about $50M for five years. They were stuck in fear, negativity, and scarcity. They embraced the Law of Attraction and invested time and money into shifting the energy and culture of the company. As a result, in 2005 they earned $65M, in 2006 earned $80M and it keeps moving up."

Where do you begin? Although we've already identified that using the Law of Attraction is not just a positive thinking program, it's a great place to begin. Making this change alone and holding people accountable for being positive, eliminating gossiping, backstabbing, and negativity will make a significant shift in those organizations where these are present.

In addition, organizations can increase their level of positive attraction through P&A, Praise and Appreciation. Frequently, the workplace environment is so busy that no one is offering Praise and Appreciation when a job is well done. This must be done religiously, not sporadically, in order to see a change in the organization.

Taking the Law of Attraction into the workplace creates an environment that is joyful and harmonious. People work more effectively together and create substantial results. Don't leave these valuable principles to your personal lives, for it's when you live the principles 24/7 that you see amazing results.

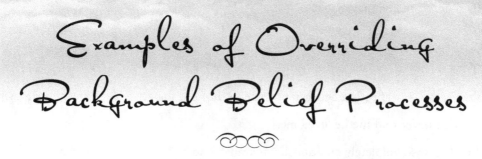

Examples of Overriding Background Belief Processes

In Chapter 10, Renew Your Beliefs, there was a suggested process for identifying and removing your negative Overriding Background Beliefs.

The four steps identified were:

1. Discover

2. Dissect

3. Discard

4. Declare

There is no right or wrong way to do this exercise as long as you eventually progress through all four steps. The six examples provided show a variety of ways to process your feelings in this exercise. The goal is to be as honest as possible so that you can remove your negative Overriding Background Beliefs and replace them with new powerful, supportive beliefs.

DAN

WHAT'S NOT WORKING

I am struggling in the area of relationships.

DISCOVER

I was able to identify the following Overriding Background Beliefs:

- I am unworthy.

- I am emotionally unavailable.

- I did not have good role models.

DISSECT

- I never saw any affection between my parents, nor did they ever share any affection with me.

- My dad never told me he loved me.

- My dad was completely emotionally unavailable to my mother, me, and my brothers.

- The environment was negatively neutral, there was no affection, but there was not any fighting or conflict going on either.

- I was happy as a child, but I was blissfully ignorant.

- I didn't date in high school.

- In my thirties I became aware of the nothingness that was in my house growing up.

- I was told I was emotionally unavailable.

- I felt unworthy, because women could find someone better.

DISCARD

I wrote a letter to my father as follows:

> How dare you not be an active participant in my childhood. It was unfair for you to leave everything to mom! Boys need a positive role model and it's unacceptable that you did not embrace that responsibility! You made many conscious decisions that excused yourself from good parenting and time with us and there is no acceptable reason or rationale for your lack of thought and effort in creating a loving and nurturing environment that every family needs.
>
> You also deprived yourself of our love and missed the opportunity to make mom feel loved and appreciated. You could have set the tone by your actions, but instead you missed the opportunity to give, receive, and teach love. Through my own experience, I know that love for children is not a burden, so withholding it is a selfish act that creates loss for everyone.

DECLARE

- I am now capable of enjoying emotional intimacy.

- I am now capable of giving emotional intimacy.

- I am attractive, outgoing, and radiate positive energy.

- I generously share my time and energy with those who are important to me.

- I am confident because of everything I have accomplished.

After finishing this exercise, I felt somewhat sad about what it revealed, but I also felt a sense of relief. The exercise was helpful because it forced me to think about my family dynamics in a new way. Perhaps for the first time in my adult life I was no longer making excuses for my Father's behavior and able to let go of some of the confusing feelings I had about our relationship and myself.

REBECCA

WHAT'S NOT WORKING

1. Financial prosperity

2. Physical – self

3. Physical – home

DISCOVER

I was able to identify the following Overriding Background Beliefs:

- I am not worthy.

- I don't deserve it.

- I am not good enough.

- I can't do anything right.

DISCARD

Experiences that support the above beliefs:

Mom used to always say "You can't do anything right!" whenever I would make a mistake. And then I would say over and over to myself, "I'm not good enough…" "I can't do anything right," "I'm stupid!" over and over while I was crying alone in my room. That would eventually lead to "I hate her" and "I hate myself."

In my 20s I was riddled with self-hate. My mom wasn't doing it to me anymore, but I sure was!

Whenever I would make a mistake, fail to keep my word, say something wrong, not say something when I needed to, I would be flooded with self-hating thoughts such as, "I can't believe I did that! How could I be so stupid? Who do I think I am? I'm such an idiot! I'm such a loser! Nobody cares what I say! I hate myself!"

And then I would be flooded with intensely negative feelings throughout my body, especially in my chest and throat. Sometimes it would feel like I was being strangled with a noose around my neck. This is how my words were creating physical feelings in my body. And this would happen almost every single day.

It stopped when I got married. My mom was constantly on my back about everything. The common theme from her was that I couldn't do anything right. How I brushed my hair, how I dressed myself, how I did an art project, how I cleaned my room, how I played with my brother, whatever I did or didn't do led to her yelling at me, constantly!

She was always pushing, pushing, pushing in a very mean, negative, and hurtful way. I remember it being more intense in my preteen years all the way up to the weeks before I got married at 28.

Something changed once I got engaged and was on the verge of becoming a wife. She started treating me like I was a grown woman and she finally stopped parenting me. It appeared that her main goal in life was to get me married, and once this happened her job was done. She completely eased up. Our relationship has changed for the positive now that I am in my forties, but I am still riddled with inner demons that mirror her words and actions toward me while I was growing up.

DISCARD

- HOW DARE YOU crush my precious spirit with your cruel and careless words!

- HOW COULD YOU do that to your innocent little girl?

- I CAN'T BELIEVE you would treat another human being that way.

- HOW DARE YOU laugh at and ridicule my growing body!

- HOW DARE YOU be so cold, angry, and distant from me when I needed you most!

- I AM DONE with your anger! It is not mine! Take it back! It is all YOURS!

- I AM DONE hiding in shame;

- I AM DONE cowering in the corner!

- I AM DONE worrying about upsetting you or anyone else!

- I AM DONE burying my precious self for fear of displeasing you or anyone else.

- I AM DONE believing the bullshit of your angry words!

- I WILL NEVER, never, never allow you to destroy my spirit again.

- YOU WILL NEVER, ever have access to my precious spirit ever again. You are done. I want my precious spirit back! You are so done!

DECLARE

1. I AM GOOD ENOUGH NOW!

2. I always have been and always will be good enough!

3. I AM a precious and loveable child of God!

4. I absolutely deserve all my good NOW!

5. I am so deserving of having the life of my dreams right now!

6. I am precious and loveable just as I am!

7. I am gentle with myself as I learn and grow!

8. I embrace all my actions with love.

9. I allow myself to make mistakes and learn as I grow.

Second Phase:

1. <u>What is the payoff?</u>

   I get to stay small. I can stay hidden and little and not risk being found out.

2. <u>What is the price?</u>

   I live a small, inadequate, unfulfilling life! I repeat my mom's qualities of negativity, constant criticism, anger, and disconnection with myself, God, and those I love.

3. <u>What is the prize for overcoming it?</u>

   My life comes ALIVE! I live in joy, peace and connection. I am free. I attract all the money that we need to own our next home, to put Sam into private school, to live near my family and friends, and to give back to my spiritual community with time and money.

MARY

WHAT'S NOT WORKING

- I am a perfectionist.

- I am very shy at times.

- I internalize my emotions too much.

DISCOVER

- I am not worthy.

- I am unimportant.

DISSECT

My parents divorced when I was three-years-old and my father re-married when I was five-years-old. My brother and I lived with our dad and stepmother. Our stepmother did not like us at all, and my dad ran a very strict house. Often, my stepmother would make up stories to tell my dad when he got home of how my brother and I had misbehaved, talked back, or didn't comply with her orders. She would literally just make up stuff. My dad always believed her and took her side, punishing us severely for the alleged acts. We were not allowed to explain that we didn't do it or give our version of what had happened because that would be talking back, and result in further punishment. My dad didn't like it when we showed emotion. My dad also believed that when in public, children should only speak when they are spoken to.

DISCARD

Instead of a letter, I came up with a list:

- I am done letting you speak over me as if I don't matter.

- I am done letting you silence me.

- I am done being perfect.

- I am done doing things your way.

Over the years I have struggled with the "un-relationship" I have with my dad. The truth is that it will never be different as long as my stepmother is around. He still takes her side and lets her whim rule. And, since I am now 33, and she still doesn't like me, she puts up roadblocks when I do attempt to have a relationship with my dad.

At one point, I felt especially hopeless and wanted to tell him what he was missing. I wrote this letter to him:

I am sorry that . . .

- You don't remember my birthday.

- You don't take the time to call me.

- You don't hug me when I see you.

- You never come to see me.

- You don't know how I am doing.

- You don't know who I really am as a person.

- You don't know what makes me laugh.

- You don't know what makes me cry.

- You don't know when I am sad.

- You don't know my friends.

- You don't know my heart.

- You always took her side.

I never sent the letter, but it helped me realize that his lack of effort in our relationship was really his choice and his doing, not mine.

Doing this process revealed many things to me:

- It wasn't okay to speak.

- It wasn't okay to be happy.

- It wasn't okay to show emotion, or you would receive more punishment.

- It wasn't okay to be me; I had to conform to others' expectations of me.

Since my father took my stepmother's side rather than mine, he conveyed that she was always right and I was wrong. I now realize that I am a perfectionist because I am trying to be right, I am shy because I was taught it wasn't okay to speak; and I internalize more than I should because I was taught that emotions are bad and that showing emotions would get me in trouble. I now realize that the negative Overriding Background Beliefs from my childhood are still impacting me in ways I never imagined.

DECLARE

- I am accepted.

- I am lovable.

- I am successful.

- I am strong, but I still have feelings and acknowledge them.

- I deserve to be happy.

- It is okay for me to have a different opinion and express it.

- It is okay for me to be upset, angry, or cry.
- I can be myself.
- I can dress how I want.

MEGAN

WHAT'S NOT WORKING

- I work endless hours with an ever-present belief that I MUST.

- I don't know how to work without suffering and being stressed out.

- I am deeply sad and unfulfilled most of the time.

- I am broke all the time, regardless of how much money I make.

- I am afraid to do what I really want to do – sing, dance, and choreograph.

- I do not know what to do with my personal free time.

- I am deeply ashamed of myself.

DISCOVER

- I must be perfect

- I am absolutely nothing without my talents and skills.

- Hard work gives you worth and can earn you the love and respect of those around you.

- There is only one way to do things – the RIGHT way.

- Life is hard.

- Money is painful.

- Everything in life must be earned, including love.

- Humility is a virtue, confidence is a liability (i.e., you're too big for your britches).

DISSECT

I remember loving my father so deeply that it hurt. His attention on me was critical to my enduring happiness. Both of my parents were "perfectionists" in EVERYTHING they did. The most prevalent memory of my home growing up were the endless rules. I remember wanting to express the explosive creativity that was bursting inside me, but I only remember being criticized or laughed at. When I was five, I remember dancing around the room and bursting with expression and joy as I moved to the music. My mother got disgusted watching me and made the remark, "Megan – stop that and do what you were taught in class." I remember thinking, even at five, "How can I create a dance out of two lousy steps," which was all we had apparently been taught. Mostly what I remember is the "looks of disgust" in my parents' faces, and it makes me ashamed to this day, though I'm not sure why.

Much of my journey through my dancing years was wrought with this type of war between who and what I wanted to become, and who and what "they" wanted me to become. Whenever I'd speak up and dare to express one of my dreams out loud, it was always shot down with laughter, serious criticism or the dismissing line, "Oh Megan, don't be silly." As I got older, I became more and more afraid to express myself and just be me, and I became utterly obsessed with pleasing those around me.

Today, I am living a life I consider to be empty and void of what I want and desire deep in my heart. I am lost and can't seem to find the way back to me. I've had years and years of practice avoiding my truth and being afraid and self-conscious to the point that it became hard to leave the house. Work was the only thing I remember consistently getting praised for, so all I know to do is work – it's the only place I'm totally comfortable and confident.

DISCARD

To EVERYONE who stomped on my spirit and made me feel like I was too much, too big, or too "whatever." I AM! SO GET OVER IT!

Mom:

- I am DONE letting you control me or my feelings.

- I am DONE saying what I think you want me to say instead of what I really feel and think.

- I am DONE being pragmatic in lieu of all that I dream is possible.

Dad:

- Let's see, how can I put this, Go to hell in a hand basket you big, lazy, drunk jerk! That about covers it.

April:

- I am DONE letting you make me feel like I stole something from you.

- I am DONE apologizing for everything I am.

- I am DONE trying to get you to forgive me for getting all the attention and talent in the family.

- I am DONE feeling sorry for you and for me.

- I am DONE saying yes when I mean NO, NO, NO!

June:

- I am DONE, DONE, DONE feeling like a loser around you.

- I am DONE apologizing for living in California.

- I am DONE begging you to accept and love me as I am.

- I am DONE pretending I'm something I'm not.

- I am DONE worrying about what you may think of me.

- And one more thing – I may not be Aretha Franklin, but I sure as hell am Megan, and believe you me I stop traffic when I want to so get used to it.

Aunt Rosie:

- I am DONE giving you all my power. And to your remark, "Oh come on, Megan, that's big time. What are you REALLY going to do?" I now say – "Well, Aunt Rosie, it has to be the big time if it's going to hold my talent, so LOOK OUT LADY!"

- This step makes me wonder why I never questioned these beliefs all along. When I look at them in writing, they are CLEARLY other people's individual problems and in the end, have ABSOLUTELY NOTHING to do with me.

DECLARE

- I am lovable just because I am alive.

- I am funny and joyful.

- I am totally successful in everything I do.

- I strive for "excellence" rather than "perfection."

- I am fulfilled and happy.

- I am honest about my thoughts and feelings.

- I am dependable and strong.

- I am a loving and supportive friend.

- I work smart rather than hard.

- I am wonderfully talented.

- I enjoy singing and dancing on a regular basis.

- I have all the personal time I want to enjoy my friends, family and ME.

- I love myself and my company.

- I am blessed beyond words in all areas of my life.

- I TOTALLY ROCK!

This process got me in touch with a deep-seeded rage that I have been stuffing down my whole life. I look back at the list of things that aren't working in my life, then I look at the volume of Overriding Background Beliefs I have been taught since childhood and I want to SCREAM. There is so much unreleased passion inside me that I feel like if you light a match around me I'll blow up. This exercise has taught me that it's time to begin releasing my passion and using my talents!

KEN

WHAT'S NOT WORKING

I want more financial freedom.

DISCOVER

- I'm afraid of failure.

- I'm afraid of success.

- I believe you have to work hard to be successful.

DISSECT

My father always made me feel as though I had nothing to offer the world. Any time I accomplished something and I told my father, he called me a liar, a cheat, and a thief, which I was none of. But as a young man I noticed myself avoiding challenges because I was afraid people would repeat my father's words.

DISCARD

I have since confronted my father about this, and sadly he wasn't too coherent. He has drowned himself in liquor and drugs and it is my personal belief that when he was telling me those negative things, he was talking about himself. With that, I was able to "disconnect" from the situation and realize that it was not me, but him that he was talking to all those years ago.

I am done thinking I have nothing to offer the world. How dare you ever call me a liar, a cheat, and a thief! I will never let your influence cause me to avoid challenges or do my very best for fear of anything.

DECLARE

- I am a success in all that I do.

- I love to take risks and enjoy the journey of life.

- I am an amazing man and I acknowledge who I am and all that I have accomplished.

- I am open to receiving all of the good the Universe has to offer me.

PRICE/PRIZE

1. **What is the payoff?**

   The payoff I get in letting this go is that I am freed from the subconscious thinking that my success or failure is a direct judgment on my character.

2. **What is the price?**

   The price I paid is years of holding myself back from the things I want most in life.

3. **What is the prize for overcoming it?**

   The prize I get for overcoming this is my ability to truly shine; to exert myself in areas of life that I want to improve. The ability to know that my success or failure is just part of life. I am honest, have integrity, and do not cheat. I have character and deserve to have success.

After finishing this exercise I felt overwhelmed with the joy of freedom. I didn't feel held down by my thoughts anymore! This exercise was helpful because it allowed me to give back the guilt and resentment that, for some reason, I felt the compulsion to hold on to. I learned what I didn't know about myself before. I have the power to control my thoughts and memories.

ANJALI

WHAT'S NOT WORKING

I am having difficulty believing in and creating a financially abundant and prosperous life for myself.

DISCOVER

I was able to identify the following Overriding Background Beliefs:

- I'm not smart enough to be successful in business.

- I am not "too late," or "too old" to increase my financial literacy.

- My parents never taught me good business or money skills.

- It's hard work (mostly physical) to make money.

- I cannot be both spiritual and wealthy.

- I am always late and behind—successful people are never late or behind. Therefore, I will never be successful.

- I don't have the right connections.

DISSECT

- My mother frequently said, "We are poor so we CAN'T AFFORD IT."

- My dad was not good with money or business.

- My dad taught me that investing is "stupid" and non-spiritual and that the best place for money is in the bank."

- Children were not included in money discussions ("Children are to be seen and not heard").

- My parents took pride in living a frugal life.

- I was not allowed to work (part-time) until college because "money is not important."

DISCARD

I wrote a letter to my father as follows:

> Dad: How could you not have taken care of the family so that we never would've had to feel poor and less than? So that mom wouldn't have had to keep telling me, every time we went shopping that we were poor and that we cannot afford it?

> You always did what YOU want to do, regardless of what the family will feel or have to go through. You were never good with your money and spent thousands of dollars on "things" and decisions that lead to no Return On Investment and lost all the money. You never taught your children how to manage money, how businesses are operated, how bills are cal-

culated and paid for, how checks are written, etc. Furthermore, you always asked the children to excuse themselves from the table because you were going to talk about "adult stuff" and that children did not need to know anything about money.

You did not teach me how to invest, how to read a bank or financial statement, how to budget, balance an account...nothing, absolutely nothing about financial things!!

How could you not show me or any of your children how to manage money?

You have taught me that investing in stock is the stupidest thing to do and that I should never think of following your footsteps. It is because you did not do your due diligence. Not because stock is greedy and will always create misery!

You frequently borrowed money from your father and even sold a couple of prime real estate properties just because you did not want to manage it from overseas. You also frequently mentioned to me that you were using your "retirement fund." You jokingly said that your Father left you too much money that created sibling rivalry and unhappiness, and that you are going to leave your children in debt instead! Although you were joking, it was disturbing and sad to hear this as a child.

DECLARE

- I AM smart. I have always been extremely clever, creative and intelligent and will always be.
- I am not old! I am very young. I have plenty of time.
- Money comes easily and frequently.
- Conscious and compassionate investors are waiting for my wonderful energy and ideas!
- I have many, many wonderful and meaningful friendships—my friends are genuine, integrity rich, fun, expressive, energetic and successful.
- I am loved!
- Financially abundant life comes to me easily and is my birthright. I claim my wealth, freedom and prosperity.
- Wealthy people ARE spiritual and spiritual people CAN be wealthy!

It was a life changing moment when I discovered this hidden belief and connection between spirituality and money/wealth! After identifying what changes I needed to implement, I immediately put it into action and was able to create a new reality—overnight! The change really can happen that quick. There are, of course, more changes to be made, but the discovery of this negative belief enabled me to move confidently in the direction of positive change, because I knew what behavior I needed to stop repeating!

HOWARD

WHAT'S NOT WORKING

Two of the things that have not been working in my life so far are my career path and my self-confidence.

DISCOVER

In retrospect, I always felt that I was being put down by my mother who always said, "That's ok BUT why didn't you do better?" and my father always told me that as long as I tried my best he would be happy. I always was the kid who was very talkative during class and found it hard to study and stay focused. After graduating college and starting in the work force, I was very restless and changed companies more than I should have. Even though I enjoyed my work I never seemed to be able to get ahead until I was tested many years later I found that I had adult Attention Deficit Disorder (ADD).

DISSECT

I realized that some of the blame can go to my ADD, and the other can be from always getting mixed messages from my parents. Growing up without self-confidence and not being able to stay focused on a task caused me much trouble in school, college, and later in changing companies often.

My parents had different reactions to this discovery. My father understood why I acted the way I did growing up and also as an adult. On the other hand, my mother would not accept the diagnosis and continued to put me down as a son "who never tried as hard as he could." This has led me to question my own abilities in relationships and work. I find that I go overboard to prove to others that I am confident, capable, and able to do anything.

DISCARD

Dear Mother,

I am done feeling that I am not good enough to do anything I want to. I am done feeling that having ADD is something to be embarrassed of, and with the help of medication I can stay focused and complete any task I start. There is nothing you can say now that will alter how I feel. My self-confidence has improved dramatically because of these realizations.

Furthermore, "I now cut the cords and break the ties that have bound me to these old, inaccurate ways of thinking, feeling, believing, and acting. I celebrate all that I am and my new life."

DECLARE

- I am now confident in my abilities to handle any situation that comes my way.
- I am now confident that I do not need anyone's approval.

- I am now confident that I can focus on tasks and complete them.

- I am now confident that I can be in a relationship and grow without being afraid of rejection.

- I am finally confident and like myself for everything that I have accomplished.

Doing this exercise was very helpful to me because it helped me to actually stop and take a look in the mirror at the person I am and how I developed some of the thoughts and feelings I live with on a daily basis. I am now certain that I can develop a strong sense of self-confidence and live a more powerful life.

APPENDIX 3

101 *Power Statements to Accelerate Your Attraction Quotient*

∞∞∞

HEALTH AND WELLNESS

1. Today, I am grateful for the miracle of my body.

2. I have the power to create the physical health and fitness I desire.

3. I now experience energy, health and vitality in every cell of my body.

4. I now choose to treat my body with love and care, giving it all of the food, exercise and rest it needs.

5. I love and admire every inch of my magnificent body.

6. I nourish my body in healthy and self-loving ways.

7. I am now filled with abundant energy and vitality.

8. Every cell in my body vibrates with positive energy and supreme health.

9. I now experience quick and immediate healing in every cell of my body.

10. I lovingly care for my body by giving it all the sleep and rest it needs.

FINANCIAL FREEDOM AND ABUNDANCE

11. I am a money magnet. Money loves me!

12. I have the power to create all of the money I want in my life.

13. Abundance is my birthright. I claim it now.

14. Money comes to me in increasing amounts through expected and unexpected sources.

15. I have more than enough money to meet all of my needs and desires.

16. My mind is open to receiving unlimited prosperity and abundance.

17. I now handle my money wisely and responsibly.

18. I now earn a substantial income doing what I love to do.

19. I pay all of my bills on time and have plenty of money left over.

20. Money flows to me in avalanches of abundance.

21. I love the work I do and I am richly rewarded for it.

HAPPINESS AND JOY

22. I deserve to experience happiness and joy every day of my life!

23. Every minute of my life is filled with pure joy and bliss.

24. I am filled with incredible joy that flows through me with every beat of my heart.

25. I now release any destructive beliefs I may have had, and joyfully embrace new powerful beliefs.

26. With every breath I take, I am filled with more peace, love and joy.

27. My happiness and joy are fully expressed without inhibitions or limitations!

28. I radiate peace, love, and happiness to all those around me.

29. I am free from my past and open the door to a happier and brighter future.

ABUNDANT RELATIONSHIPS

30. I love and accept myself as I am in this very moment.

31. I am open to experiencing new heights of intimacy with those I love.

32. I have the marriage of my dreams.

33. I practice unconditional love with myself and everyone around me.

34. I rejoice in the love I encounter every day and extend it to those around me.

35. I attract only healthy and positive people.

36. All my relationships are loving and harmonious.

37. I now look for and find the good in every person with whom I interact.

38. I express myself fully with clarity and confidence.

39. I am open to receiving the love, support and encouragement others want to give me.

ELIMINATING OBSTACLES

40. Nothing can stop me from achieving my goals and desires.

41. I move through any and all obstacles with ease. I am unstoppable!

42. I am bigger than any obstacle I may face.

43. I now look at all obstacles as opportunities to grow.

44. I now maintain the focus necessary to achieve my goals and desires.

45. I believe with all my heart and soul that it is possible to have what I want.

46. I release all sources of negativity in my life.

47. I choose to embrace and claim my power every day.

48. I have the courage to let go of the person I have become in exchange for the person I am becoming.

TAKING ACTION

49. I enjoy doing what it takes to achieve my goals.

50. I am a master at manifesting all of my dreams and desires.

51. I structure my time effectively so that I achieve maximum results.

52. Today I maximize my efforts and focus 100% on my highest income earning opportunities.

53. I say "good-bye" to procrastination and take action now.

54. Through my actions and attitudes I am a source of inspiration for others.

55. Every day I am taking positive actions to make my dreams a reality.

56. I create a home filled with peace, joy and beauty.

57. I am a powerhouse! I set goals, make plans and take action everyday!

RECEIVING YOUR GOOD

58. I am so happy and grateful now that …(fill in with your desires).

59. My arms are wide open to receiving all of the good the Universe has to offer me.

60. I joyfully welcome all of the unlimited possibilities before me.

61. I boldly ask for what I want and I receive it with gratitude and grace.

62. I deserve and welcome all my good now.

63. I feel the feelings and experience the joy of all my desires being fulfilled!

64. I easily and openly accept all of my abundance now.

65. I face each day with an attitude of gratitude and abundance.

66. My heart is overflowing with gratitude and joy for all of the good that is in my life now and coming to me in the future.

67. I now allow others to love and be supportive of me.

EXPANDING YOUR THOUGHTS

68. I manage what I think at all times. If it is not powerful, I don't think it.

69. I raise my consciousness and expand my thoughts to attract all that I desire.

70. I have everything I need right now to manifest everything I want.

71. I feel the feelings and think the thoughts that attract my good in record time.

72. I am being shown everything I need to know to create and fulfill my mission and purpose in life.

73. I am aware of all of my beliefs and I only hold on to those beliefs that serve me.

74. I fully accept that something bigger and better than what I expect is on its way.

75. Since like attracts like, I keep the frequency of my thoughts on the highest good in life.

DEEPENING YOUR SPIRITUALITY

76. God is my source, my safety, and my security.

77. I am Divinely guided to take right action at all times.

78. I believe in Divine timing and I trust that everything comes at the perfect time in the perfect way.

79. I let go and let God take care of every moment.

80. I make it a priority to find meaningful ways to connect to my Higher Power every day.

81. I notice my Higher Power all around me throughout the day.

82. I slow down and create more "white space" in my life to deepen my connection to my Higher Power.

FACING YOUR FEARS

83. I am bigger than any fear or obstacle I face.

84. I have the courage and confidence to move forward in my life.

85. I eliminate any worry or fear and act with conviction.

86. My confidence increases more and more everyday.

87. I take action in spite of my fears.

88. I breathe in strength and confidence and breathe out fear and doubt.

89.   I trust in my intuition and take action based on what is true for me.

90.   I act as if I already have all the confidence I need and desire.

91.   I acknowledge any fears and realize they are only False Evidence Appearing Real.

92.   My fears have no power over me.

93.   I joyfully overcome every fear I face.

NURTURING YOUR SELF-ESTEEM

94.   I love and accept myself unconditionally.

95.   I value myself and give priority to my needs creating greater happiness in my life.

96.   I forgive myself for any harm I may have caused myself or others, knowingly or unknow-ingly.

97.   I am the most important person in my life and I treat myself like royalty.

98.   I love myself and give myself permission to make mistakes and learn as I go.

99.   I am worthy to experience all that I desire in life.

100.   I speak gently, kindly and lovingly to myself at all times.

101.   I celebrate my uniqueness and individuality.

101 *Actions to Accelerate Your Attraction Quotient*

❧❧❧

YOUR PHYSICAL HEALTH AND WELLNESS DESIRES

1. Give your body all the sleep and rest it needs regularly.

2. Be aware of what you put into your body and portion sizes. Give your body the most nutritious options possible.

3. Start eating organic and eventually eliminate foods with chemicals, preservatives and additives.

4. Keep your body and brain fully hydrated by drinking plenty of water throughout the day.

5. Do some form of activity for a minimum of 30 minutes every day.

6. Get all of the suggested checkups for your age range.

7. Power walk and power talk. As you are walking briskly, declare your chosen Power Statements for the day. Say them out loud and with conviction!

8. Always appreciate how wonderful you truly are by thinking self-loving thoughts about every inch of your physical being - your body, your face, your hair, your weight, etc.

9. Have fun! Make sure to take time and laugh, rent a funny DVD, lighten up, do activities you enjoy regularly.

YOUR MONETARY DESIRES

10. Be grateful every time you pay for something.

11. Write "Thank You!" on all your checks. "Thank You!" that I can buy this wonderful product or service. "Thank You!" for providing for me. "Thank you!" that I have the money to buy it – and that the check is good. *

12. Put pictures of money all around you to represent the money flowing to you from all directions. Get play money from the store, take a picture of a $100 bill, purchase $1,000,000 bills online, or take a dollar bill and make it into whatever denomination you desire.

13. Tithe your time and money to the place(s) you are spiritually enriched.

14. Identify your beliefs about money. What did your parents teach you about money when you were growing up? Write them out and replace any negative beliefs with positive prosperous thoughts.

15. Read the bestselling books on money and money management.

YOUR EMOTIONAL DESIRES

16. Perform a Resentment Releasing ceremony. Write down all your resentments of people, places or things. Take the time to do this thoroughly and completely. Release these resentments by declaring "I am NOW done with these!" and burning them in a fire pit or barbeque, disintegrating them into nothingness.

17. Develop an "I can do it!" mindset. When doubts creep in, counter-act them with a Power Statement such as, "I can do whatever I set my mind to!"

18. Play music as often as possible. Music lifts your soul to new heights and is known to have therapeutic value. It is also a great way to raise your vibration.

19. Plan and take regular vacations for much needed rest and relaxation. You'll come back revitalized, happier and more productive.

20. Choose to live in joy versus struggle. Actively pursue ways to bring more joy into your life.

YOUR RELATIONSHIP DESIRES

21. Open your heart to love. Visualize your heart opening and being filled with the white light of pure love.

22. Commit to forgiving everyone for everything. If this step seems too big be willing to keep on open mind and consider it.

23. Forgive yourself for any real or perceived harm you have caused yourself or others.

24. Ask all of those you love, "What do I do that makes you feel loved the most?" And "What do I do that makes you feel unloved the most?"

25. Plan regular date nights with your spouse or partner.

26. Make a list of 101 things you're grateful for about your partner.

27. Read personal development books with your partner and discuss what you've learned.

28. Express gratitude to everyone around you (partner, family, friends, etc.) throughout the day.

29. Stop trying to control others. Embrace the phrase, "Live and let live!" Live your life to its fullest and let others do the same as they choose to.

30. Make it a priority to bring romance into your life. Romance equals fun, excitement, love and joy which are high frequency emotions that will bring more of the same into your reality.

31. Hold positive and loving thoughts about everyone in your family and especially for anyone who seems to have irritated or hurt you. The more love you send to each person, the more love will come back to you.

32. Make time to play with your children daily. Allow yourself to laugh and be silly with your children.

33. Be real, honest and open with your children.

ELIMINATING OBSTACLES

34. Commit to limiting the negative influences of TV, radio and newspapers. Turn them off and fill your free time with more positive influences.

35. Eliminate clutter from your environment. Spend just 15 minutes every day clearing away clutter, unwanted items, and items that no longer serve you.

36. Be persistent with how fully you practice *The Seven Steps to AWAKENING* and *The Five Keys to Accelerate Your Power of Attraction*. Don't give up before the miracle happens.

37. Remove complaints from your repertoire. Focusing on the negative of any situation brings more of the same.

38. Commit to do the inner work necessary to release Overriding Background Beliefs.

TAKE MEANINGFUL ACTION

39. Commit to taking focused action towards your dreams and goals everyday.

40. Journal everyday and focus on gratitude, releasing frustrations, connecting to your Higher Power, connecting to your True Self, identifying goals and action steps, etc.

41. Keep a Gratitude Journal and write a minimum of five things you are grateful for every day until you have a list of 101 things.

42. Do Power vs. Fear writing. Draw a line down the middle of a page. On the left side write down all your fears, insecurities, things you don't want. Keep writing until you have nothing left to write – get it all out. Then on the other side of the page take each fear/insecurity or thing you don't want, draw a line through it and rewrite it into a powerful, positive, affirmative statement. For example, "I'm afraid I won't have enough money

to pay my utility bills this month." Change this to, "All my utility bills are paid in full and I have plenty of money left!" By the end of this process you will feel fantastic, energized and ready to take on the world.

43. Practice stream of consciousness writing regularly. This is where you put pen to paper and just let your thoughts flow. It doesn't matter what you write about, because it's all about the action of writing and getting words to paper. For best results, use these guidelines; 1-2 pages to get by, 3-4 pages to make progress, and 5 or more to accelerate your progress. When done consistently, this process will open doors to your subconscious like nothing else. Some people find that through this writing they get deeply and intimately connected to their Higher Power.

44. Create a vision board and look at it everyday visualizing and feeling as if you already have what your heart desires. Remember to generate the positive feelings and energy associated with having everything on your board.

45. Write out your goals, post them everywhere and review them daily.

46. Discover what it is that you desire and write it out clearly, as though you have already attained it. "I am happy and grateful now that I earn $200,000 or more annually; I now enjoy my healthy, fit body; I'm excited that I now have a big, beautiful home; etc."

47. Define the specific action steps you need to take to attain these goals.

48. Move forward with massive action. A little action will get you little results, massive action will get you massive results. Which would you rather have?

49. Focus on creating results that bring you closer to your goals every day. To do this, remove distractions, interruptions, and obstacles as much as possible.

50. Place pictures all around you of the things you desire so that you see them throughout the day. Take time to stop and look at them and feel how wonderful it is to already have them.

51. Experience your desires first hand; i.e. test drive your dream car, visit open houses, try on designer clothes, etc.

52. Create a support system of like-minded people who are on the same path of manifesting their dreams and experiencing THE AWAKENING.

53. Spend time in nature, among the flowers, plants and trees. When you are connected to nature, ideas, information and healing energy tends to flow more freely to you.

RECEIVE YOUR GOOD

54. Commit to focusing on gratitude every day. Visualize opening your heart and filling it with the golden light of gratitude.

55. Throughout the day say the Power Statement, "I am filled with infinite love and gratitude," repeatedly.

56. Receive your good openly, gratefully and gracefully.

57. Genuinely express appreciation for everything you receive, whether it is a free cup of coffee, lunch or dinner, a traffic-free drive home, or kindness from a stranger.

58. Always accept when someone offers help as a practice of opening up to receive your good.

59. Practice asking for help and say "Thank you!" all day long.

60. Infuse your whole life with appreciation and playfulness for all the abundance you currently have.

61. Believe with 100% certainty that your good is already in existence and is on its way to you right now.

62. Visualize your "Three Minutes of Magic" every day. Create a three minute scene for every one of your desires. Imagine it all-out, over-the-top, fun, exciting, and engaging all of your senses. Studies have shown that the mind cannot tell what is imagined and what is real. So when you spend quality time visualizing your "Three Minutes of Magic" your mind believes it is true. First you practice "receiving your good" in your mind, and then you "receive your good" in reality.

63. Keep a log of all the ways you see the Law of Attraction working positively in your life. This will help you focus on all of the good you are receiving in many different forms.

EXPAND YOUR THOUGHTS

64. Do the written exercises in Chapter 10 to discover and discard your Overriding Background Beliefs.

65. Monitor every word you think and say. Catch yourself in any negative thought or comment. Stop and replace each negative thought or comment with a Power Statement. The more Power Statements you can replace the negativity with, the faster you will move yourself forward.

66. Commit to spending at least one half hour every day on personal development – reading books, articles, listening to recordings, etc.

67. When you catch yourself focusing on things you don't want, create the habit of asking yourself what you DO want.

68. When you ask yourself, "Why is this happening to me?" ask instead "How can I go about creating what I DO want?" And pay attention when the answers start flowing.

69. Look for the positive side or lesson in every situation. Instead of, "I can't believe that is happening to me again!" ask "What is my lesson here?"

70. Dream big! Let go of small thoughts about yourself! See yourself being incredibly successful and happy.

71. Practice quieting your ego's demands. Stay heart-centered and not head-centered.

72. Become the expert at knowing exactly what it is you want. Dedicate time every day to get intensely clear on what you desire and what you are passionate about. Keep a journal just for this and take it with you where ever you go.

73. Give up "getting even" with others. Surrender to peace at all cost.

DEEPEN YOUR SPIRITUALITY

74. Slow down and create a soul-filled lifestyle.

75. Share your gratitude abundantly.

76. Do "soul work" every day through prayer, meditation and developing your dreams.

77. Catch yourself feeling happy and take note of what made you feel that way.

78. Express joy and wonderment at all of the miraculous creations in our Universe.

79. Make "soul-searching" a regular part of your day. Ask yourself, "Who am I? Do I like the person I am? Do I treat myself with respect? Do I treat others with respect?" Depending on your answers, start making changes without delay.

80. Focus on your breath frequently throughout your day. Be still and breathe deeply.

81. Identify your values. Do you lead a stress-filled life or a soul-filled life? If so, how does that match your values?

82. When praying for Divine intervention regarding a challenging situation, make sure you ask for clear, easy to understand guidance and direction. And trust that the support you are seeking is on its way.

83. Spend time alone, meditating upon what you truly desire. Focus on simply breathing, relaxing and centering yourself. Have pen and paper on hand and ask yourself, "What's my heart's deepest desire right now?"

84. Focus on developing the belief that you can have what you desire without a shadow of a doubt, with complete and total confidence.

85. Create a sacred space for meditation and contemplation. Fill this space with things that have special meaning to you. Include pictures, symbols, books, music, art, etc. Commit to spending daily time just for yourself in this inspiring space.

86. Create "white space" in your life by reducing the things you are currently responsible for. If you're always flying around in a frenzy you have a difficult time deepening your spirituality.

87. Say "No," to some activities so that you can create a soul-filled life.

FACE YOUR FEARS

88. Take at least one small action everyday toward the achievement of one of your goals.

89. Replace fearful thoughts immediately with positive Power Phrases. Repeat the positive Power Phrases out loud with enthusiasm until the fearful thought and associated feelings are released.

90. Visualize your way into action. Spend time everyday visualizing yourself in the situation that brings you fear. See yourself as calm, confident, energized and poised. Practice your part in this scene over and over again in your mind. Your mind doesn't know the difference between so called "real" and "imagined" experiences. Practice perfection in your mind first and then take the action in real life.

91. When you catch yourself in a downward spiral of catastrophic thinking, STOP and write down your fears. The key is to look deeper than the surface fears and to go deeper to discover what is really going on.

NURTURE YOUR SELF-ESTEEM

92. Get into the habit of speaking kindly and positively to yourself at all times. Refrain from absolutely any negative self-talk.

93. Commit to being honest with yourself at all costs.

94. Be true to yourself by listening to that small quiet voice inside. Trust your instincts and follow them.

95. Shower yourself with love and kindness.

96. Make sure you do things that make you feel good about yourself.

97. Be attentive to apologizing quickly for any mistakes you make that hurt other people's feelings. Be careful to avoid being defensive.

98. Focus on creating a life of integrity, being counted upon, and caring.

99. Commit to using your Power Statements throughout the day. Start first thing in the morning in front of the mirror for five minutes with additional time and places throughout the day, e.g. while waiting in line, driving in the car, washing dishes, taking the dog for a walk, etc.

100. Do three things each day that soothe your soul. Yes, it can be cleaning out a drawer, but all three things can't be in the same category.

101. Accept yourself fully as being a Divine creation and a magnificent being.

* Action #11 is from Chellie Campbell's book, *The Wealthy Spirit: Daily Affirmations for Financial Stress Reduction"*

APPENDIX 5

The Awakening Mastery Community

You are an amazing creator! Your ability to create what your heart desires far supercedes your ability to comprehend it. However, fear and procrastination prevent more people from realizing their dreams than anything else. Don't let your dreams fall victim to these two culprits. Join **THE AWAKENING Master Community** today.

It's been said that the bigger your dream and vision the more people you will need to help you achieve it. **THE AWAKENING Master Community** will help you succeed faster and go further than you would on your own through the additional guidance and support of experts and people who have traveled the same road as you.

Through **THE AWAKENING Master Community** you will be inspired to achieve greatness; you will learn how to embrace the Law of Attraction so that it works in your favor, creating greater abundance and joy in your life.

The secret to creating results using the Law of Attraction is two fold:

1. You must learn the specific strategies to harness the incredible power of your mind. Without knowing these strategies you will create lackluster results, if any.

2. You must also learn how to sustain your focus long enough to achieve your desired results. Life is full of obstacles and distractions that take you off-course everyday.

To create breakthroughs in the areas of your life you would like to change, you need the additional support to guide you and help you stay focused on your goal and move forward with confidence and speed. **THE AWAKENING Master Community** will help you do that.

- You will learn how to dream bigger dreams and make them a reality with ease.

- You will learn how to establish systems for success that would otherwise elude you.

- You will tap into a live community of other successful individuals practicing **THE AWAKENING** principles.

- You will have regular coaching opportunities with **THE AWAKENING** author, Alicia Ashley, and other authors and experts who will inspire you and teach you how to be all that you are capable of becoming.

These are all powerful benefits of being a member of **THE AWAKENING Master Community.**

YOU'RE A CREATURE OF HABIT

It is a fact, we are all creatures of habit. If you are not completely living the life of your dreams then the habits that currently control your life are preventing you from doing so. Changing these habits is not easy. If it was there would be a lot more success every January when people make New Year's resolutions!

Typically most people who set goals sooner or later (usually sooner!) get distracted, or become filled with fear and derail. And this scenario is repeated over and over again delaying the process of ever experiencing happiness and success. You deserve to live a life of joy and satisfaction, where you set goals, achieve them and then fully enjoy the many rewards of an abundant life.

As a member of **THE AWAKENING Mastery Community** you will be able to build support systems to help you establish new habits of success that will help you stay focused on your goals and live your hearts desire! Life's distractions will no longer stand in your way and you will be able to overcome fear, uncertainty and doubt.

Can you change your habits overnight and achieve all of this on your own? For most people, if they could have, they already would have. If you haven't, why not? There are many excuses, but what would you rather have, excuses or results?

Being a member of **THE AWAKENING Mastery Community** is a gift you give yourself so that you can create results and begin to fully realize your unlimited potential.

WHAT WILL YOU RECEIVE?

With **THE AWAKENING Mastery Community** membership you will receive unlimited access the following exclusive programs and resources:

1. Two Power Thoughts eLessons each week. These eLessons will help you stay focused on the principles of the Law of Attraction as presented in THE AWAKENING. They will help you get on, and stay on the path of achieving maximum results using the Law of Attraction.

2. Participation in four TeleClasses each month. You may join each of these calls live or you may download them and listen to them at your leisure.

   A. Two calls are with authors and experts regarding the Law of Attraction and other related topics.

   B. Two calls are group coaching calls with THE AWAKENING author, Alicia Ashley. You may email your questions prior to the calls and listen in for the answer.

3. Exclusive resources through the **Mastery Community** website that includes a variety of articles, ebooks, audio recordings on topics relating to your success.

4. Exclusive member offers on learning information and seminars from **Mastery Community** partners.

5. Invitations to exclusive "Member Only" **Mastery Community** events held quarterly.

6. VIP seating at select events open to the public.

7. Free attendance and price reduction on select events open to the public.

So what is your hearts desire? What vision of the present and future moves you? No matter what you have tried before, whatever it is you are seeking, right now is your chance to transform your dreams and vision into a beautiful new reality.

Sign up today at and receive your first month absolutely FREE! Join **THE AWAKENING Mastery Community** and begin receiving the guidance, insight, and mentorship you've been searching for.

GO BEHIND THE SCENES OF THE AWAKENING WITH 4 "READERS ONLY" BONUSES!

Although you have just finished THE AWAKENING your journey toward living an unlimited life is only just beginning. Waiting for you at are a set of exclusive resources for your eyes and ears only. These incredible resources pick up where THE AWAKENING book leaves off. Designed to further awaken your mind and soul author Alicia Ashley has provided readers additional steps and insights into living an abundant life, rich with love, prosperity, freedom, and joy.

Immediate Access to 7 Audio Programs FREE!
($79 Value!)

After reading the book you know *The Seven Steps to AWAKENING*. Now hear from the author of THE AWAKENING herself as Alicia Ashley personally guides you through all seven steps. Once you access the "Reader's Only" section of the site you can immediately download over 70 minutes worth of life changing principles and insight from Alicia.

Hear from the Masters of THE AWAKENING FREE!
(Priceless!)

You've read their inspiring and uplifting stories now hear from the masters of THE AWAKENING. During her research for the book Alicia set out to interview some of the leading authorities on THE AWAKENING and the Law of Attraction. Now you can go behind the scenes and access excerpts from the actual audio interviews Alicia conducted. These exclusive interviews are being made available only to readers of THE AWAKENING. Here's just a sample of the incredible group of authors, experts, ministers, doctors, and teachers you will personally hear from:

- Chellie Campbell
- Hale Dwoskin
- Rev. James Golden
- Scott Hunter
- Alex Mandossian
- Marci Shimoff

- Dr. John Demartini
- Dr. Masaru Emoto
- Mark Victor Hansen
- David Koons
- Stephen Lewis
- Rev. Jim Turrell

Are you ready to AWAKEN to your new life?
Go to www.TheAwakeningBook.com/bookspecial
to access your FREE Bonuses!

GO BEHIND THE SCENES OF THE AWAKENING
WITH 4 "READERS ONLY" BONUSES!

7 Week AWAKENING Course for FREE!
($495 Value)

You've finished reading THE AWAKENING. You feel awakened, ready to live in a state of amazement. If you're a fan of THE AWAKENING book, you cannot afford to miss this course as it picks up right where the book leaves off.

During this unforgettable seven-week email course, author Alicia Ashley will personally guide you through *The Seven Steps to AWAKENING* and *The Five Keys to Accelerate Your Power of Attraction*. You will learn to put these steps to use in your life right away and be on your way to living an abundant life, rich with love, prosperity, freedom, and joy.

One Month Membership in THE AWAKENING Mastery Community FREE!
($24.95 Value)

THE AWAKENING Mastery Community is a community driven environment where you get to connect with like minded people who share your same passion for living an abundant life and practicing the Law of Attraction. You will be guided by some of the world's greatest teachers as they share the insight and knowledge for putting what you have learned from THE AWAKENING to work in your life.

As a member you will be able to participate in four exclusive TeleClasses each month, two with an author or expert in the area of the Law of Attraction or related topic, and two with THE AWAKENING author, Alicia Ashley. Please see Appendix 5 for additional information.

Are you ready to AWAKEN to your new life?
Go to www.TheAwakeningBook.com/bookspecial
to access your FREE Bonuses!

ABOUT AUTHOR

Alicia Ashley, M.A.

A licia Ashley is a former psychotherapist who has become an award-winning speaker, successful entrepreneur, and record-setting author. Her mission is to empower all men and women to experience more love, prosperity, freedom and joy by using the Law of Attraction. Alicia shares her boundless enthusiasm and success secrets through her popular teleclasses, dynamic live seminars and transformational weekend intensives.

After practicing psychotherapy for over five years in Southern California, Alicia closed her practice to pursue her love of public speaking and traveling. As a result, her training and management consulting has inspired thousands of individuals to achieve greater levels of excellence and productivity. Her impressive list of Fortune 500 clients includes: American Express, Autoglass U.K., Microsoft, GTE, Dow Chemical, Bank of America, Ritz Carlton, Marriott, Hilton, Starwood, Renaissance, MGM Grand Hotel and Casino, and many other well-known organizations.

In addition to her professional endeavors, Alicia includes being a successful single Mom to a lively eight-year old boy, walking on fire twice, completing 11, 26.2-mile marathons, and numerous 5K and 10K races as some of her greatest accomplishments. No, she has never taken home the purse, and her picture has never graced the front page of a single newspaper, but she definitely practices what she preaches about using the Law of Attraction to make your goals and dreams come true!

You can find out more information through the following websites:

www.TheAwakeningBook.com

www.PolishedPreCons.com

www.BeAwesomeNow.com

Printed in the USA
CPSIA information can be obtained
at www.ICGtesting.com
JSHW052015140824
68134JS00027B/2492